THE
WINDSOR
KNOT

THE WINDSOR KNOT

CHRISTOPHER WILSON

CITADEL PRESS
Kensington Publishing Corp.
www.kensingtonbooks.com

CITADEL PRESS BOOKS are published by

Kensington Publishing Corp.
850 Third Avenue
New York, NY 10022

All Kensington titles, imprints, and distributed lines are available at special quantity discounts for bulk purchases for sales promotions, premiums, fund-raising, educational, or institutional use. Special book excerpts or customized printings can also be created to fit specific needs. For details, write or phone the office of the Kensington special sales manager: Kensington Publishing Corp., 850 Third Avenue, New York, NY 10022, attn: Special Sales Department, phone 1-800-221-2647.

First Citadel printing: September 2003
10 9 8 7 6 5 4 3 2 1

Printed in the United States of America

Cataloging data may be obtained from the Library of Congress.

ISBN 0-8065-2386-7

Contents

Foreword

———◆◆◆———

By the fall of 2002, Prince Charles and Camilla Parker Bowles had been lovers for thirty years. Princess Diana strayed into their lives for little more than half that time, yet the seismic shift which occurred when all three collided altered the course of history. One life was shattered beyond recall, the reputations of two others remain badly mauled, the effect upon two young boys, Prince William and Prince Harry, is as yet unquantified but likely to be significant.

Was it all a dreadful accident of fate which left the twentieth century's most famous woman dying in a Paris underpass? Or were darker forces at work all along, forces which connived at Diana's horrific end? In the following pages Prince Charles's obsession with Camilla dominates all else; driving the action, pushing aside all objection, breaking the rules, and finally, it can be argued, slaying his wife. But why did he become obsessed?

Was it the sexual hold Camilla had over him? Did she use it to further her own ambition to be near the throne? Did Charles run from his wife through feelings of inadequacy and shame? Did Diana, who never placed the act of love near the top of her personal list, drive her husband back to Camilla through her scant attentions? The story which follows is no accidental lovers' triangle, nor yet is it a cynical *ménage à trois*. It is, however, shot through with personal ambition—Diana's clear-eyed wish to be a princess, no matter what; Charles's dream of a satisfactory dynastic alliance; and Camilla's lust to follow in the footsteps of her own great-grandmother's royal dalliance.

This story exonerates nobody: The consequences of it are that the Western world has been robbed a twentieth century icon, possibly the most famous face of the century; and an ancient royal house has been permanently weakened. None of the participants could have realized the ultimate consequences of their actions, and yet slowly and inexorably the story winds forward to death and disillusion. It is indeed a tragedy worthy of ancient Greece, with each figure magnified by history in the retelling of the tale.

Diana was the brightest shining star in the British royal family in nearly 500 years: In her time as a princess she brought luster, freshness, and a new sense of purpose to a tired and rudderless institution. The grown-up world can live perfectly well without the existence of royalty, as the United States demonstrates so very well; yet by wearing those famous designer dresses and priceless jewels, Diana was able to use the fascination people retain for credible royalty to draw attention to other matters—the plight of AIDS sufferers, the isolation of old age, the horrors of land mines. Her celebrity was a positive force for good—that much cannot be denied, despite the revisionist theories which have been floated (mostly by Prince Charles's camp) since her death in 1997. She gave a new zest and a new meaning to royalty.

Charles has, in his professional life, unquestionably distinguished himself. No other future monarch has provided so much for the youth of his country in terms of jobs, hope, and self-respect; nor spoken with a voice of reason against worrying trends, nor attempted to check the blind arrogance of politicians by word and action. There is no other candidate for the job of King of England, but if there were, it would have to be a startlingly accomplished person: Charles has done the work, and he has earned the plaudits. Yet some might argue, after reading these pages, that he remains an isolated figure, selfish and morally weak—one whose actions above and beyond the other two players caught in this Windsor knot can be held responsible for the calamities which followed, both to himself and to others. It was Charles who cold-bloodedly chose Diana as a wife; Charles who cuckolded a brother officer in the early years of that officer's marriage; Charles who committed adultery in his own marriage when the going got tough.

And Camilla? So determined is Charles to marry his greater love that a remarkable whitewash job, connived at and involving the British press, is under way at the time of this writing. History has been rewritten in Fleet Street so as to conveniently forget that the woman who may, one day, sit beside Charles at his coronation was also the woman who used a honey trap to lure her former lover back into her bed, once her first ambition in life, to marry a cavalry officer, had been achieved. There is little doubt, from the evidence of the following pages, that she could have resisted Charles's attentions at a time when she had a small baby and planned to further increase her family. Married to a Roman Catholic, she was, more than most, aware of the dangers involved in the route she chose to take—not from a moral standpoint, but from a purely practical one. Once she had the besotted prince back in her grasp, it made the task allotted him—to find a suitable bride—well-nigh impossible. He only had eyes for Camilla. She did nothing to push him away.

Princess Diana believed that her husband should have been faithful to her, a jejune and foolish notion given the long history of marital infidelity in the ruling British house; Indeed, she herself descended from an adulterous liaison between King Charles II and his mistress Nell Gwynn. Nonetheless, Diana clung to the idea that her marriage vows, delivered before the nation and the world, should be honored. Charles, after a feeble but well-intentioned attempt to remain faithful to her, turned once again to the only woman he truly loved—and slowly, piece by piece, the royal castellations started to crumble and fall.

The act of revenge—willful, mad, and bad—by Princess Diana in collaborating with the author Andrew Morton in producing his book *Diana—Her True Story* may single-handedly have put paid to royalty in Britain. There have been few signs, since that book's publication in 1992, that public opinion has wanted to put the House of Windsor back on the pedestal it happily occupied for centuries.

Diana confessed that on her honeymoon, "At night I dreamt of Camilla the whole time . . . obsessed by Camilla totally. I had tremendous hope in me (for our marriage), which was slashed by day two." And so her resentment grew, finally exploding with all the ferocity of a petrol bomb thrown through a plate-glass window.

The publication of *Diana—Her True Story* allowed Charles to be publicly condemned for his adultery, but the effects went much further than that. Hidden between the lines in Diana's story were vignettes of daily life within the royal family—something that writers had only guessed at before; now, it was as if there were a closed circuit TV camera in

Buckingham Palace which we were invited to come and watch. It drastically altered the perception, both of the world's press and the public, toward the royal house. Suddenly there was a desire to expose royal weakness, and an equal desire to read those exposures.

The marriage of the queen's second son, the Duke of York, was exposed as a sham, with the lusty Fergie having sex with her Texan boyfriend in the room next to where her husband sat on the sofa, watching TV.

The queen's youngest son, Prince Edward, who took a job in the theater, was accused of being homosexual. The queen's daughter Princess Anne was exposed as having had not one, but two affairs with Camilla Parker Bowles's husband. Prince Philip, the iron-hard head of the family, was accused of bedding Lady Romsey, the wife of his cousin.

And that was just the sex. Windsor Castle, the royal family's home since Norman times, caught fire. The queen was pilloried for not contributing a single penny toward its multi-million-pound repair, while appealing to her subjects to help pay the bills. It finally led to clamorous calls for Her Majesty to pay income tax—and the moment she capitulated on this point, though it was seen by everyone as a right and proper thing to do, Queen Elizabeth II lost much of the mystique referred to above. She had, at a stroke, become a mere mortal in the eyes of the public. As a direct consequence, the debacle after Diana died was laid at the queen's feet. The once-omnipotent sovereign had lost much of the respect she spent her whole life earning the hard way.

Though royalty has ruled absolutely in Great Britain since 1066, with one short break, it is probably now at its weakest ebb. If Charles and Camilla had not fallen in love, and Diana had not revealed it, the press and public in Britain would have been less ready to condemn the royal family as a whole. Yet the following pages all too clearly demonstrate that Camilla was the one person in Prince Charles's loveless life who truly understood him, who answered his needs, and who listened to his thoughts.

The prince has almost a sixth sense about his destiny which may yet confound his critics, both within and without the palace walls. During the years since 1997 he has undergone a very public period of rehabilitation; it may well be that this humbling process will make for a stronger, yet more amenable monarch when his time comes. Certainly there was a danger, before the fall, that arrogance and myopia were beginning to infect his princeship.

In January 1993 a six-minute fragment of a conversation he had shared with Camilla Parker Bowles three years earlier surfaced, in an eerie and sinister way. Whatever its genesis, the effect on Charles of the publication of the so-called Camilla-gate Tapes was to effectively blow away forty-four years' work—a lifetime of making himself acceptable to the people who one day he would rule.

For this act of duplicity—apparently loving one woman while secretly devoted to another—the Prince of Wales took an unprecedented public mauling. Opinion polls showed, again and again, how the British nation could not stomach the thought of Charles cheating on their number-one cover girl.

With the prince's declaration that the royal marriage was over, and the emerging evidence that it had been a complete sham, the historians began sharpening their quills in readiness for their epitaphs on the House of Windsor. It does not take much to puncture the pundits' faith in an outdated institution whose power base has been eroded and whose function is now almost entirely ceremonial; indeed, suddenly there were some very good reasons to believe the monarchy might not survive the death of Queen Elizabeth II.

But history has a way of soothing fears and healing wounds; and it was not unreasonable to suppose that soon natural anger at having been so wilfully cheated would give way to a better tolerance of Charles's unusual circumstances and apparently discreditable behavior. But forgiveness can only come with understanding, and a clear understanding is only possible if those who care about royalty are furnished with the full facts of Charles's affair with Camilla Parker Bowles.

This I have attempted to do, as it is my conviction that the incomplete versions which have appeared to date have all distorted the facts by concentrating on Diana, her life and problems. Interestingly, the one person who finally understood it all said in the months before her death, in a private conversation with a BBC reporter: "Let's face it, Camilla is the love of Charles's life, and always has been. I don't feel any animosity toward her anymore. In fact, I really think she deserves some form of recognition. After all, she's been loyal to him and extremely discreet for such a long time."

Charles and Camilla exist; they will continue to do so. Those who have a certain sympathy for thwarted love may be encouraged by the following chapters, but the story is no cozy romance. People, both children and adults, have been hurt by this Cupid's accident. Many others, millions maybe, feel cheated for one reason or another by what has happened.

More than any other, Diana was cheated. But as the following pages amply demonstrate, she knew about Camilla all along—she was warned of the married woman's existence even at the moment when she first met Charles. Camilla was too omnipresent, and Charles's courting of Diana too chaste, for the penny not to drop—even for a girl who was far from being a woman of the world.

With the benefit of hindsight it is possible to see that there is a version of events other than the one which has been put forward so forcefully over the past few years. It is generally supposed that if Diana considered Camilla at all, it was only as the vague threat which all former girlfriends pose to a future wife. Innocently, she walked up the aisle of St. Paul's Cathedral believing that, from now on, Charles was all hers.

The reality is somewhat different. It was clear from the outset that this was a dynastic match, one which was wanted by Charles in order to perpetuate the line and silence the critics—including his own father—who claimed he neglected his duty by remaining unmarried. Equally it was wanted by Diana for reasons of ambition: She was determined to turn it into a love match if possible, but it never happened.

Charles's obsession with Camilla barely wavered under the onslaught of his young wife's charms, but then Camilla always looked to her great-grandmother Alice Keppel as a role model. Alice's tenure as King Edward VII's favorite mistress—La Favorita—was long and uncontroversial. But in those early dalliances at Smith's Lawn she cannot have known that her place in the history of Britain's monarchy would be even greater than that of her illustrious forebear: For with her love and affection for Charles she is still in danger of dealing a mortal blow to the monarchy in Britain, should she accept his proposal of marriage.

What is left, now that the cat is out of the bag, is for the royal machinery to make the Charles-Camilla imbroglio an acceptable fact of life, yet in this they have signally failed. Successive royal biographers have pointed to the sorry lack of talent in the present "management team" of the House of Windsor, or "the Firm," as they like to call themselves. In these pages are detailed instances where misleading information has been disseminated, apparently in order to buttress the Prince of Wales's position with regard to his relationship with Camilla. A franker, bolder approach is what is required in order to assuage an affronted public who feel that the royal wedding of 1981 was an expensive sham, and that they were made to look fools by waving their Union Jacks while Charles stood at the altar thinking about Camilla.

Furthermore, as history's wheel turns and Prince William becomes a bigger player in the royal show, there are dangers that the public's disillusion over the Charles-Camilla question may be forgotten in the headlong dash by the people to anoint William as their number-one royal figure. William has his own views about Camilla, views which are shielded from the general public at this time. However, one thing is known, and that is this wholly admirable young man will not act as a pawn in the game of Charles's quest for public acceptability. William has had his own large helping of heartache, with the breakup of his parents' marriage, his mother's increasingly fretful ways, and finally her sad, ugly death; it is to be expected he will do little to publicly embrace Camilla, no matter what the palace spin-doctors would have us believe.

This is an imperfect story, which has its origins in a child who knew very little love and found it increasingly hard, as he went through life, to gather any more to him.

As the boy became a man he found in the shape of Camilla Parker Bowles someone in whom he could put his trust, with whom he could share his fears, and under whose watchful gaze he could carry out the loneliest job in Britain.

It is an imperfect love story, but then we live in an imperfect world.

London, April 2002

Chapter One

Four in the Morning

———⟨◦◦◦⟩———

Berkeley Square in late October

With the first frost still a week or two away, Mayfair clings on to the last vestiges of summer warmth. The huge plane trees have been stripped bare, the thick carpet of leaves underneath swept away.

In the country, among the higher reaches of British society, the season has moved on. Pheasants have replaced grouse as a prime target, fishing rods have been put away. Huntsmen have hauled their pink coats out of the cupboard and burnished their boots.

In London, though by now the debutantes have scattered to the four winds, the party season has begun. Though fashions alter, the immutable London season goes on; it has barely changed in half a century.

In October 1972, the war in Vietnam was on the verge of ceasefire; Dr. Henry Kissinger was holding secret meetings with the North Vietnamese in Paris, flying on to talks with President Thieu of the South in Saigon. Britain's political leaders, Edward Heath and Harold Wilson, had come to an uneasy truce about Britain's membership of the European

11

Community. Britain was involved in an unedifying scrap with Iceland: The Cod War erupted with fishing boats and Royal Navy frigates firing on one another. A flight to New York cost $87 and a bottle of Pol Roger champagne $4.50.

The queen, together with Prince Philip and Princess Anne, toured Croatia as part of their visit to the Communist-ruled state of Yugoslavia, while at home a memorial service was held for the sovereign's libidinous cousin, Prince William of Gloucester, who had died two months earlier in an airplane crash.

The most eligible bachelor in the world was a twenty-four-year-old sublieutenant in the Royal Navy, if not quite a man of the world, then someone who had already seen more of it than most of his contemporaries.

Charles Philip Arthur George, Prince of the United Kingdom and possessor of an elegant array of subsidiary titles, had been known by the title of Prince of Wales for three years, and while both he and the nation still relished the novelty of this new appellation, to many he was still known simply as Prince Charles.

Though much had been written about the boy, little was known of the man. From a remote Scottish public school he had disappeared into the anonymity of Cambridge University and thence, a year earlier, into the Royal Navy in the tradition of his father, grandfather, and great-grandfather.

To satisfy the diktat of the Duke of Edinburgh, Charles also learned to fly, spending some of the summer months of 1972 familiarizing himself with Royal Naval Wessex helicopters and aircraft of the Queen's Flight. Soon he was to return to the navy to endure the low point of his service with them—as a humble officer on the coastal minesweeper HMS *Glasserton*. But that autumn, the sober-sided prince allowed himself a little light relief. He was young, fit, not unhand-some—and ready to fall in love.

In the pursuit of women, he pictured himself as a younger version of the man he most admired—his dead cousin, Prince William of Gloucester. William was everything a prince should be—tall, dark, staggeringly good-looking, and formi-dably attractive to women. He broke all the rules: While in Tokyo he lived with an older woman who was a double divorcee and mother. She was an artist who painted him in the nude—then displayed the picture in an exhibition. Soon she was supplanted by another older woman, also a divorcee and mother. Prince William of Gloucester could take his pick of beautiful women, and regularly did.

Charles, in awe of his older relation, wanted to follow suit. William's heroic death in an air race near Wolverhamp-ton in the Midlands that summer only served to strengthen Charles's resolve in that regard—he would take up where William had left off. He would find beautiful women, woo them, conquer them, leave them . . .

That was the fantasy. The reality was that his conquests so far were neither exciting nor numerous. While an under-graduate at Trinity College, Cambridge, he discovered the pleasures of the bedroom with Lucia Santa Cruz, the glam-orous daughter of the Chilean ambassador to London. Three years older than the prince, she was employed by the master of Charles's college, Lord Butler, as a research assistant on his memoirs, *The Art of the Possible*. Butler later recalled: "The Prince asked if she might stay in our lodge for privacy, which request we were very glad to accede to"—and so to bed. But the relationship came to an end at about the time Charles graduated.

He then entered a brief and unsatisfactory liaison with

Lucinda Buxton, later to became a notable filmmaker but in preference to marriage, choosing a single life in the company of women. Charles also enjoyed a friendship, though hardly a passion, with Sibella Dorman, the daughter of the governor-general of Malta, Sir Maurice Dorman. An invitation to the George Cross Island, where the couple were spied rubbing each other with suntan oil, was reciprocated with an invitation to Sibella to join Charles on the royal yacht *Britannia* after he was crowned Prince of Wales. But the relationship soon fizzled out.

And that was about it. Charles's biographer Penny Junor observed: "He had a number of girlfriends . . . but the relationships were mostly platonic. Not a natural womanizer, he was far more likely to present a girl with some hideous practical joke—like the envelope he gave to one which exploded with rubber bands when she opened it—than a single red rose.

"Like most public schoolboys who have been cloistered in an all-male preserve for five years of their adolescence he was awkward with the opposite sex, unsure of himself, and had never had much opportunity to overcome his diffidence. His peers could practice and make fools of themselves in anonymity. He could never be anonymous."

He also lacked opportunity. In the months leading up to October 1972 he had toured Canada and the U.S.A.; sailed to Fiji, Bermuda, and Barbados—then went on, at different times, to France, Kenya, Germany, and Gibraltar. This was in addition to his military duties in first the RAF, then the Royal Navy. Meeting girls was a problem.

But not in Berkeley Square. Not in Annabel's.

Considered by many to be the best nightclub in the world, it was then, as now, an unflashy place which boasted neither hostesses nor floor shows nor gaming tables. Instead it comprised a dark set of basement rooms decorated in discreet English country-house style, with paneled walls hung with pictures by Augustus John, Sir Edwin Landseer, Sir Alfred Munnings, and the royal court painter, Sir Oswald Birley, father of the club's founder, Mark Birley. There were separate bars decorated in dark green, a dining room and dance area, a vaulted ceiling held up by brass columns which were polished daily: The ethos was one of sophisticated seclusion.

Its critics would argue that there is a smugness about its denizens, a self-congratulatory ease in the knowledge that they are part of an English inner circle which excludes the socially ambitious, the untrustworthy, and those of lesser birth. In addition the only journalists ever allowed through the doors are those who accept the vow of silence over events which take place inside: It took many years, for example, for the story to leak that Sandra Paul, now married to former Home Secretary Michael Howard, had been propositioned—to her disgust—by Ted Kennedy in there. The mustachioed Lord Lucan was a regular, but that was another story altogether.

Into these surroundings royalty may venture, sure in the knowledge that they may safely let down their hair; and in the 1970s Annabel's was a perfect launchpad for those early steps into adulthood where the young could flirt and enjoy the heady scent of cheap music far away from the curiosity of the common herd.

There, in the dark, in the basement of the house where King George III's lady of the bedchamber, Lady Isabella Finch, made her home, history was about to be made. Under the awning and down the steps came a party which included the twenty-two-year-old Princess Anne, newly back from her tour of Yugoslavia, followed by Prince Charles, snatching a rare night's carousal after a dreary shore posting at HMS *Dryad* at Portsmouth.

It was a unique sighting of the prince and his younger sister out on the town together, but it was those accompanying the royal siblings who would have given anyone gifted with foresight a special frisson. These escorts included the suave Gerald Ward, a Berkshire landowner whose father commanded the Household Cavalry and was appointed Silver Stick in Waiting to the queen—dual posts which one day would become familiar under the custody of another officer.

And then there was the twenty-five-year-old Camilla Shand, a relatively unknown girl-about-town with an interest in horses, clear blue eyes, and a nicely rounded figure. Miss Shand, when she had a job, was a secretary, but this description should not to be confused with someone of lowly rank who needed to work in order to live. Her lineage was aristocratic—some said royal. She had been a debutante in 1965 and had enjoyed the fruits of the London social round for the past six years. Most of her friends were married, but for various reasons this sexy but unremarkable-looking woman remained single.

Camilla lived in an unusual place for one of her wealth and social standing—the Cundy Street flats at the back end of Belgravia. Though one of her forebears had made his name and family fortune from building the estate for the Dukes of Westminster, she herself occupied the only part he did not build—an ugly postwar seven-story block which, with its three neighbors, had taken the place of elegant stuccoed terraces bombed flat in the war. Mozart wrote a symphony yards from where she lived; yet the sight of the tall and drably constructed towers set against the pillared, white-painted mansions of Belgravia was about as inharmonious as it was possible to get. Victoria Coach Station, with its rumbling coaches belching black fumes, was the nearest landmark.

Miss Shand had no obvious royal connections, but her landlady in the two-bedroom ground-floor flat was Lady Moyra Campbell, the daughter of the fourth Duke of Abercom, who had been a maid of honor to Queen Elizabeth II at her coronation, and whose mother was a close friend of the Queen Mother and Mistress of the Robes in that royal household. Lady Moyra moved out when she married an Irish landowner, and Camilla's new flatmate was Virginia Carrington, beautiful daughter of the Conservative politician and former Guards officer, Lord Carrington.

Camilla was no stranger to Annabel's, though it had only lately become attractive to the young. Across Berkeley Square, ten minutes' walk away in Swallow Street off Piccadilly, lay the deserted remnants of the only challenger for the blue bloods' nocturnal attentions, Sybilla's.

Opening in 1966, this nightclub had been named after Camilla's cousin Sybilla Edmonstone. She was all Camilla was not—beautiful, celebrated, deeply fashionable. The contrast between the girls' lives was best demonstrated by two almost simultaneous events that year. On the one hand there was Camilla's rather staid coming-out dance at the Surrey home of her uncle, Lord Ashcombe, where the most exciting event was a car crash involving two silly debutantes. On the other hand, there was the opening of Sybilla's.

Co-owned by George Harrison, then a godlike figure by virtue of The Beatles' worldwide acclaim, and baronet Sir William Pigott-Brown, its first night was a sensation, the greatest manifestation yet of the Swinging Sixties. All four Beatles were present; The Rolling Stones had held back their tour of America to be there. It was a blessed moment of synchronicity, when for a brief moment class barriers were breached and pop stars of lowly birth mixed with the earls of Lichfield and Shelburne, Lord Eliot, the children of Lord Harlech, and such figures of the moment as Vanessa Redgrave, Julie Christie, and Rudolf Nureyev.

And there, center stage with all eyes on her, was Sybilla. At twenty-two she had the face and figure of a model, the adulation of the *beau monde,* and an impressive fortune stemming from her great-grandfather Marshall Field's Chicago stores empire. Her name and face had become synonymous with the freewheeling spirit of the age; her very presence was enough to make grown men go weak at the knees.

So very different from the fledgling Camilla Shand, whose charm for the opposite sex was a rumbustious earthiness, rather than a goddess's aloofness. But then her upbringing lacked the cosmopolitan élan of her older cousin.

However, as we shall learn, there were hidden depths to her family. Camilla seemed on the face of it an unlikely date for the Prince of Wales that night in 1972. Her father, who described himself as an "educational films representative" when she was born, lived in London but preferred the country, where he pursued the fox with vigor and his business interests with rather less success.

She was not related to the dukes of England, nor to any foreign royal houses—the two areas where Charles might expect to find a future bride. She was not then the possessor of a personal fortune, and of the girls in her debutante year she was possibly one of the least photogenic. In addition she was known to have enjoyed a lively love affair with an army officer called Andrew Parker Bowles, at thirty-two eight years her senior, which those who knew the couple predicted would end in marriage.

But Parker Bowles, a serving major in the Blues and

Royals cavalry regiment, had been posted to Germany. And in the preceding summer months Camilla had spent much time at the Guards' Polo Club at Windsor, together with her friend Carolyn Gerard Leigh and Andrew Parker Bowles's sister, Mary Ann Paravicini, whose husband, Nick, was a Life Guards officer and polo-playing friend of Prince Charles.

The connection had been established. It was at a party soon after Charles and Camilla met that, with typical *joie de vivre,* she made her historic proposal: "My great-grandmother and your great-great-grandfather were lovers. So how about it?"

Factually, she was accurate. Between 1898 and his death in 1910, King Edward VII enjoyed a close physical and intellectual relationship with the Honorable Mrs. George Keppel, a woman twenty-eight years his junior. Of all the king's extramarital relationships, this was the most profound and Charles, well versed in his family's history, knew of the special role Alice Keppel played in the life of his ancestor as confidante and hostess.

Had he studied more closely the photographs of Alice Keppel, he would have seen an eerie resemblance between the two women. But there were more similarities—many more—between Alice and Camilla. And in the end, Camilla would achieve a greater footnote in history than her celebrated great-grandmother.

Ahead of him the prince faced the prospect of the chilly wastes of Lincolnshire, where he would undertake a week's refresher course flying RAF Jet Provosts, and beyond that the even less congenial surroundings of the RAF's Advanced Flying Training School in Anglesey. But that night in the warmth and dark of Annabel's, Camilla Shand's proposal echoed again in his ears. Champagne corks popped and romance was in the air.

Princess Anne and Gerald Ward danced to the hits of the day, Eric Clapton's "Layla," the Bee Gees' "Run to Me," Michael Jackson's "Ain't No Sunshine," Roxy Music's "Virginia Plain," and when things slowed down, Charles and Camilla took to the floor for Python Lee Jackson's "In a Broken Dream" and Faron Young's "It's Four in the Morning."

At four in the morning they were no longer in Annabel's, but in the ground-floor flat of Stack House, Cundy Street, discovering a passion which was to last many long years; years of joy and sometimes of adversity, but years where never once would the love die.

Chapter Two

Part Lover, Part Mother

It was history repeating itself. Though there are similarities between Charles and Camilla's affair and that of the Prince of Wales and Mrs. Simpson, it is the relationship between Camilla's great-grandmother, Alice Keppel, and Charles's great-great-grandfather, King Edward VII, which casts the most light over subsequent events.

Alice Keppel was born in Scotland in 1869, the youngest daughter of Admiral Sir William Edmonstone and Mary Elizabeth Parsons. Edmonstone, the fourth baronet, was descended from the royal house of Stuart by a fifteenth-century marriage: King Robert III's daughter Mary married Sir William Edmonstone of Culloden, and in 1445 they were given the family seat of Duntreath Castle on the Stirlingshire side of Loch Lomond.

Set in uncompromising Scottish moorland and with the backdrop of two austere, bald hills, Duntreath appeared a forbidding edifice with a courtyard and tower at each corner. Yet its stark exterior belied the comforts within, and its solidity and history were arguably a proper setting from which a king's mistress might emerge. "It was romantic, of a standard of luxury without equal in those days; gay with a touch of Frenchness in its *salons en enfilade* and premeditated perspectives. The atmosphere of the place was complex: half medieval, half exotic," wrote one member of the family.

As Alice passed from childhood into adolescence, her personality became more pronounced: Honest, energetic, practical were the adjectives used, mirroring those of another woman almost a century later. She was noted for exceptional kindness—"her nature was without pettiness, prejudice, or malice," wrote one biographer. "Even as a girl her tact was remarkable." In a different age, when only the chosen few were privy to the king's infidelities, her charm and good nature uniquely shielded Alice from attack once she became Edward's mistress.

Her upbringing was aristocratic, but as a younger daughter she was unlikely to bring a great dowry to her future husband. Nonetheless she made the choice to marry for love, not money, accepting the proposal of the Honorable George Keppel, third son of the seventh Earl of Albernarle. He was twenty-six and an officer in the Gordon Highlanders, she was twenty-two, when they married in 1891.

Despite a lack of money on both sides, contemporaries thought she had done well—for Alice, like her descendant, was not one of the celebrated beauties of the age. Dame Rebecca West noted: "Her charm was not in her looks; George indeed was the only real beauty of the two. Alice had no distinctive characteristics of face or figure. She was endowed with a bright pale skin, and those Scottish eyes that have the quality of a clear stream but with a noting, concerned quality, as if she were a theater sister in a well-run hospital." Just as with Camilla, her charms lay elsewhere than in striking physical beauty, though both were the possessor of an ample bosom. Hugh Walpole noted: "Mrs. Keppel is great fun. I do like her. She's like the sergeant in the guard with a sense of humor."

Her husband's family, despite their Dutch origins, were by the late nineteenth century an intensely grand English family. Arnold Joost von Keppel joined the Prince of Orange on his first trip to Britain in 1688, and remained one of his closest allies after he ascended to the throne as King William III the following year. He was created Earl of Albemarle and made Knight of the Garter—"for his *beaux yeux*," observed Sir Harold Acton dryly.

This intimacy with the monarch extended, unusually, over three generations, with the second and third earls also being made Knights of the Garter. The connection with the throne was maintained, albeit in a watered-down form, through succeeding generations—George Keppel's own father, the seventh earl, was treasurer to Queen Victoria's household as well as twice being Under Secretary of State for War. His mother, Sophia Macnab, was an unusual choice of wife for an established aristocrat and courtier in that she was the daughter of a Canadian, Sir Allan Napier Macnab. A soldier, lawyer, businessman, and politician, Macnab owed his massive fortune to speculation in real estate, and his knight-hood to the zeal with which he suppressed the Canadian Rebellion of 1837.

A contemporary described Alice's husband thus: "one of those tall and handsome Englishmen who, immaculately dressed, proclaim the perfect gentleman." He was also a wom-anizer and, though from a grand family, was perpetually short of cash—a situation which remained unrelieved until King Edward got him a job in trade, working as an agent for his friend Sir Thomas Lipton, the grocer. On the face of it, and in the light of subsequent events, the youthful match did not augur well. Yet it lasted more than fifty years, from 1891 to 1947, when the couple died within weeks of each other.

Three years after their marriage at St. George's, Hanover Square, their first child, Violet, was born. In adulthood she was to become notorious in her own right when, as Violet Trefusis, she embarked in 1918 on a turbulent love affair with the writer Vita Sackville-West. Lesbianism, a form of love not acknowledged by Queen Victoria to exist, was still deeply shocking, even in the sophisticated salons of Mayfair.

When Violet was not quite four, an incident occurred which was to change her mother's life. On 27 February 1898, the Prince of Wales came to dinner with the Keppels at their Wilton Crescent, Belgravia, home. In the words of his biographer, Sir Philip Magnus, "An understanding arose overnight"—and an affair started that would continue until the king died. The historian Richard Hough put it more graphically; the relationship "warmed with the speed of a bonfire."

The couple had already met: while inspecting the Norfolk Yeomanry, of which he was colonel-in-chief and in which George Keppel served as an officer, the prince saw Alice and asked his friend Lord Leicester to introduce them. They subsequently met at Sandown races when she was accompanied by Sir John Leslie. Then, wrote Leslie's granddaughter, Anita: "HRH gave Leslie to understand that his presence was no longer required. Whimsically, my grandfather used to describe that certain look—blending shrewd appraisement and admiration—that crossed the prince's face as his eyes traveled over Mrs. George Keppel's lovely face and fashionably curved figure."

"She was attractive enough to interest him sexually;

entertaining when he was bored, patient when he was can-
tankerous, sympathetic when he was ill, unobtrusive when he
appeared in public," noted the writer Theo Aronson. "Like all
successful mistresses Alice was part lover, part wife, part
mother," and no more accurate description could be found of
Alice's descendant.

Less than two years after the royal love affair began, a
second daughter was born to Mrs. Keppel. Successive historians have balked at addressing the question of the child's
parentage—but certain factors point compellingly toward
Edward's being the father. Alice's marriage, by this stage, was
nine years old. From the beginning of the affair the king was
virtually a daily visitor at the Keppel houses in first Wilton
Crescent, then Portman Square. From the outset George
Keppel was a quiescent player in this ménage à trois, and
indeed had romantic interests of his own. It would not be
unreasonable to assume that the physical side of the Keppels'
relationship was by now dormant, even though to the end
the pair maintained a devoted affection for each other.

Furthermore, it is highly questionable whether Keppel
even fathered Alice's first child. Violet was generally assumed
to be the daughter of an earlier paramour, the recently
widowed Ernest William Beckett, the future Lord Grim-
thorpe, and in later life Violet's lover, Vita Sackville-West, told
the writer Philippe Jullian that Beckett was indeed Violet's
father.

Additional evidence of the platonic nature of Alice's relationship with her husband may be found in the caustic aside
of the Marchioness Curzon to her husband: "Mrs. Favorite
Keppel is bringing forth another questionable offspring!
Either Lord Stavordale's or H. Sturt's!" Since Alice gave birth
to no further children it may be supposed that she suffered a

miscarriage soon after, but clearly the multiplicity of sexual dalliances she enjoyed does tend to point to a conjugal inactivity between husband and wife.

One further, and telling, piece of evidence came sixty years later when the child born to Alice in the first months of sexual intrigue with the king decided, in old age, to write her memoirs. Sonia Keppel entitled the book *Edwardian Daughter,* the neatest of double entendres and the most illuminating pointer to her true parentage.

If Sonia Rosemary Keppel were Edward's daughter—a theory subscribed to by Theo Aronsen—that would make her King George V's half sister. It would make Sonia's daughter Rosalind a first cousin of King George VI, and her granddaughter Camilla a second cousin of the queen. It would also make Camilla a second cousin, once removed, of Prince Charles. The serendipity of this would not be lost on either.

Edward's affair with Alice Keppel was barely three years old when he ascended to the throne as King Edward VII. He was sixty, she was thirty-one. Their way was made easier by George Keppel's good-natured complaisance: "He was an extremely handsome, tall army officer with a bristling mustache, an aquiline nose, and a hearty laugh. Very fond of women himself, he raised no objection to the prince's friendship with his wife, to whom he was deeply attached; and when his income proved inadequate for the sort of life he was called upon to lead—and his wife's bank managers, to whom she was, as her daughter said 'irresistibly attractive,' could help no more—he cheerfully went to work for Sir Thomas Lipton, who obligingly found him employment at the prince's instigation," wrote the historian Christopher Hibbert.

Mrs. Keppel fulfilled more than a mere bodily need for the king and, such was the graceful and unassuming way in which she conducted herself, her presence by his side was accepted at all levels, including, grudgingly, by Queen Alexandra herself. By the time Edward and Mrs. Keppel met, the royal marriage was thirty-five years old; the queen was aged fifty-four and had become isolated in her deafness.

Anita Leslie, in her book, *Edwardians In Love,* observed: "When Edward's niece Princess Alice came to stay at Sandringham, she found Mrs. Keppel delightful. She never flaunted herself or took advantage of her position as the king's favorite. Queen Alexandra was very fond of her and encouraged the liaison. There was a lot of gossip about their relationship and unnecessary sympathy for Aunt Alex who didn't need it, as she welcomed the relationship."

Just as her great-granddaughter would do eighty years later, Alice hosted dinner parties for her royal paramour: On one occasion she was famously placed next to the kaiser "so she might have the opportunity of talking to him." The Keppels and the king would make annual trips at Easter to Biarritz, and the Keppels also regularly visited Sandringham.

The king, benevolent in incipient old age, took great delight in Alice's two daughters, and it was said that they had grown up "rolling their hoop with a scepter." As the younger daughter—Camilla's grandmother Sonia Cubitt—later recalled: "Sometimes Kingy would come to tea with Mama, and was there when I appeared at six o'clock. On such occasions he and I devised a fascinating game. With a fine disregard for the condition of his trousers, he would lend me his leg, on which I used to start two bits of bread and butter (butter side down), side by side. Then, bets of a penny each were made, and the winning piece of bread depended, of course, on which was the more buttery."

This indulgence was repaid by the dedication with which Alice Keppel served him, as mistress and helpmeet. Lord Hardinge of Penshurst, permanent head of the Foreign Office and Viceroy of India, noted in a private memorandum: "Everybody knew of the relationship which existed between King Edward and Mrs. George Keppel . . . I used to see a great deal of Mrs. Keppel at that time and I was aware that she had knowledge of what was going on in the political world. I would like here to pay tribute to her wonderful discretion, and to the excellent influence which she always exercised over the king. She never utilized her knowledge to her own advantage, or to that of her friends; and I never heard her repeat an unkind word against anyone. It would have been difficult to find any other lady who would have filled the part of friend of King Edward with the same loyalty and discretion."

Friends of Camilla Parker Bowles would echo those sentiments at dinner parties and in private conversations almost a century later. As Sir Philip Magnus noted: "The truth is that in Alice Keppel the king had found not only a woman who . . . would excite him physically as well as relaxing him mentally (a rare combination in itself). On top of that he had found a mistress who could cherish him as fondly as a wife. No man, not even a monarch, could have asked for more."

There were other mistresses, of course—the Princesse de Sagan, the Countess of Warwick, and the actress Lillie Langtry among them—but it was with Alice that Edward was able to find the most profound relationship: She was universally known as La Favorita. What was remarkable was the tolerance of both Queen Alexandra and George Keppel—only once did the queen slip from saintly forbearance, as the historian Christopher Hibbert reported: "One day . . . glancing out of the window at Sandringham, she caught sight of Mrs. Keppel returning with the king in an open carriage. Mrs. Keppel had become rather stout by then and the sight of her imposing bosom alongside the rather corpulent figure of the king suddenly struck the queen as ludicrous. She called her lady-in-waiting to come and share the view and burst into peals of laughter"—not something Princess Diana was able to do in a later generation.

Until Edward's death in 1910, Alice Keppel occupied an equal place in the king's innermost circle along with his financial guide, Sir Ernest Cassel; his adviser on military affairs, Sir William Esher; Lord Fisher, the First Sea Lord; Lord Hardinge; his private secretary, Sir Francis Knollys; and the Portuguese ambassador, the Marquis Luis de Soveral. Remarkably, not only did the upper echelons of society open their arms to accept her, but so too did the queen. At a house party at Chatsworth, the Duke of Devonshire's seat, in January 1904, the king and Mrs. Keppel, "with lovely clothes and diamonds," played bridge in one room while the queen was entertained with songs and music elsewhere. Nor, judging by the queen's unusual liveliness, was she in the slightest put out to be sharing a roof with her husband and his mistress.

Though Alice—like Camilla—hosted private dinners for her paramour, her public self-effacement was complete. Only when she ventured abroad with the king could she be treated as an equal. Edward's biographer, Gordon Brook-Shepherd, declared that in Biarritz, "Alice Keppel was Queen." For a month or so each year, from early March to early April, the couple would hold sway in the French seaside resort, he staying in a suite of rooms in the Hotel du Paris while she was welcomed at the Villa Eugenie, the luxurious home of Sir Ernest Cassel.

They would meet each day at a quarter past twelve and together would stroll along the promenade, recognized by all and hindered by none. Indeed, some illustrated French papers even went so far as to airbrush out the features of Mrs. Keppel whenever she was photographed with the king.

Then they would invariably lunch in his suite at the Hotel du Paris where, according to one historian, both drank copiously. The soft Atlantic weather, the French cuisine, and the absence of protocol allowed the king to unwind and give his full attention to his companion, paying her the compliment of treating her as an equal.

"Edward VIII thought too highly of Alice to subject her to the indignity of a clandestine existence," wrote Theo Aronson, though perforce this courtesy could only be extended in a sympathetic environment. The king could never take Alice on his annual visit to Marienbad, where in the course of his so-called "spa diplomacy" he would meet political and royal figures from all over Europe, and where a veil would have to be drawn over her presence. But he did take her on several occasions to Paris, where she forged an alliance with the ex-Empress Eugenie, widow of Napoleon III.

It was in Biarritz, however, where the king's life started toward its close. He arrived there in March 1910, after an unusual altercation with Queen Alexandra over the excursion which, by now, was as regular a fixture as the Glorious Twelfth was for him to pick up his gun. He had caught a chill in Paris, and Alice nursed him until his health returned. Their sojourn in Biarritz was much longer than usual—seven weeks—and the longest continuous period the couple had ever spent in each other's company.

His arrival back in Britain in late April prompted another chill, which turned to bronchitis: Within a week his life was all but over. Perhaps because of the exceptional intimacy they had shared on their recent holiday, perhaps because of the lengthening years of their relationship—they had been insep-arable now for twelve years—Alice vehemently asserted her rights, as she saw them. For six days while the queen, alerted to the emergency, was hurrying home from a holiday in Corfu, Alice attended the king at Buckingham Palace. On Alexandra's arrival Alice sent her a letter which Edward had written her at the time of his appendix operation in 1902, which stated that "if he were dying he felt sure that those about him would allow her to come to him."

Alexandra, faced with the unexpected demise of her husband, was violently opposed to the idea, but the clamorous Alice was eventually allowed into the room where the dying king lay to see her lover once more. Edward insisted that the two women kiss as an act of reconciliation, to which the queen frozenly assented. But as the monarch's condition deteriorated, a resistant and by now hysterical Alice was removed from the room.

Lord Esher wrote afterwards: "Altogether it was a pitiful and rather theatrical exhibition, and ought never to have happened." The queen added, bitterly: "I would have not have kissed her if he had not bade me."

In bereavement Alice was inconsolable—her daughter Sonia wrote: "A pall of darkness hung over the house, blinds were drawn, lights were dimmed, and black clothes appeared, even for me, with black ribbons threaded through my underclothes." The king had made provisions, through Cassel, for his mistress to buy a villa in Italy, but it was to be fifteen years before she did so. Instead she took her entire family on a tour of Ceylon and the Orient, returning two years later to a new house in Grosvenor Square.

Life without her lover went on for another thirty-seven years—in 1925 she finally purchased a house in Florence, escaping to England when the Second World War broke out and returning when peace was declared. On 11 September 1947 she died, aged seventy-eight, of cirrhosis of the liver.

She had never once been known to be indiscreet about her relationship with the king, and never kept a diary. Her dedication to him was utter and complete.

George Keppel followed his wife to the grave within weeks; it was said he could not see the point of living without her. They had been married for fifty-six years.

As one famous life came to its close, another had just begun. Alice Keppel's granddaughter Rosalind, married to a dashing army officer called Bruce Shand, gave birth on 17 July 1947 at King's College Hospital in London to a daughter, Camilla. History was about to repeat itself.

Seventeen years later, when the gossip columnists were looking round for a suitable label for the debutante Camilla Shand, they came up with the phrase "building boss Lord Ashcombe's niece." The Ashcombes, whose family name is Cubitt, were known as the people who built Belgravia and made the Dukes of Westminster rich. As with all legends this was only partially true, but it served as an identity tag for those who were unfamiliar with Camilla's rich ancestry.

Back in the eighteenth century in the little town of Buxton in Norfolk, documents first recorded the existence of the Cubitt family: The name derives from the Anglo-Saxon, meaning "elbow." Thomas Cubitt, one of a widespread Norfolk yeoman family, was a tenant farmer living at Mayton Hall and working for Lord Yarmouth. It was debated whether his son William was "prodigal or incompetent," but either way by 1772 he was poverty-stricken and moved to Swannington, five miles away.

By the end of the eighteenth century records were more comprehensive and there emerges a Thomas Cubitt, described as a master builder and "the penniless son of a Coltishall farmer." Having trained as a carpenter he married and fathered twelve children, as well as establishing a thriving builder's business which was ultimately responsible for the construction of some of London's finest streets in Belgravia and beyond. Much of the Grosvenor estate, including the ultimate in grandeur, Eaton Square, together with Pimlico and a portion of the lesser suburb of Clapham, was his responsibility, though a great deal of the work was subcontracted: Cubitt's aspirations rose above mere construction and focused more on the social quality of the work. Grander commissions followed, including the creation of Osborne, Queen Victoria's palatial summer house on the Isle of Wight, and the remodeling of Buckingham Palace.

Cubitt's origins were humble, his ascent quite breathtaking. He became an adviser to Prince Albert and, unusually for one in trade, was recommended for a peerage. He died before it could be conferred, and the title was given instead to his son George. The family's arrival in the nobility took two generations, by which time they had settled in Surrey. It was Roland, the third Lord Ashcombe, who wedded Alice Keppel's and King Edward's daughter, Sonia: They were married for twenty-seven years until the union was dissolved in 1947, the year that Alice and George Keppel died, and Camilla was born.

But if Camilla's ancestry on her mother's side, with its roots in Scottish royalty and Dutch nobility, was gilded and wreathed in the aroma of love and intrigue, her father's ancestors had an equally fascinating tale to tell. The Shands started life in Scotland, too—though as merchants, not kings. By the late eighteenth century John Shand was established in a minor way in business, to be followed by his son Alexander Garden Shand. As Camilla's Edmonstone ancestors were being raised to the baronetcy, Alexander was making his own way upward by marrying an heiress, Isabella Morton, on 5 June 1809. She brought to the marriage an estate in Banff- shire, and after six years of marriage produced a son, Hugh Morton Shand.

But the wealth Alexander had so assiduously cultivated during his lifetime, and might reasonably have passed to his son and heir, disappeared overnight. Isabella having prede- ceased him, he made a deathbed marriage to his housekeeper and effectively dispossessed the son. So Hugh joined the army and sailed for India, as so many of similar backgrounds and financial circumstances did in the high days of Empire. Imbued as he was with his father's business acumen, it was not long before he established a trading company which brought the inevitable profits from the cornucopia of the Indian subcontinent. Returning to London, he bought a complete terrace of houses in Edwardes Place, Kensington, and the wealth he generated has effectively kept the family ever since.

For Hugh, marriage could wait—fortune came first; so it was not until he was forty that he took a wife. He chose Edrica, the daughter of the portrait painter Joshua William Faulkner, and the wedding took place in London in 1855. By now the family was firmly based in London and three sons were born in a short space of time. The eldest, Alexander Faulkner Shand, was born on 20 May 1858 in Leinster Gardens, Bayswater. Educated at Eton and Peterhouse, Cambridge, where he read law, he went on to train as a bar- rister, picking up an honorary LLD at St. Andrews. But he was never called to the Bar: instead his life took a bohemian turn. His life became increasingly hedonistic, and soon he joined the set which evolved around Beatrice and Sidney Webb. Economists and social reformers, the Webbs laid the foundations of the Britain's Fabian Society and set out to alter the country's sociopolitical system, and while in this they may have failed, they did succeed in creating the *New Statesman* as a voice of the intelligent left.

Under this influence Alexander Shand became interested in the nascent study of psychology and wrote a book, *The Foundations of Character,* outlining his theories. He became engaged to Constance Lloyd, a slim, graceful, and violet-eyed English beauty; but at the age of twenty-four she met and fell in love with the notorious homosexual Oscar Wilde. Constance and Wilde finally married when she was thirty-three, but Alexander had already found another wife in the form of Augusta Mary Coates, whose paternal family had been doctors in Bath for five generations and whose mother was a member of the Hope shipping family from Liverpool.

The marriage was not a happy one: Alexander's lifestyle was that of a dilettante while his wife, who bore him a son, Philip Morton, was religious, straitlaced, and energetic. Constantly engaged in the pursuit of good works but personally "vague and hopeless," according to some who knew her, she expressed concern over the upbringing of her son but then largely left that responsibility to nannies.

Philip Morton followed his father to Eton and went on to King's College, Cambridge, before starting a lifelong love affair with France at the Sorbonne. He went to visit his grandfather in Florence, where Alice Keppel was soon to make her home, before embarking on a multifaceted career which saw him become one of the most influential writers on modern architecture of the age, and one who was instrumental in introducing modern architecture to Great Britain. He counted among his friends many of Europe's leading architects, including Walter Gropius, Le Corbusier, and Wells Coates. Philip was a prolific writer and an acclaimed authority on food, and in particular wine—an enthusiasm he shared with his father and grandfather, and which he was to pass on to his son. He also wrote copiously about apples, and set up the Fruit Group at the Royal Horticultural Society. His character, like his career, was ever changing—his friend Sir John Betjeman, later Poet Laureate, described him as "a man of compelling charm," but there was also a collection of enemies and broken marriages.

An extrovert, raconteur, and eccentric, he annoyed many of his associates with his outspokenness: His impatience and intolerance were legendary. His politics were described as "red" by some—he voted for Labour in the 1945 election—but as "right wing" by others. Certainly he bore all the hallmarks of upper middle class intolerance—he was racist, sexist, and anti-Semitic—but in matters of intellect he was said to be enlightened.

His rackety existence, numerous affairs, and general disregard for life's rules inevitably caused a falling-out with his father, and ultimately led to his being disinherited. In fact a clause in his father's will specified that if any of the grandchildren gave money to their father they themselves would be disinherited.

He was married four times, first to Edith Marguerite Harrington, in April 1916. Exactly nine months later a son, Bruce Shand—Camilla's father—was born. Philip returned to the war—he served "a brief and undistinguished service" in the Royal Field Artillery—and that, effectively, was the end of the marriage. Edith remained close to Philip's parents, and Bruce was brought up by his grandparents with the assistance of a number of boarding schools.

In 1920 Bruce's parents were divorced—whereupon Edith, the daughter of an accountant, became engaged to a golf course designer and left for the United States. The child, still only three, was thus effectively deserted by both parents.

By the time Bruce was six his father was living in France; father and son were not to meet again until 1935 when he was eighteen, and then only by reason of Alexander Shand's death.

At the time of the 1920 divorce Bruce's father met and married Alice Tunnere. Within a few short months a daughter, Doris, was born—but the marriage was soon over. By 1926 he was living in Lyons and obtained shares in a velvet-making mill. That year he married a Frenchwoman, Georgette Avril, whose family owned the mill, but that, too, ended in divorce with a great deal of publicity in the French press and the judge directing Shand to "turn his attentions to another country."

He swallowed the rebuke and headed for England. There, in 1931, he married Sybil Sissons, the daughter of a Wey-bridge solicitor, and at last found contentment. With his wife he served during the Second World War at the admiralty in Bath before returning to Lyons, where he died in 1960.

His stepdaughter from this marriage was to become Lady Stirling, wife of the architect Sir James Stirling; and with Sybil he had a daughter, Elspeth Rosamund Morton Shand. To her he dispensed a single piece of advice: "It does not matter whom you marry as long as he isn't a politician, a lawyer, or a Welshman." Elspeth's husband, the future chancellor of the Exchequer Sir Geoffrey (now Lord) Howe, was all three. As a privy councillor and uncle by marriage to Camilla Parker Bowles, Sir Geoffrey was able to offer firsthand advice in the crises which were to billow up in the years ahead.

By comparison with his father's wayward lifestyle, Bruce Shand devoted himself to a life constrained by convention. Though he may have expected to go to Eton, the decision was taken by his grandmother to send him elsewhere. "She was anxious that I should not go to Eton where both her husband and son were set on the road to modest intellectual prowess," Bruce Shand later recalled. "Rather illogically, and I think unfairly, she attributed the plethora of wives, four in all, that my father collected to the influence of that seat of learning."

His grandmother Augusta may have been right. Bruce went to Rugby ("a school I cordially disliked") and his life thereafter was a model of rectitude. After Rugby there was a brief spell in France before he went to a crammer in Pimlico. He was accepted by the army and joined the Royal Military Academy in 1935.

His heroic exploits with the 12th Lancers, a cavalry regiment, in the Second World War are racily described in his memoirs, *Previous Engagements*. He earned the Military Cross twice, and was wounded and taken prisoner by the Germans in 1942. On his release from Spangenburg Prison at the end of the war he met the twenty-four-year-old Rosalind Cubitt, whose father would shortly become the third Lord Ashcombe, and in the euphoria of a capital city released from the constraints of war, the couple married at St. Paul's, Knightsbridge, in the bitter chill of January 1946. Typically for this gallant soldier, based at Bovington Camp, no close members of his family turned up for the ceremony.

In the space of the next five years three children were born—first two girls, Camilla and Annabel, then a boy, Mark. In adulthood Mark Shand was to lead an unstructured life more reminiscent of his Shand ancestors than the Cubitts or Keppels. Born when Camilla was four years old, he was educated at Milton Abbey, a substitute for the academically more demanding Eton, before plunging with enthusiasm into London life: His quite exceptional good looks and laconic style made him an essential adjunct to every fashionable party.

Eschewing the university and the armed services, Mark Shand took a fine arts course at Sotheby's before adopting a freelance career as an art dealer, at one stage specializing in the art deco period. By the time he was twenty-two, according to the London gossip columnists, he was enjoying a liaison with Princess Lee Radziwill, sister of Jacqueline Onassis, who was twenty years his senior. The relationship evolved from a 1971 house party in Barbados given by Mark's uncle Lord Ashcombe for Jackie, Lee, and others; the month-long sojourn among close friends was otherwise most notable for the near drowning of John-John Kennedy, then aged ten, in Glitter Bay.

The house party was also attended by Camilla, who took along for company her flatmate from Ebury Street, Virginia Carington—a decision which resulted soon after in Lord Ashcombe, known as Mad Harry, proposing marriage to Virginia, despite a twenty-two-year age difference: Clearly the Barbadian air had special qualities for dissolving the generation gap.

While staying at Princess Lee's house in the West Indies, Mark met Caroline Kennedy, then a schoolgirl, and encouraged her to come to London to undertake the same fine arts course he had studied. When she arrived in Britain, the free-wheeling Shand was enjoying a relationship with an American actress called Barbara Trentharn, who was later to marry John Cleese. But while the eighteen-year-old daughter of the assassinated president was in London—and just about the time his sister Camilla, then still single, was falling in love with the Prince of Wales—Mark embarked on a romance with her.

If alerted to their children's latest fancies, and not every parent is, Major Shand and his wife Rosalind must for a moment have marveled that, of three children, one should be dating the offspring of a queen and another the offspring of a U.S. president.

The relationship flourished despite Miss Kennedy being involved in two bomb incidents—first when a car bomb exploded outside the house where she was staying, then again when she moved to the Onassis family flat in Mayfair where another explosion occurred. Mrs. Onassis was reported to have pleaded with Caroline, halfway through the Sotheby's course, to come home. When she refused, Jacqueline requested special protection for her daughter, through the American Embassy. She was said to have been beside herself with anger when Scotland Yard informed her that only top-risk targets enjoyed personal protection, and that Caroline must walk the streets unguarded like anyone else.

Caroline stayed the course, enjoying Shand's attentions so much she sewed him a pair of boudoir slippers, but the relationship did not survive her return to the United States. Nevertheless Mark remained friendly with the family while moving on to his next conquest, Bianca Jagger, whose marriage to Mick Jagger had recently ended in divorce.

By now he was the hottest ticket in town, and in February 1979 the *London Evening News* asked: "Is This the Sexiest Man in London?" It pointed out that Bianca Jagger, who had been his date for the past year, was fascinated by his expertise in aikido and the tattoo of a snake on his body; the newspaper raved about "his shaggy locks, Nureyev hips and casual, bored manner." These attributes then earned the attentions of American heiress Avril Payson Meyer, whose mother Sandra had been married to the British publisher Lord Weidenfeld, and the actress and model Marie Helvin, who had recently separated from the photographer David Bailey.

But as he matured Mark Shand sought out new conquests

of a different variety. His life had changed after a dangerous canoe trip into the headhunting backwaters of Indonesia and before long he had become immersed in the plight of the elephant. Riding across India on one convinced him of their endangered nature and he wrote *Travels with My Elephant*. It was a best-seller, earned him the title Travel Writer of the Year, and moved him toward a different class of writing and away from a previous stab at authorship, a travel book called *Skullduggery,* with photographs by world-famous war photographer Don McCullin, described by one reviewer as "a boys-together book—lots of drinking, hangovers, constipation, nights on the town."

In 1990 Mark married the actress Clio Goldsmith, niece of the financier Sir James and the daughter of the ecologist Teddy. An article in a London newspaper in 1994 suggested that, at forty-two, he had finally found a purpose in life. "Now it's time to put something back," he mused. "I've taken all my life."

Her critics, Princess Diana foremost among them, might say that Mark's sister Camilla had yet to learn that particular lesson.

Chapter Three

From Birth to Ambition

<hr/>

Though later she adopted the additional Christian name Rosemary in deference to her Cubitt grandmother—Edward VII's daughter—she was named at birth as plain Camilla Shand.

Her recently demobilized father, Bruce, no doubt too busy during the summer of 1947 with a new and unprofitable career as an educational films representative, left the task of registering the birth to his wife, Rosalind. Up to and about five days after the birth at King's College Hospital, it was she who walked to the Lambeth Central office to fill out the necessary paperwork to register her firstborn. The couple had yet to celebrate their second anniversary.

Handsome and urbane, Shand cut a raffish figure prior to his marriage, running with a much faster set than his Rugby contemporaries. His new friends were higher-born, but such was his natural charm he was soon absorbed into the sleek existence of St. James's club land, becoming a member of the two-hundred-year-old Boodle's in his early twenties. This life of splash and dash brought him into financial difficulties from "frequent and expensive dinners at the Mirabelle, nights at the Four Hundred, and considerable sociable drinking at the Ritz Bar" and a committee of friends were forced into sorting out his shaky finances while he once again headed for war. But he never lacked companionship: "One seemed to see friends everywhere and it would have been difficult to be lonely," he observed, adding wryly, "and anyway the Americans had not yet arrived"—the inference being that London's best girls were still available.

But marriage to the Honorable Rosalind Cubitt, daughter of the third Lord Ashcombe, followed swiftly on his return to England. Both individuals brought a private income to the marriage, but future employment was always going to be necessary. The couple settled in to a rented home, the Manor House at Westdean, set high in the Sussex Downs above the English Channel.

Camilla was four months old when the nation finally shook off the burden of war to celebrate the marriage of Princess Elizabeth to Prince Philip of Greece. In London, such was the frenzy of excitement over the forthcoming spectacle—somehow an embodiment of all that the nation had been fighting for—that seats on the processional route were being resold for the modern-day equivalent of £35,000. At Buckingham Palace, a series of glittering parties, the like of which had not been seen for a decade, took place: At one, an Indian maharajah became belligerently drunk and physically attacked the Duke of Devonshire, and Field Marshal Smuts, casting his eye across a sea of tiaras, turned to Queen Mary and enthused: "You are the big potato; all the other queens are small potatoes." At another, Princess Juliana of the Netherlands, dancing with Elizabeth's uncle, the Duke of Gloucester, slipped to the floor "large and plump and gasping" so that everyone froze, including the royal family, until she was hauled into a vertical position once again.

In Sussex, the population celebrated at a rather more sedate pace, with a telegram from the Mayor of Lewes, Alderman Whittington, deemed as the most fitting way to mark the occasion. A thousand local schoolchildren crammed into the town hall for tea; and near the Manor House a celebratory bonfire was lit, though in the aftermath of war there was some difficulty in finding material worthy of the occasion. Gabriel, the ancient bell in the market tower, was rung for an hour during the wedding, distracting the denizens of the Crown Hotel who were trying to watch the proceedings, without too much success, on a prototype television set.

The royal wedding, which so instantly set the nation aglow after the long dark years, had been engineered by Lord Mountbatten, who, a generation later, was to play a part in providing sanctuary for Queen Elizabeth's as yet unborn son and the blond-haired little girl still too young to recall any of these heartwarming events. From the obscurity of rural Sussex, this child would, thirty-four years later, share the bed of another future sovereign in the hours running up to an even more famous royal wedding.

When Camilla was sixteen months old, the nation celebrated the birth of an heir to the throne. Prince Charles arrived on a cold, raw, moonless November evening in the Buffi Room of Buckingham Palace, in marked contrast to the efficient but overcrowded and under-resourced surroundings in which Miss Shand had been born. But like Camilla, as a citizen of the welfare state, he received his ration card, free milk allowance, Ministry of Food orange juice and cod liver oil—and he was inoculated against diphtheria.

Barely had the nation settled down from the excitement of a future king's birth when another baby girl, Annabel, was born to Bruce and Rosalind Shand, again at King's College Hospital in London. A few weeks later—after the birth had been registered—another name was tactfully remembered and added, so that she became Sonia Annabel Shand, after her grandmother. Two years on, a brother, Mark Roland (named for Lord Ashcombe), was born. The family was now complete.

Pretty and with long blond hair, Camilla was a lively child who made friends easily. Her first school—Dumbrells, at Ditchling—was three miles from the Shands' new home, a former rectory at Plumpton called the Laines.

The regime at Dumbrells corresponded with the age: tough, resolute, unswerving; yet its driving force was Victorian. And with good reason—the influence of its co-founders, Edith and Mary Dumbrell, who started the school in 1885, still hung in the air sixty-five years later when Camilla was first pushed through its doors. Their protégé, Miss Knowles, was now headmistress, but their indelible presence was everywhere. Nothing had changed—the place was a time capsule, frozen in the days of Queen Victoria, grimly hanging on to values and virtues which had long since perished. One of Camilla's teachers, Miss Vera Clarke, chillingly summed up the school and its pupils: When the children came at four and a half, she asserted, the first thing they had to learn was the meaning of the word no.

Today's children, vouchsafed Miss Clarke soon after Camilla had fled the school, were more independent, much noisier, and lacked consideration. They were inclined to be superficial, lacking in depth of thought, and, living in a perpetual rush, tended to act on impulse. They spelt badly, were unable to retain knowledge, and on no account was one ever to curry favor with them.

"Discipline was strict," recalled one old girl. "It was decreed that any possession found lying about must be worn by the culprit for a whole day, including mealtimes. One of the older girls came to lunch wearing three hats; a younger one was sadly hampered by a large sewing basket tied to her waist."

The five-year-old Camilla was terrified by a large "crucified" bat with wings outstretched which had pride of place in the entrance hall of the school, which was furnished with a wide variety of stuffed animals in glass cases. Old girls talked with bravado of the days when they were turned out of bed at 6:30 and forced to take a cold bath. There was no central heating in the bedrooms, on winter mornings the ice had to be cracked in water ewers, and chilblains were a regular occurrence. At 7:30 the bell would ring for "some violent exercises" which continued for twenty minutes until there was a respite for prayers.

Spartan is an insufficient description of this kind of regime for young girls newly away from home; but instantly the young blonde showed her mettle. Contemporaries particularly recall the cold, and her ability to withstand it. Because of the lack of heating, pupils wore Wellington boots all year round—a youthful fiction at the time was that this was because snakes permanently infested the orchard.

A fellow pupil from that period remembers: "A school inspector came and was dumbstruck. He never knew such a place could exist. The school was so harsh I used to say that a child who could cope with Dumbrells could cope with anything."

Back at home, life at the Laines revolved around horses: Bruce Shand had lived up to his cavalryman's calling in the years leading up to the war, owning a chestnut horse called the Bashaw upon which he hunted with the Cottesmore: Indeed his regiment was filled with ardent huntsmen. By the time Camilla was nine, Major Shand had sufficiently impressed the members of the Southdown Hunt by his dedication that he was made joint master. Camilla had her own pony and very soon was introduced to the debatable pleasures of fox-hunting over some of the most beautiful countryside in the whole of the south of England. The Southdown Hunt's highly individualistic master at the turn of the century, Norman Loder, was commemorated in Siegfried Sassoon's *Memoirs of a Fox-Hunting Man.*

At the age of ten, at the same time that Prince Charles was making his first tortured steps into boarding-school life at Cheam in Berkshire, it was decided that Camilla—now that she had mastered the brutal hair-shirt regime which characterized so much of the country's postwar private education—should be allowed to continue her schooling in London.

This rather unusual choice for an aristocratic country-based family—boarding school in the counties surrounding London would have been a more obvious choice—was made easier by the Shands' possession of a second home in South Kensington. The decision had little to do with her aversion to the excesses of Dumbrells for, from the start, it was clear that she shared Bruce Shand's courage under pressure. If her stay at Dumbrells seemed to resemble his own sojourn in Spangenburg a decade earlier, it only served to draw father and daughter closer together.

This was in marked contrast to Prince Charles, who, made of altogether different stuff, hated Cheam. One biographer noted: "The queen remembered him literally 'shuddering' with terror on the journey there. For nights after she left him he cried himself to sleep—quietly, into his pillow, hopeful that no one would hear him—in his wooden bed which, as his mother had observed before she left him, was too hard to jump on. The memory still hurts; it was, he said many years later, the unhappiest time of his life."

These two contrasting experiences give an early indication of the nature of the relationship which was to develop in adulthood between a resolute woman and a shy, self-questioning man; the one confident in her capacity to cope and make friends, come what may, the other forced by his position to lack spontaneous reaction or friendship. In addition the warmth of Camilla's home life, where she enjoyed a close and loving relationship with both her parents, contrasted sharply with the emotional wilderness Charles endured during those formative years, when he would greet his mother with a bow or a handshake; in later life he would bitterly observe that sometimes a whole day and night would pass before he could see the queen or she asked to see him.

So at the age of ten, with Charles miserably installed at Cheam, Camilla Shand set off for the fashionable Queen's Gate School in South Kensington, described at the time as "an establishment which provides wives for half the Foreign Office." Smart, but not the sort of place from which you might expect to meet a prince. Her father would take the bus from their South Kensington house to South Audley Street, Mayfair, where he had become a partner in the blue-chip wine merchant, Block, Grey and Block.

The sixth-form English teacher at Queen's Gate was Penelope Fitzgerald, later a Booker Prize–winning author. "When I arrived the school was changing," she recalls. "It had been a place where girls were taught how to write checks and play bridge, but by then academic standards were improving."

The ever-sporty Camilla—now briefly but trendily known as Milla—excelled at fencing and quickly improved her riding skills. London was an open door, and as the new decade of the 1960s approached she started to taste the daily freedoms which are only available to upperclass metropolitan children: tea at Fortnum's, a stroll with friends to Harrods, a walk on summer days through Hyde Park to watch the Household Cavalry ride by, their breastplates and medals gleaming in the sunlight. In rural Norfolk, many miles from such sophistication, a little girl named Diana Spencer was learning to walk and talk.

Even further removed, Charles was now stuck at Gordonstoun, the Scottish public school near Elgin, of all the brutal schools in an age of brutalism, the worst. Ross Benson, a contemporary, recalls: "He was bullied. He was crushingly lonely for most of his time there. One coterie of ruffians hanged the cat belonging to their housemaster, Major 'Hebbie' Downton, in retaliation for his attempt to curb their unruly behavior. At another house the seniors made a practice of greeting new boys by taking a pair of pliers to their arms and twisting until the flesh tore open. In all the houses boys were regularly trussed up in one of the wicker laundry baskets and left under the cold shower, sometimes for hours."

While Charles may have escaped falling victim to some of these wilder excesses he was by no means inviolate; and often psychological torture replaced the more customary physical torture the boys inflicted upon each other.

In one other respect, too, Camilla's and Charles's schooling differed. From the moment she arrived at Queen's Gate it was clear that the spirited Miss Shand had an eye for the boys; and they for her. Though it was a girls' school, it was perfectly possible in the course of the day to bump into boys from Westminster School or St. Paul's, as well as those not privileged enough to receive a London public school education. Camilla may not have been the most conventionally pretty girl in her class but she possessed "an inner glow," as one of her contemporaries described it: "When a boy hove into view she could turn on the headlights—and how!" In this, Camilla shared something with another royal mistress, Wallis Warfield. Fifty years earlier, noted Wallis's biographer, Charles Higham, fellow schoolgirls of the Baltimore belle "asked each other how she, the least pretty of them all, had managed to hook the handsomest boy they knew. Her secret was that she researched her prey. She knew how to praise, to build the adolescent male's ego." Here, indeed, was an eerie echo.

But at a time when teenage thoughts turn to the opposite sex, Charles found himself in an establishment where the very idea of sex was treated as a perversion. The philosophy of Gordonstoun's sexually repressed founder, Kurt Hahn, was "to kindle on the threshold of puberty nonpoisonous passions which act as guardians during the dangerous years."

A contemporary of Charles recalled: "There was little homosexuality at Gordonstoun . . . but there was very little heterosexuality either, and the school gave the prince no experience of dealing with women. Quite the contrary: To keep the royal virtue intact the usual sources of female companionship had been carefully closed off."

That included visits by younger sisters to the still all-male establishment; visits to or from nearby girls' schools; or exeats (weekend trips) to places with a promising female population. While Camilla was in London practicing, as all adolescent girls do, her charms on the opposite sex, Charles was four hundred miles away in a cold and cheerless community with not a girl in sight. In retrospect, it was a disastrous way of going about trying to raise a well-rounded, balanced, and gregarious child.

Back in London, Milla Shand was turning into what one former classmate described as "a bit of a tearaway." Another contemporary, later to rise to prominence as the sixties pop star Twinkle, recalled: "I always thought she was the coolest girl in the school. I remember her best when she was fifteen and a half. She was a very hoity-toity little madam, and she always looked great. She was what you would have called a Sloane Ranger type. We didn't get on that well because she was very into hunting and shooting and that kind of thing. We used to have mammoth rows about all that because I was totally against it.

"She knew that I wanted to be a pop star—she didn't have to say what she wanted to be. She had a confidence that I envied. She was someone who didn't need to be anything other than she was."

While some of the pupils were destined to become debutantes, traditionally virgins at that time, others took off on the hippie trail down the King's Road, eating in the Chelsea Kitchen just opened by a man called Terence Conran, or trying, and usually failing, to score some hash—as the phrase went—in the Picasso café.

But despite her undeniable sex appeal Milla wore unhip twin-sets and tweed skirts and appeared thoroughly conventional: She was not in the vanguard of girls excitedly pushing through the magenta doors of Biba's clothes shop in Kensington. "She didn't seem to mind being different from the others. It was odd, in a way, because girls can be cruel, but there was an inner something in Milla that others recognized as stronger," recalled a friend from that time. "She was looked up to by the other girls—a lot of them wanted to be her friend. She had a certain magnetism—I think simply because she knew she was going to be a success in life."

Compare that experience with Prince Charles, who found himself followed wherever he went at Gordonstoun by boys making slurping noises—anyone who socialized with him was accused of "sucking up" and therefore he found himself despised, and cocooned in isolation—and it is plain to see who at the end of their secondary education was equipped for adult life. "She would live the life that she wanted," said a Queen's Gate contemporary. "That's what Milla exuded."

In the summer of 1964, as Charles grappled with his O-level exams—he scored passes in English language and literature, Latin, French, and history—Camilla prepared to leave Queen's Gate. As academic careers go, it was not an outstanding one, and she would not be staying on for her A levels. Instead the plan was for her to travel, to Switzerland and to Paris, a city her father and paternal grandfather adored, to be "finished."

Though despised by educationalists as an upper-class cop-out, to persons of an inquiring mind, international travel and exposure to foreign languages and culture was a valid learning experience. Paris in the mid-sixties was a hotbed of revolution: The OAS, the right-wing Secret Army Organization led by outlawed French generals and colonels of the failed putsch in Algeria, started a bombing campaign against leading intellectuals. Their purpose was to blame the subsequent protests and demonstrations, which came in wave after wave, on the Communists. Once the atmosphere of protest was triggered, demonstrations became the fashionable thing: Cars were burned, pavements ripped up. On the Boulevard St. Michel one morning, a student coolly directed the traffic while the CRS riot police sat helplessly by: The students had gained control.

As Camilla traveled back to England, the protests followed her—there were riots in Grosvenor Square, and The Rolling Stones captured the spirit of the age with their song "Street Fighting Man." The Beatles wrote "Revolution," but it transpired that the song was against, rather than for, radical change. Bob Dylan played the Royal Albert Hall, round the corner from Camilla's house, and was booed hysterically when he put aside his folk songs, strapped on an electric guitar for the first time, and crashed into the opening chords of his anthem "Like a Rolling Stone."

Camilla's return was followed, inevitably, by her debut in the London season. This strange, complex, and once courtly ritual had diminished somewhat in status since its heyday in the Edwardian era. The fact that the debutantes were no longer received at court by the queen had taken away some of its prestige, yet if there was a focus and a purpose, it was toward the House of Windsor and the continuity of the class system. Whatever reduced status it may have enjoyed in the new egalitarian Britain of socialist premier Harold Wilson, those white-clad virgins who trooped the large, wheeled cake into the ballroom of the Grosvenor House Hotel in Mayfair on the occasion of Queen Charlotte's Ball would have thought themselves a cut above the debutantes who, fifty-one years before, attended the Bachelors' Cotillion at the Lyric Theater in Baltimore. But they were wrong, for from both events emerged into the world a mistress, and more importantly a lasting love, for an emotionally deprived Prince of Wales.

Camilla's official introduction to society occurred on a chilly March day in 1965 when her parents gave a cocktail party for her at 30 Pavilion Road, Knightsbridge, just behind Harrods. These hired rooms were a popular venue for parents whose London home was insufficiently large to cater for the 150 or so debutantes, debs' "delights," relations, and friends who traditionally attended this steppingstone. This was a time-honored ritual which started with tea parties, then progressed through cocktail parties, dinners, dances, and balls into the early autumn, when it was considered that the girls were sufficiently "out" to cope in the adult world.

A contemporary account, giving a flavor of the age, survives of this first step into the outside world. Mrs. Betty Kenward, the social diarist of *Harper's,* under her awesome nom de plume of Jennifer, intoned: "The Honorable Mrs. Shand's cocktail party for her attractive debutante daughter Camilla was another successful party.

"This was one of the very first of the debutante cocktail parties and might have been a bit sticky as, at the beginning of any season, the young people have not yet got to know each other, but both the hostess and Camilla did plenty of introducing and it went with a swing."

Outside, in the real world, India and Pakistan went to war over Kashmir. General Franco, pressing Spanish claims to Gibraltar, enforced a landward siege of the Rock. Ian Smith, the new prime minister of Rhodesia, issued a unilateral declaration of independence from Britain and its Commonwealth, and United States forces became even more deeply involved in the war in Vietnam, initiating a series of bombing attacks on North Vietnam. In the U.S., Malcolm X, the extremist black leader, was shot dead in New York, and civil rights agitation took hold with outbursts of violence in Watts, the Los Angeles suburb.

But in gentle Knightsbridge, champagne was poured and Camilla Shand came out. Among her guests were Rupert Hambro, of the banking family, who was shortly to become her lover, and a host of girls who in the fashion of the time wore scoop-neck dresses, pearls, and too much mascara. Lady Mary Gaye Curzon, the drop-dead blond daughter of Earl Howe who was generally agreed to be Deb of the Year, was there too. That year, 311 girls took part in the London season, dressing themselves in Mary Quant and making their miniskirted presence felt in the King's Road and Carnaby

Street. They danced to the old-fashioned music of Confrey Phillips and (down in the discos which were now de rigueur at every deb dance) to the headier sounds of The Beatles, The Stones, and The Walker Brothers.

But 1965 was the end of the old world. Sir Winston Churchill died, so too did T. S. Eliot and Somerset Maugham; The Beatles were made MBEs, collecting their medals from Buckingham Palace and smoking a joint in the lavatory while waiting for their moment with the queen; and Russian and American astronauts met in space.

The contraceptive pill became more generally available, and the sexual habits of a generation changed virtually over-night. According to the London diarist Nigel Dempster, it was during this debutante year that Camilla lost her virginity, to Kevin Burke, an independently wealthy nineteen-year-old who was then a handsome fixture on the deb scene. "She was terrific fun, immensely popular, and although she wasn't a beauty like Mary Gaye Curzon, she was attractive and sexy," Burke, son of the aviation chief Sir Aubrey Burke, recalled. "She was never tongue-tied or shy, and she always had some-thing amusing to say."

He added: "I remained with Camilla all that year. I suppose we were in love. Then she ditched me."

It may well be that Mr. Burke was the first, but a friend from Sussex wryly observed: "Camilla had been fooling around from an early age," and in any case it was time to move on from her first steady relationship. The next person she saw was the one she really wanted.

The Royal Horse Guards, commonly known as the Blues, were an integral part of the Household Cavalry—one of the great tourist attractions of London as they mounted guard in Whitehall on their black chargers. Alongside Bruce

Shand's 12th Lancers, the Blues had fought valiantly at El Alamein in the Second World War, but their battle honors went back to Waterloo and beyond.

Among their blue-blooded officers were numbered Viscount Somerton, shortly to become the Earl of Normanton, Lord Chetwode—and Lord Fermoy, whose sister Frances was about to divorce her husband and lose a bloody battle to keep her four children, who included a four-year-old called Diana Spencer.

All these soldiers, and others in the regiment, had been educated at Eton. But one who by virtue of his being Roman Catholic had not was Andrew Henry Parker Bowles, a twenty-seven-year-old lieutenant, recently promoted to the rank of local captain.

Possessed of striking, almost beautiful looks, Andrew may not have been an Etonian but his credentials were impeccable. His father, Derek, who had also served in the regiment and lived at Donnington Castle House near Newbury, was said to be the closest male friend the Queen Mother had. Certainly at her daughter's coronation in 1953, a place was found for the fourteen-year-old Andrew as a page to the Lord High Chancellor Lord Simonds: a deft genuflexion, at the Queen Mother's behest, to his ancestry.

The earls of Macclesfield emerged in the reign of King George I when Sir Thomas Parker, Lord High Chancellor of Great Britain, was first made Lord Parker, Baron of Macclesfield, then advanced five years later in 1721 to become Viscount Parker and Earl of Macclesfield—though this success was later tainted when he was tried by his peers on charges of corruption, and found guilty.

The sixth earl's son Algernon married the daughter of Lord Kenyon, who had the distinction of being a lord-in-waiting to Queen Victoria, King Edward VII and King

George V. Their son Eustace married in 1913 an heiress called Wilma Bowles, daughter of Sir Henry Ferryman Bowles, upon whose death the Parker Bowles name emerged. But by bloodlines and marriage Andrew Parker Bowles was also connected to other great families—the earls of Derby and Cadogan, the dukes of Marlborough, and, indeed, the Queen Mother herself through the earls of Strathmore. His mother, Dame Anne, was a close friend of the queen, and Chief Commissioner of the Girl Guides, and through her family, the de Traffords, Andrew was able to trace his ancestry back to the twelfth century.

All this was handy for a serving cavalry officer in a senior regiment and was in marked contrast to Bruce Shand's humbler—though more interesting—ancestry. It also helped when it came to the London season, for only young men of gentler birth were admitted to the parties given by the parents of each year's debutantes.

By the time he met Camilla, Andrew Parker Bowles was a little long in the tooth to be doing the rounds of the deb circuit again, and in the normal course of events would never have bumped into his future wife. But while he had been in New Zealand serving as an aide-de-camp to the governor general, Sir Bernard Fergusson, his younger brother Simon had escorted her to several parties: He had been working for Bruce Shand at Block, Grey and Block. Their relationship was platonic; but when Andrew met his brother's date it was a *coup de foudre*.

Nigel Dempster recorded: "In London, Andrew lived in a small bachelor apartment in Portobello Road in Notting Hill, and it was there that he and Camilla began what friends remember as 'a very hot affair indeed.' Andrew was already an accomplished lover and quickly proved himself to be an unfaithful one, too. He had a penchant for beautiful titled women, including Lady Caroline Percy, who was already the steady girlfriend of a baronet, and Lady Amabel Lindsay."

This aristocratic merry-go-round was a very sophisticated world indeed, far removed from the icy wastes of Gordonstoun where Prince Charles labored on in numbing isolation, desperate to escape the cheerless and antisocial environment into which his father had plunged him. Indeed, by the beginning of 1966, he had had enough. Despite much acclaim for his starring role in the school's production of *Macbeth,* he had done averagely or badly in virtually all other spheres, failing to make any of the school sports teams and promising little hope of an outstanding academic success when it came to A levels. His escape to Timbertop, an outstation of Geelong Grammar School 200 miles north of Melbourne, was a welcome relief. As Camilla Shand and Andrew Parker Bowles made their name as a dazzling couple around "swinging" London, the heir to the throne, still only seventeen, was living in the Australian outback learning for the first time in his life how to fend for himself. His chores included chopping and splitting wood, feeding pigs, cleaning out fly-traps, and sheep-shearing. Had Camilla met him in this passage between boyhood and manhood, there is little doubt she would have dismissed him from her mind: He was no match for a dashing cavalry officer and man of the world who was ten years his senior.

And yet, and yet . . . Kevin Burke, the jilted lover, remarked that during their yearlong association he was struck by how much store Camilla placed by the fact that her great-grandmother had been Edward VII's mistress. "She was always mentioning it, as if it were something almost talismanic," he later recalled. That part of her history was a deeply motivational force.

But all that was in the future. Parker Bowles, a gifted amateur jockey, took the same devil-may-care attitude toward his love life as he did toward his racing. Soon he was to break his back in a fall at Ascot, but as much damage might have befallen him from the way he conducted his love affairs.

Once he and Camilla became entangled in 1966 he ran her against his current love, Lady Caroline Percy, and everybody knew it. "I certainly knew I wasn't the only person being taken out by Andrew at the time," Lady Caroline said. "There were always other girls and older women. I never knew Camilla very well when we came out, but when I was with Andrew she would come up to me at parties and ask me what I was doing with her boyfriend. She was always doing this to girls at parties. But I got fed up with it and said to her, 'You can have him back when I've finished with him.'"

Nigel Dempster, in his book, *Behind Palace Doors,* shines considerable light on the army officer's helter-skelter love life whose complexity and variety meant that the couple had been lovers—on and off—for seven years before they finally married. While Camilla wore white for the wedding at the Guards Chapel, followed by a reception at St. James's Palace, she had participated in a love imbroglio worthy of a French farce or a cheap sex novel, depending on the reader's tolerance of those times. For it truly was the era of free love; and while its more vocal advocates tended to come in kaftans and long mustaches or miniskirts, it was not their province alone. In the Age of Aquarius, anyone could join in.

Certainly Andrew Parker Bowles, no hippie he, breathed the scented air of the sixties with relish. Possessed of a dazzling charm, outstanding looks, a brave athleticism, and private means, he found that few women could resist him. Before being seconded to New Zealand he had been engaged to Sue

Morley, the daughter of a brigadier, but it was a short-lived arrangement. Now he dropped Camilla Shand and picked her up at will, and she was powerless to do anything about it.

"Andrew behaved abominably to Camilla, but she was desperate to marry him. When I was with him I discovered he was also having an affair with a married woman," recalled Lady Caroline Percy. Camilla responded by bedding banking heir Rupert Hambro. "Rupert knew that their affair was futile because of Camilla's obsession with Andrew, but he liked her and knew they would always be friends," wrote Dempster. "He still remembers the masochistic glee she took in telling him about tricky situations Andrew's unfaithfulness sometimes caused. But she often saw the funny side of things afterward; her girls' talk always had the funniest lines and the best anecdotes."

In 1969 Parker Bowles was posted to Hobart Barracks near Hanover in Germany, which gave Camilla time to draw breath and look around. On his brief returns home over the next couple of years he was off again—this time in hot pursuit of Princess Anne, who at nearly twenty was eleven years his junior, and at the time involved with Brian Alexander, the son of war hero Earl Alexander of Tunis.

Anne, with a libido which matched the cavalry officer's, caved in to his charm and enjoyed a torrid relationship which gave both much cause for pleasure. But Parker Bowles's absence in Germany on duty and the fact that, as a Roman Catholic, he knew that he could never marry Anne without creating painful inner turmoil within the royal family, put a dampener on the relationship.

With time on her hands, Camilla started to spend her days at polo. Her friend from debutante days, Carolyn Gerard Leigh, was the daughter of the chairman of the Guards Polo

Club at Windsor, Colonel Gerard Leigh, and encouraged her to come along to matches.

Shortly before going up to Cambridge, Charles had played in his first polo tournament at Smith's Lawn, his side beating Captain Ronald Ferguson's in the final. While an undergraduate he joined the University Polo Club, as much out of his combination of reticence, natural introspection, and remoteness of position as because his father dictated it. He gained his half blue, and by the time he graduated, his handicap had gone from minus two to plus two.

He once explained: "I love the game. I love the ponies. I love the exercise. It's the one team game I can play. It's also a very convenient game for me—you can't just nip out of Windsor Castle and enjoy a soccer game."

What he omitted to add was that polo is an aphrodisiac, that the sport itself heightens sexual tension in the participants, and the women who follow it are fully cognizant of this, and that a secret language develops between player and spectator at the close of play which, fueled by Pimms or champagne, has provided many memorable encounters.

In addition polo was something at which the prince almost instantly excelled, and for once he was allowed to show off without inviting criticism from the press—indeed, such was the recondite nature of the sport that at Smith's Lawn, certainly in the early days, Charles was pretty much left alone by a puzzled Fleet Street who did not understand the rules and weren't interested enough to find out.

One further factor brought Charles to love the polo field: The women who watched were the right sort: well bred, tight-lipped, admiring, discreet. After the ham-fisted fumblings of his undergraduate days when he felt too embarrassed by the thought of who he was to proceed in the way that young men should, suddenly he was admired by beautiful women for himself, for his body and his horsemanship. Being Prince of Wales was just the icing on the cake—what the women were looking at was a fit, tough player in tight jodhpurs who clearly had a taste for danger.

And one of the women who was looking, and looking hard, was Camilla Shand.

Chapter Four

Sex, Lies, and Also-Rans

<hr/>

When Charles and Camilla finally met in 1971, at Smith's Lawn in the shadow of Windsor Castle, it was as if they had known each other for ever: certainly they already knew a lot of people in common. For example, Charles's first-ever "date" was with Marilyn Wills, the daughter of the queen's cousin Jean Wills, when they went to see *The Sound of Music,* at the age of fourteen. Marilyn went on to be one of the principal guests at Camilla's coming-out party at 30 Pavilion Road in 1965, and the pair remained close friends.

On taking up foxhunting, Charles had become devoted to the remarkable Ulrike Murray-Smith. This redoubtable huntress was the wife of one of Bruce Shand's closest friends at Sandhurst, George Murray-Smith, and between them this couple managed to foster a consuming passion for hunting in two generations—Shand and the Prince of Wales.

Another connection between Charles and Camilla was Nick Paravicini, a swashbuckling former Life Guards officer who was a towering presence on the Smith's Lawn turf and a friend of the prince. He had married, ironically, Andrew Parker Bowles's sister Mary Ann, who, while the cavalryman was abroad, had become good friends with Camilla. These were just three obvious connections—conversation came easily because of the many other friends and acquaintances they had in common, and it took very little time for the mutual attraction to grow. In addition to all this, Bruce Shand had made his own way to the fringes of the royal family by being nominated as a member of the Queen's Body Guard of the Yeomen of the Guard, the ancient group of stalwart former soldiers whose nineteenth-century uniform forms a colorful backdrop to the sovereign to liven up many a state occasion.

It was a fallow time in the prince's love life. After Lucia Santa Cruz and Sibella Dorman, his first two conquests, there had been no further sexual experiences. Since graduating from Cambridge in 1970 he had been pressed into service by a queen who at last felt she could show him off to the world—a visit to Ottowa was followed by a tour of Canada; then he was dispatched with Princess Anne to be guests of the U.S. president, Richard Nixon, in Washington. A tour which included Fiji, Gilbert, and Ellis Islands, Bermuda, and Barbados was followed by a trip to Paris to represent the Crown at the funeral of President de Gaulle. A brief trip to Kenya on safari with his sister was followed by further single-sex incarceration in the RAF at its Lincolnshire officers' college, Cranwell—so that by the summer of 1971 the young, fit, handsome prince was desperate for congenial and obliging female company. He was twenty-two, and had less experience of the opposite sex than the majority of males his age. Coupled with this a painful shyness, an inbuilt caution against being snared by an adventuress, and a general lack of knowledge of women's ways (which arguably he still possesses) stayed his hand when it came to making advances to the opposite sex.

"For the prince real life began with Camilla," says another Smith's Lawn fixture from that time, the Argentinean polo player Luis Sosa Basualdo. "He either met girls at polo or took them to polo. A favorite place was the Guards Polo Club."

With Charles's active support, polo was enjoying an upswing. Though still a fledgling spectator sport with a heavy emphasis on the military, it was, during the next decade (and particularly with the arrival of the Princess of Wales) to turn into a champagne-drenched, sponsored jamboree, adored by people who have never had the slightest intention of climbing onto horseback; but in the early seventies it was still the child of Earl Mountbatten, his nephew Prince Philip, and a few postimperial devotees.

But its popularity was growing: Within a couple of years polo would become an unofficial arena where the queen and her family could mix in informal circumstances with relatively ordinary people—those with a penchant for equine pursuits and who could follow the more esoteric aspects of the game, at least—and it was at Smith's Lawn that Captain Mark Phillips was to make his debut as a future member of the royal family.

Charles made a creditable show on the turf, encouraged by his father and Captain Ronald Ferguson (ultimately to rise to prominence as father of the future Duchess of York), and in 1972 was made captain of the Young England polo team. It was a consolation prize for Prince Philip losing his place in the England polo team through a wrist injury, which put him permanently out of the game. The pressure was on Charles to perform on the polo field, and he obliged. The girls loved it.

One of the stars of Smith's Lawn was the accomplished horseman, Andrew Parker Bowles. Often he would find himself drawn against Prince Charles's side in low-goal matches.

A habitue of the Guards Polo scene from that time recalls: "Andrew would often come to Smith's Lawn—he was an excellent player. About once a week he'd bring Camilla down by car. If Andrew was playing against Charles, she'd watch; otherwise she'd just go and watch Charles. She wasn't that interested in the game. She was very interested in hanging round Charles.

"What was astonishing was that he took any notice of her. There were plenty of glamorous women around, but she had holes in her jeans and looked a mess. Not exactly an oil painting."

"The relationship developed almost straight away—it took no more than a casual glance to see that something was going to happen," says another friend from that time. "There was an electric magnetism between them and even if they were standing some way away, you could tell from the intensity of their conversation and the way they looked at each other what the upshot would be. It was like watching two steam trains heading toward each other at full pelt."

Ironically the British press, determined to find a future bride for the prince, missed it completely. Charles's exploits in the saddle were covered sporadically, but so much was going on in his life at that time that the hallowed turf at Smith's Lawn was quite often given a miss. "And there was no one there who was going to call up the *Daily Mail* and tell them, 'Come quick, Charles looks like he's got himself a woman,' " said one polo regular. In addition royal coverage, as opposed to court reporting, had yet to develop as a tabloid art, and its greatest exponent, the *Daily Mirror*'s James Whitaker, had only just come on the scene.

But even before the 1971 polo season came to a close, Charles was forced back to duty. The regimen his father worked out as preparation for kingship which, as all recognized, was only a heartbeat away and could come soon or late—was tough, demanding, leaving little room or time to woo. As Whitaker reported: "[Charles] is a man who courted with flowers, tender words, a lot of hand-holding, and soft candlelight. At the end of the evening he would drop off a girl at her flat and then get on the telephone to her as soon as he returned to his own apartment at Buckingham Palace. For the next hour he would talk softly and lovingly to the girl. He would say how much he loved her, how much he savored the color of her eyes, the smell of her hair." All the things, in fact, he found impossible to say to the person direct—an unfortunate trait that would expose itself two decades later in the Camillagate Tapes.

But for now, there was no time for wooing. In the autumn of 1971 as he faced his twenty-third birthday alone and, he thought, unloved, he set out on the next stage of his hair-shirt career preparation. In the autumn he joined the Royal Navy as a sublieutenant and after a six-week induction course at the Britannia Royal Naval College at Dartmouth in Devon he set off for Gibraltar to join HMS *Norfolk*. For the next nine months if his thoughts were of Camilla Shand they had to be shared with the incessant noise and grinding turbines of the 5,600-ton guided missile destroyer.

The following May he earned a brief respite, being allowed by his senior officers to accompany his mother and father on a state visit to France. And, coinciding with the start of the polo season, Charles found himself ashore again undertaking courses at HMS *Dryad*, a shore establishment at Portsmouth. From there to Broadlands, the stately home of his "honorary grandfather," Earl Mountbatten, was a fifty-minute drive in his Aston Martin Volante. Throughout this period, in reaction to his father's persistent questioning over navy life, he preferred to seek refuge with Mountbatten—

himself an Admiral of the Fleet—and it was during this time that their relationship, adult to adult, flourished. Charles was able to discuss his love life (or lack of it) with Mountbatten, and though the old seadog had an eye on a self-aggrandizing dynastic alliance with one of his Knatchbull granddaughters, she was still too young and Charles had had no chance to sow his wild oats.

The polo season of 1972 allowed Charles further respite, and that was when the relationship with Camilla Shand was at last allowed to develop. But it was short-lived. Within months of his return from Germany, Andrew Parker Bowles realized that there was no future in his relationship with Princess Anne, and by the autumn she was seeing Captain Mark Phillips, an officer in the 1st Queen's Dragoon Guards. Charles's affair with Camilla, when it finally happened, was short, vigorous, and a dazzling revelation. "It finally made him a man," was the comment of one of Camilla's friends.

But despite all the lengthy telephone calls and whispered tendresses it became eminently clear that there was no future in it. Camilla's seven-year, on-off affair with Andrew Parker Bowles was too well known ever to remain a secret for very long, and the questionable mores of the time would not allow for a Princess of Wales who was "secondhand goods." That, almost singlehandedly, killed the idea of their having any future together; though in addition there was the question of Camilla's pedigree to be considered.

Although, in the New Elizabethan age, there were no apparent hard-and-fast rules about whom the young royals should marry—King George V had relaxed them sufficiently during his reign to allow his daughter to marry into the aristocracy rather than to some foreign prince, and the Duke of York did similarly, bringing the blood of the earls of

Strathmore into the royal line—it was assumed, if Charles were to marry an English girl, she would be highborn.

Though Camilla Shand was an aristocrat by virtue of her mother's lineage, there were discrepancies along the way, not least the rabid lesbian Violet Trefusis. And Bruce Shand's wayward ancestors, particularly his four times married father, would inevitably prove an embarrassment upon discovery.

These factors, together with the rather cruel fact that though possessed of a magnetic charm, Camilla was unphotogenic, meant that there was little future in the affair at that time. Camilla was aware of it from the moment she invited the prince into her bed—and in any event Andrew Parker Bowles, now putting all thoughts of Princess Anne from his mind, was ready for marriage.

"There was a school of thought at that time which said that Camilla only seduced Charles because Andrew had seduced Anne," one polo source said. "She was determined to show him that she could do as well in the royal pulling stakes as he'd done. There was always that element of pursuit by her, the feeling that she was determined to show him that she was as good as him, in no matter what."

If the affair between Andrew and Camilla, which had started so many years ago, was a battlefield, then a truce was called on 15 March 1973 when the couple announced their engagement. Andrew spent the day in a Berkshire nursing home hobbling around with the aid of a walking stick after a riding accident.

Four months later the couple were married at what one society magazine described as "the wedding of the year." The Guards Chapel in Birdcage Walk, a stone's throw from Buckingham Palace, was so crowded that three hundred extra chairs were added to its normal capacity of five hundred—

even then, late guests were forced to stand at the back. The groom appeared to have recovered from the effects of his stag night at White's, the superexclusive St. James's gentleman's club. "I've paid the damages bill," Andrew's brother Simon revealed nonchalantly. "The party got slightly out of control—there was a lot of broken crockery and glass, and chairs."

Princess Anne, now infatuated, however briefly, with Captain Mark Phillips—they would marry four months later—was present to see her former lover marry. If there was a twinge of regret, she would in the fullness of time ease its pain by returning to Parker Bowles's side after the collapse of her marriage.

Present at the ceremony too was the Queen Mother, Andrew's distant relation, and though Princess Margaret missed the service, she attended the reception across the park at St. James's Palace. On a boiling hot summer's day, Camilla looked cool and self-possessed as she finally achieved what she had waited seven years for. "She was wearing lashings of tulle, and diamonds in her hair," recalled one guest. "She sparkled as much as they did."

For the time being at least, it was over between Charles and Camilla. "There was never any question then of Charles marrying Camilla," recalled her friend, the former Carolyn Gerard Leigh. "He was much younger, simply a nice boy . . . Camilla was conscious of her select status but she never wanted to be queen." Not then, anyway.

One person not present at the wedding was Prince Charles himself. By early July he was aboard HMS *Minerva*, a Leander-class frigate, cruising the waters of the West Indies. If his thoughts dwelt on his lost love—and despite other versions of this tale it was Camilla who dropped him, not vice versa—they could not do so for long. At one stage *Minerva* called at Hamilton, Bermuda, and Charles strolled on the lawn of Government House with Sir Richard Sharples, the British governor. Within a week Sharples had been assassinated by terrorists on the same spot, and with *Minerva* due to call again for repairs, Charles was transferred briefly to the survey ship *Fox*.

The voyage went on to the Bahamas, where the prince represented the queen at their independence celebrations, and he put all thoughts of love from him by deep-sea diving in the shark-infested waters of the Caribbean or dancing until 5:00 A.M., with his ship due to sail at 6:00 A.M., in the nightclubs of Caracas, Venezuela.

While the newlyweds honeymooned, plans were being made at the admiralty for Charles which were likely to prove the prince's greatest alibi in the years to come, when a scurrilous and potentially damaging rumor emerged at the Guards Polo Club: that Prince Charles was the father of Camilla's son.

If true, the story would have a terminal effect on the future of the monarchy. Other kings and princes have fathered illegitimate children—only two generations before, both the Duke of Kent and, less convincingly, the former Prince of Wales, were supposed to have fathered bastards. Even the godson of Prince Philip, the Maidenhead-born Max Boisot, was rumored for over forty years to be the prince's natural son—a rumor which swirled along unchecked until 1988 when, with her son now forty-four and a professor of economics at the Euro-Chinese Business Center in Beijing, Philip's wartime girlfriend, the former nightclub owner Helene Cordet, issued a denial. She said that, although Philip had paid Max's fees through Gordonstoun, it was simply because at the time she was virtually destitute.

But it was unthinkable that such a thing could happen now (though why, it is hard to fathom: The bastard descendants of King Charles II are perfectly respectable figures in British society, carrying the dukedoms of St. Albans, Grafton, and Richmond and Gordon).

To those with a nose for scandal, however, it was perfectly possible. Camilla—as everyone at Smith's Lawn knew all along—had an affair with Prince Charles before her marriage. Before too long, within the space of a few months, she was once again engrossed with the prince: And since royal bastards are such a part of the fabric of British history, it seemed hardly surprising to those sophisticates in the know, barely worthy of note. Within this circle, the rumor spread and took wings.

Except this. It is true that Camilla gave birth to her son, Thomas Henry Charles (that last name another clue for the rumor mongers) on 18 December 1974, seventeen months after her wedding. It is also true that Charles agreed to be the boy's godfather. But that is where the connection ended, for exactly nine months before the child's birth, while Camilla was making Bolehyde Manor in Wiltshire a home for herself and her new husband, Lieutenant the Prince of Wales was halfway through a tour of duty as communications officer on HMS *Jupiter* on the other side of the globe. There is no evidence, in a period when he also accompanied the queen and Prince Philip to the opening of the Commonwealth Games in New Zealand, to support the notion that he found time to fly halfway round the world for a secret tryst with a woman who had rejected him for an older man—any more than there is evidence that she flew out to Australia and New Zealand to meet him at the various ports of call made by the *Jupiter*. But just because it wasn't true didn't mean the rumor went away—and by the time it emerged into the light of day, the public were ready to believe anything about Charles's relationship with Camilla.

In the early days of the Parker Bowles marriage, an attempt was made to conform to the idea of marital fidelity. But old habits die hard, and Andrew was not a man to turn aside the many opportunities that came his way. More importantly, close friends of Camilla could discern an ambition in her to maintain the powerful royal connection she had forged with her sex and her sympathy. Though only fifteen months older than Charles, she was both mother figure and sexual fantasy to the inexperienced prince—and she knew it.

But the couple lacked opportunity in those days and Charles became the "moving target" figure suggested by Earl Mountbatten. The honorary grandfather had already chided him about getting too serious about Camilla, according to his private secretary John Barratt, and encouraged him to sow his wild oats. There followed a period during which Charles experimented freely with women, almost never to their satisfaction. It has been suggested that, in order to increase his power over the prince, Mountbatten set up a "slush fund" in Nassau to take care of any difficulties arising from unfortunate entanglements with women—a fund which was said to have been called upon two or three times between late 1974 and mid-1979. While this cannot be entirely discounted—students of British royal history will recall similar arrangements made for Charles's wayward, bisexual great-uncle, the Duke of Kent—it is unlikely that Mountbatten would have raised the hundreds of thousands of dollars himself. In this late period of his life he was strapped for cash, with holes in his bedroom carpet and a rusting and dangerous car to transport him about. But it was a story people liked to tell, implying as it did that Charles was a wild sexual athlete.

Whatever the arrangements, Charles was now about to move into a restless period where his preparation for kingship was at the cost of personal happiness. From the insecurity of his own refugee childhood, Prince Philip was determined his son should be perfect in his appropriateness for kingship— that all matters, including personal happiness, should be put to one side in pursuit of this goal. In many senses this was an admirable ambition, despite its merely being fueled by the memory that a dilettante monarchy, such as the one into which he was born, is a short-lived monarchy. The fear that his son could turn out like some of his Greek royal relatives drove him on, and in the end Charles, though at the cost of mutual friendship with and respect for his father, came to see his point of view.

The rootless years between 1972 and 1980, looked at with the advantage of hindsight, bear witness to the lack of care and understanding devoted by parents and advisers to Charles's personal happiness. Some observers say that his haunting search for alternative philosophies and remedies was simply an outlet for his feeling of being unloved.

Between 1972 and 1980 Charles had a number of identifiable girlfriends, and sexual relationships with a number of other women. None of them, ultimately, was satisfactory. Those he felt strongest about sexually he cared less for personally. Those who seemed more on his spiritual wavelength failed to entrap him sexually. His relationships were a sorry mess, but instead of earning sympathy from his family, each new failure (described paradoxically by the press as a conquest) brought an increasing irritation from his father, who was anxious that the royal line should multiply without delay.

One woman who knew him well at that time reported: "He was excruciatingly shy (with women). I don't think he was happy doing what he was doing. He was using women, and he knew it."

Another woman who knew the prince then said: "He was a gentle, melancholic soul. There seemed to be such a loneliness, a strange desolation trapped inside him." It did not stop him falling in love—a quite usual reaction by those who feel themselves unloved. He had a nine-month relationship with Georgiana Russell, the daughter of Britain's ambassador to Spain, Sir John Russell, and a kinsman of the Duke of Bedford. Georgiana had a certain exotic quality by virtue of her mother's Greek background—she was contemporaneous with Prince Philip, though, being a commoner, she lasted longer in her homeland—and Charles was attracted by her sophistication: She was eighteen months his senior and worked for *Vogue* magazine.

This relationship was doomed to failure because Charles had yet to learn that women required more than an early declaration of love, followed by an unswerving march down his own particular path. He may have told them he loved them, but Charles had been alone so long he had lost the art of unselfishness. Georgiana Russell went missing after a freezing fishing trip to Balmoral where Charles carried on with the routine he had developed for himself over the years, one which he saw no reason to vary.

Stephen Barry, Charles's valet, recalled: "She was freezing cold and eating scraps because the prince was on one of his economy drives. I think she thought the week would be rather glamorous—a romantic interlude in the Highlands with her prince. Nothing of the kind. He was standing with his feet in icy water all day, while she was bored out of her mind. I thought then she was not going to last the course and I was right."

Georgiana was followed by Lady Jane Wellesley—a likely princess if ever there was one, or so Fleet Street thought. She was beautiful and poised and had known Charles since child-hood. Her father was suitably grand, being the eighth Duke of Wellington and direct descendant of Britain's most valiant soldier. The duke and the queen were close friends; Lady Jane had all the outward and visible hallmarks of a future Princess of Wales.

While this relationship endured, over three years or so, Charles's star remained in the ascendant with the nation. It looked as though he would be making his marriage vows before his thirtieth birthday, the period of grace he had ordained for himself. But in the end the relationship failed, despite the turnout of a crowd of ten thousand at Sandringham for the New Year of 1975 when an announcement seemed imminent.

"She appeared to pass muster on most counts, being aristocratic, lively, attractive, and thoroughly discreet, but Charles was never entirely sure about her," wrote his biographer Alan Hamilton. "He found her emancipated, tough, and radical in her views; indeed, she went on to work in the highly competitive world of television, and combined her BBC researcher's job with being her office representative of the National Union of Journalists. For Charles, in the end, she was too outspoken, too articulate, and too unwilling to accept a subsidiary role, although had she married the Prince of Wales her effect on his outlook would have been fascinating to behold."

Lady Jane's attitude was best summed up when she was subjected to the same kind of press interest which was to characterize Lady Diana Spencer's entry into the public awareness five years later. Instead of a demure smile, a bashful lowering of the eyes, and a helpful pause for the photographers before getting into her car, Lady Jane snapped when asked if she was to marry Charles. "I don't want another title," she said. "I've already got one, thank you." And with that, she was gone. Some thought Charles had proposed marriage and this had triggered her departure.

Charles's situation was a complex one. He had found his perfect partner in Camilla: In just about every respect she suited his selfish needs, shrewdly never asking anything, always giving. Their sexual relationship had resumed quite soon after the birth of Camilla's son Tom. But the affair was illicit and could never be condoned, and it was Charles's duty to soldier on and find himself a wife. If he took a cynical view of this aspect of his royal duty, it can hardly be surprising. Too much pressure and not enough freedom within British society was condemning him to a course he would later deeply regret.

The demoralizing search went on. And none came more demoralizing than Laura Jo Watkins. In March 1974 HMS *Jupiter* paid a courtesy visit to San Diego, home of the U.S. Pacific Fleet: Laura Jo was a tall, blond, stunning-looking part of the welcome committee. The daughter of Admiral James Watkins, an acquaintance of Earl Mountbatten whom he had met in Malta while serving with the U.S. Sixth Fleet, she fell for the prince and he for her. Mountbatten decided to improve the shining hour by inviting her to London to accompany Charles to the farewell party for Walter Annenberg, departing U.S. ambassador.

Charles then went on to invite her to hear his maiden speech in the House of Lords—a milestone for him, in that this would be where he put down his marker for history. The speech was about the better coordination of leisure facilities across the land: apparently uncontroversial, and certainly avoiding the major issues of the day, but actually a reasonably important long-term issue to which successive governments wished to apply neither policy nor resources. It was tailormade for Charles's burgeoning philosophy of looking after the nation's spiritual well-being.

But whatever effect he hoped to achieve was wrecked by

the presence of the delectable Miss Watkins in the gallery of the House of Lords. Leisure facilities do not make headlines; but a stunning blonde, and an American at that, do. And so the newspapers turned their magnifying glasses on the admiral's daughter, and before too long she was being described as "an unmarried Wallis Simpson"—a not very accurate parallel which stressed her nationality and the fact (which was left unsaid) that she was sleeping with the Prince of Wales.

This kind of crude analogy drove the Queen Mother, a lifelong foe of Mrs. Simpson, into paroxysms of rage. She blamed Mountbatten.

By now, nothing was going right—until Charles met another spectacular blonde, Davina Sheffield. If the nation was to have a chocolate-box Princess of Wales, this surely must be she: From whichever angle she was photographed, she was stunning. During the first nine months of 1976 she came increasingly to be seen on Charles's arm, after meeting the prince at a dinner party at Jane Wellesley's Fulham house in the summer of 1975.

A few weeks later, Charles invited her up to face the "Balmoral test" and she passed with flying colors. "Jane and Davina had been close friends, but they have not spoken since," said a friend at the time. Between that summer meeting and the New Year, Davina flew to Vietnam where she worked hard looking after sixty orphaned boys until Saigon fell to the Communists.

When she reemerged on Charles's arm, she was about as eligible as they came: always beautifully dressed, always ready with a smile for the cameras. But then, in September, came the crash—her former boyfriend, Old Harrovian powerboat designer James Beard, with whom she had lived in a cottage near Winchester, opened his mouth. He confessed they had a full sexual relationship, then added disingenuously: "I think

Prince Charles is a very impressive man and I am sure they will be very happy. I think she will make an extremely good queen and a magnificent wife."

With this last thought, Beard destroyed a nation's irrational hopes for a virgin bride, and the relationship was over. It is worth noting in passing that Davina had enjoyed the same circular relationship with Charles and his sister Anne as the Parker Bowleses: Her former boyfriend, Old Etonian Robert Rodwell, also used to escort Princess Anne. It was not enough to save her.

And so the escorts came and went. Those logged by an increasingly bewildered press included Lady Leonora Grosvenor and her sister Lady Jane, both sisters of the Duke of Westminster; Lady Victoria and Lady Caroline Percy, daughters of the Duke of Northumberland; Bettina Lindsay, daughter of Lord Balneil; Lady Cecil Kerr, daughter of the Marquis of Lothian; Lady Henrietta FitzRoy, daughter of the Duke of Grafton; Lady Charlotte Manners, daughter of the Duke of Rutland, and her cousin, Libby Manners; Angela Nevill, daughter of Lord Rupert Nevill; Louise Astor, daughter of Lord Astor of Hever; and Lady Camilla Fane, daughter of the Earl of Westmorland.

Though, at the time, these women must have seemed startlingly different from each other, they were drawn from one section of English society. They were all public-school-educated scions of aristocratic families, all imbued with the same conservative values, and all, ultimately, dull. The only exception was a brief tangle with Fiona Watson, daughter of the Yorkshire landowner Lord Manton, who, it subsequently emerged, had revealed all of her glorious 38-23-35 figure in *Penthouse* under an assumed name. It would not take a royal expert to calculate her fate once the news came out.

With Camilla he shared the intimate details of these fainthearted attempts to find a wife. "In a sense, because she was beyond that pressure, she could laugh and joke about it in a way that no one else could—and he needed that because, frankly, it was becoming an embarrassment all round, this inability to find someone to settle down with," said a friend. "And of course the further down the road he went, the more the pressure to settle for this one or that one, the more resistant he was becoming. It wasn't getting any easier for him."

He rewarded this intimacy by inviting Camilla and Andrew Parker Bowles to his thirtieth birthday party. He danced with her, with the Countess of Lichfield—a former date when she had been Lady Leonora Grosvenor—and another former flame, Lady Jane Wellesley. It seemed that all the people he danced with that night were old flames, except one. She was the actress Susan George, who subsequently enjoyed candlelit dinners with the prince at a secret address in St. James's, and though on at least one occasion she stayed all night, this was merely the fulfillment of one of Charles's fantasies. Albeit perfectly charming, Miss George had already had a number of male partners, and in any event the nation would never countenance as their future Queen an actress who had had her clothes ripped off and been raped in Sam Peckinpah's *Straw Dogs*. The relationship didn't last long.

The years were rolling on. By now it was 1977, the year in which, Charles had predicted for himself, a bride would come along. There was no one in sight, though for a moment the matchmakers held their breath when Charles attended a charity event in Monte Carlo and was seated next to Princess Caroline of Monaco. They loathed each other on sight, and dreams of a great dynastic match dissolved amid claims from both sides: He "bored" her and she "irritated" him. In a rare and frank aside, Charles added acidly: "Before I arrived the world had me engaged to Caroline. With our first meeting the world had us married—and now the marriage is already in trouble."

In July, playing polo at Cowdray Park in Sussex, Charles was introduced to a beautiful Colombian socialite, Cristabel Barria-Borsage. His official companion that day was yet another sprig of English aristocracy, Lady Sarah Spencer, sister of his future wife. "But," said one report, "although Sarah was Charles's date that evening, it was clear he fancied Miss Barria-Borsage tremendously and had no hesitation in exercising his princely rights. They danced together for hours and Sarah wasn't very happy."

The prince drove back to London: In the front of his car was his Colombian firecracker, in the back a very disconsolate Sarah Spencer, jammed up against the detective. A few days later the not entirely gallant Miss Barria-Borsage confessed to a friend that Charles had seduced her. "As they got into bed she asked the prince: 'What shall I call you—Sir, or Charles?' went the report. "As he started to make love to her, he replied, 'Call me Arthur.' "

Sarah was treated more seriously. Picked out of the blue to attend the traditional Windsor Castle house party for Royal Ascot week, she drove herself there in trepidation: she was suffering from anorexia nervosa. Unlike his chilly response when faced with Diana's bulimia, Charles showed sympathy and understanding, but then the girl he saw before him was in poor shape. In just a few months, standing five foot seven, her weight had plummeted from 112 to seventy-seven pounds. She confessed her figure had gone down from 34-24-34 to 27-20-28. "I looked like something out of a concentration camp—I couldn't find any normal clothes to fit me, and I did my shopping in the children's department of Marks and Spencer—the bit for ten-year-olds."

She went on: "In such circumstances you behave like an

alcoholic, you just will not admit there is a problem. Worse, you end up believing you are beautiful, looking so thin." It was a forerunner of what Charles could expect, in a different form, from his wife. The girl who had been thrown out of her school, West Heath, for drinking ("I used to drink because I was bored. I would drink anything: whiskey, Cointreau, gin, sherry, or most often vodka because the staff couldn't smell it") had lost the enamel from her teeth because of the slimming disease.

But Charles persisted, taking her skiing to Klosters that winter where they shared a bedroom. Next summer, however, Sarah overplayed her hand when Charles planned a polo trip to Trouville on the northern French coast. As the week approached she more and more obviously let it be known that she wanted to be taken along. "She kept going on and on about how she would love to go, how she could speak almost perfect French, and how she knew so many people who'd be there," said a friend. But Charles opted for a French girl called Chantal—"not the kind of girl who was likely to become the Princess of Wales," remarked a seasoned royal watcher dryly, as he watched the couple bop the night away at a discotheque in Trouville—and once again Sarah was on the back burner, this time for good.

There were a couple of flirtations and a grand passion left to come. After the death of Lord Mountbatten, killed by a terrorist bomb in Ireland in 1979, all the old seadog's hopes of a dynastic match between Charles and his granddaughter Amanda Knatchbull evaporated; and the prince went on to romance Jane Ward, a pretty and wellborn assistant manager at the Guards Polo Club. She was briefly followed by a scion of the brewery clan, Sabrina Guinness, who had been friendly with Jack Nicholson and Mick Jagger and was hated on sight by the queen and Prince Philip when she turned up at

Balmoral. When she remarked that the vehicle which brought her from the station reminded her of nothing so much as a Black Maria, Prince Philip barked: "You'd know all about Black Marias." And when she sat down in a chair and the queen snapped: "Don't sit there—that is Queen Victoria's chair!" she realized the futility of the whole exercise—particularly since her stay went unconsummated. Nonetheless, before she went on to become nanny to the young Tatum O'Neal, Sabrina made an attempt to revive the relationship by writing twice to the prince. He did not bother to reply on either occasion.

Increasingly during this period Charles had taken to visiting Bolehyde Manor, the Parker Bowleses' country home. He would do so when Andrew was there, and he would do so when Andrew was not. "He was eating there regularly," recalled a friend. "This was before he'd set eyes on Highgrove. Outside the royal houses he had no place to call home.

"He was very conscious about his public image, and even at that stage if the affair hadn't been rekindled physically, he just wanted to hang around Camilla. And Camilla certainly didn't mind that. Often he had nothing else to do and he'd hang round the kitchen while she was cooking for a dinner party—then when the guests turned up, he'd disappear upstairs and have his supper on a tray. When they went, he'd come down again and carry on where he'd left off."

Andrew Parker Bowles became used to finding Charles in the house, accepted the situation, and in doing so lost points among his colleagues at the Guards Polo Club over his keenness to be hospitable to the prince. One member complained: "When he was asked to umpire after he had played himself, he would often say, 'Terribly sorry, I am needed by royal appointment,' and off he would go to pour Charles's drinks."

But still the prince was single, apparently pursuing no active course to find himself a wife—until along came Anna Wallace.

Anna, daughter of a Scottish landowner, was at twenty-five both beautiful and clever. In addition she was a passionate horsewoman, wellborn, discreet, and with an iron will of her own. In their extended romance she was accorded special treatment, as if Charles knew he was now on the home straight, coming to the end of his bachelor days.

"But it was a complete nonstarter. She'd had boyfriends like Davina Sheffield had boyfriends—she had a track record," recalled a friend. "And she would speak up for her rights."

Nevertheless Charles, by now more than a little desperate to marry and under intense pressure from all sides to show himself willing to an increasingly impatient nation, did offer his hand in marriage to Miss Wallace. She was rich enough and old enough and wise enough to refuse. Their well-publicized row at a party given for the Queen Mother's eightieth birthday—where having been abandoned in favor of other guests she lashed out at the prince: "Don't ever, ever ignore me like that again! No one treats me like that, not even you!"—was followed by an equally vicious exchange at a polo ball at Stowell Park, the Gloucestershire estate of Lord Vestey. Anna walked out of his life forever.

For that night, Charles had spent all evening dancing with Camilla Parker Bowles.

It was on again, and neither of them cared who knew it.

Chapter Five

Kissing Camilla

———⊰◦◦◦⊱———

In fact it had hardly ever stopped. Up till now, Charles and Camilla had convinced themselves they had been discretion itself, but for some time the mask had been slipping.

In early 1980 Andrew Parker Bowles, now a lieutenant colonel, was in Rhodesia where, in the run-up to independence, the situation had become volatile. Lord Soames, son-in-law of wartime leader Winston Churchill, had been appointed governor and the ambitious Parker Bowles, newly promoted, was posted to the colony as chief liaison officer.

In early March, there was the first public sighting of Charles and Camilla together since that night in Annabel's nearly eight years before. The *Daily Mail* reported:

> *While Household Cavalry officer Lt. Col. Andrew Parker Bowles, 40, is helping keep the peace in Rhodesia, his wife was at Plumpton yesterday cheering on her old boyfriend Prince Charles.*
>
> *Camilla, 32, was brought up next to the race-course, and she has been back home with her parents for Charles's visit. Andrew, personally selected by Governor Lord Soames,*

*has been one of the greatest successes of the British presence
in the former rebel colony—so much so that he is known to
Premier-elect Robert Mugabe as "Comrade Parker."*

Soon the satirical magazine *Private Eye* and its gossip
columnist Grovel were on the scent:

> *No sooner had Lord Soames been appointed Governor
> of Rhodesia than the subject of jobs for the boys arose.
> Among the lucky ones, Major Andrew Parker Bowles, now
> a colonel and in charge of British liaison with the guerrilla
> forces.*
>
> *Andrew, 39, is married to a former (?) Prince Charles
> fancy, Camilla Shand, and if I should find the royal Aston
> Martin Volante outside the Parker Bowles mansion while
> the gallant colonel is on duty overseas, my duty will be clear.*

The word was out. Yet the libel laws being particularly
ferocious in Britain, and with no direct evidence beyond the
constant wagging of wellborn tongues that the prince was
once again bedding his old love, it was left to the cognoscenti
to read between the lines and learn what was going on in
Charles's life—even while he was still supposed to be in love
with Anna Wallace and still trying to make her his wife.

The subtle digs had not escaped Ms. Wallace. Maybe she
was ready to put up with the charade, maybe she was prepared to entertain the idea of becoming Princess of Wales
despite all this—particularly since Charles had pressed his
case so convincingly, though, it has to be said, so dispassion-
ately . . . for Anna can have been left in very little doubt what
the deal would be. In their relationship which had lasted the
better part of a year—and one that seemed to have a purpose,

after all—they had never once slept together. Anna may have made her own arrangements on that score, but so had Charles: He was utterly satisfied in that department.

It was an abnormal relationship for two grown adults, though successful marriages have been built on less. But that night at Stowell Park was more than any self-respecting woman could take. "Dancing with Camilla Parker Bowles at Stowell Park that night—I mean, Camilla Parker Bowles!" uttered a friend. "Anna wasn't stupid, she knew how Camilla vetted all his women. Camilla dangled him like a trout—HRH knew that Anna would never put up with that."

Another story appeared in the newspapers during the period that Charles was wooing Anna Wallace—one that would have given her even more cause for alarm. The *Daily Mail* reported on 11 April 1980:

> *Prince Charles can expect a mixed welcome in Rhodesia next week when he presides over the Zimbabwe Independence Celebrations. Former prime minister Ian Smith, who once vowed that "never in 1,000 years" would blacks rule his country, is slipping off abroad to fulfill a "long-standing engagement."*
>
> *But there will be a familiar face for the heir to the throne—old flame Mrs. Camilla Parker Bowles, 32, is expected in Salisbury to act as an official escort for Charles.*

The report went on:

> *Paradoxically [Andrew] Parker Bowles is now back in England after making a great success of heading the liaison forces under Soames and will not be returning with his wife, the niece of Lord Ashcombe.*

Buckingham Palace officials have always been happy to see Charles in the company of happily married women, because such sightings cannot give rise to rumor.

This last sentence was another warning shot across the prince's bows, but he was not to be deterred. Camilla had let him back into her life full-time, and he was besotted.

Their rekindled passion was dangerous and, for a time, out of control. Despite the well-timed press report—no informed person believed the "official escort" tag for a second—Charles insisted that she should still accompany him to Zimbabwe. This drove senior officials into paroxysms of rage. "The hauling down of the British flag was a humiliating enough circumstance without everyone knowing the royal family's envoy had brought his popsy along with him," a Foreign Office source said later. "The lack of tact was indescribable. It just made a joke out of the whole thing."

Lord Soames, Britain's most successful postwar ambassador to Paris and as seasoned a diplomat as they come, reacted with horror at the thought of sharing a table with Charles and Camilla, together with Andrew Parker Bowles and the Soames's daughter, Charlotte, with whom Andrew—just to complicate matters even further—had fallen in love during his tour of duty in Africa. Eventually Charlotte was persuaded by her parents to fly home to London. Calling for assistance from the Almighty to overcome the dinner party from hell, Lady Soames added dryly: "And pray God may the claret be good."

Back in London and with the Anna Wallace affair apparently going strong, the matchmakers were now pinning their hopes on an early engagement announcement. But now that the relationship with Camilla, sealed in the heat and dust of Africa, was on again, the prince could hardly care less. "He was aware that something would have to be done sooner or later about finding a wife, but the person he turned to for advice was Camilla," says a former courtier. "It was most bizarre.

"Camilla felt that, now her family life was established, she could act in pretty much the same way as her great-grandmother. All that stuff about Alice Keppel was coming true for her. It's what she'd always wanted. And make no mistake—in *this* affair, there were two very determined people, each out to get what they wanted. Nothing was going to stand in their way."

Camilla slipped into her advisory role with consummate ease. With time on her hands and her husband away for long periods, she could devote herself to Charles and his problems. Often they would meet in Sussex, and it was at this stage that Camilla's parents became aware of their daughter's double life. Major Shand, though himself happily married for nearly a quarter of a century, took an urbane view of this accident of history: After all, he had seen his own father fall victim to a fickle heart several times. Friends say the relationship worried Mrs. Shand far more. But they were able to see for themselves that after so many years in the wilderness, without a friend and helpmeet, Charles had finally found a safe haven— someone in whom, for the first time, he could confide. The relief was indescribable, the consequences unthought of . . . but those who knew and cared for Charles thanked providence for his having found someone who could help him shoulder the burden of life.

Charles and Camilla's shared interests—apart from their renewed and overwhelming passion for each other—were manifold. Both were accomplished on horseback and enjoyed the thrill of the chase; Camilla insisted he should come to hunt in Gloucestershire. Both were fascinated by architecture—and Camilla was able to draw on the life of her grand-father, Philip Morton Shand, the lively proponent of the Bauhaus movement and friend of Walter Gropius. Both were amateur water-colorists seeking to improve their technique, and both had developed a passion for Italy, its architecture and art. Later critics derided Camilla for her lack of academic qualifications and her addiction to the hunt; they sought to delve no deeper to discover what else lay there for Charles to adore. But there was plenty.

To most of the population, theirs was a passion which simply did not exist. But a privileged few were witness to an astonishing display of the almost animal attraction that the two now had for each other.

The Cirencester Polo Club Ball was, as always, a private affair with no members of the press or public allowed. A biannual celebration, it was remarkable that year only because it was exceptionally hot: A marquee was built on the lawns of Cirencester House, a large Cotswold stone edifice, set in fifteen thousand acres, belonging to Earl Bathurst, and around three hundred and fifty black-tied and bejeweled guests were expected.

The guest of honor would be the Prince of Wales, a man who adored the turf of the Cirencester ground and played there regularly. Among the other guests were Andrew and Camilla Parker Bowles. It was a glittering occasion where the wine flowed and the hot summer evening raised the temperatures of all but the dullest reveler.

"But what happened was quite astonishing," recalled one guest that night, Charles's former girlfriend Jane Ward. "Charles and the Parker Bowleses shared the same table, and Charles spent the whole evening dancing with Camilla. They were kissing passionately as they danced—on and on they went, kissing each other, French kissing, dance after dance.

"Andrew wasn't quite sure how to react—he sat there smiling and saying to people: 'HRH is very fond of my wife. And she appears to be very fond of him.' He seemed not uncomfortable with what was going on, but other people were, especially the older ones. Some were embarrassed and shocked and upset because the whole thing was so blatant," went on Ms. Ward. "It's bad enough, in such company, to monopolize one woman all evening. It's worse if it's someone else's wife. But the way they were behaving was completely beyond the pale."

Another example of Charles's lustful and insensitive behavior among trusted friends is cited by those who remember a favorite dress of hers. "It was brown, very short, made of some nylon-style material and with a plunging neckline which showed off her best assets," recalled one. "Charles took one look at it, plunged his hands down the front, and grabbed her breasts. Now in mixed company that is not the done thing—but in fairness to Camilla, she was prepared to laugh it off. Charles didn't care, and everyone just looked the other way. It was pretty crass, but then I think that's his way with women—poor Diana, is all I can say."

These episodes do more than anything to illustrate the difficult line Andrew Parker Bowles chose to tread, and the decorous manner in which he attempted to overcome the difficulties (if indeed there were difficulties) he faced in his marriage. In common with Alice Keppel and her husband George, neither Parker Bowles partner was faithful to the other, and yet an intensely strong bond held them together. If, as seems clear, Andrew was prepared to tolerate the *liaison dangereux* between his wife and the Prince of Wales, he was paying a very high price in terms of public esteem. Later he would have to endure the public jeers at Royal Ascot when he was publicly dubbed "Ernest Simpson"—a reference to the man who so willingly allowed himself to be cuckolded by the previous Prince of Wales; but by then he was inured to the whispers and cackles which followed him wherever he went.

It is impossible to ascribe motives to this kind of behavior, but the fact is that at the very latest from 1980 onward and probably much earlier, Andrew Parker Bowles was aware of the rekindled sexual relationship between his wife and the Prince of Wales. When that relationship finally started to break surface in the press, a friend commented: "Andrew's not that unhappy. He's got his own fish to fry."

For some years the prince had been looking for a home of his own. In 1974, while still serving in the navy, he had been offered—and had accepted—a red-brick pile in Kent called Chevening. It had 115 rooms and three and a half thousand acres of Kentish downland, and he hated it. His visits were rare and became rarer.

With his heart and mind now very firmly in the West Country, and encouraged by the firm guiding hand of Camilla, he ordered his Duchy of Cornwall staff to start looking for a proper home for him. It had to be in Gloucestershire or Wiltshire—in other words, not too far from Bolehyde Manor—and before too long, they came up with a suitable suggestion, the home of a government minister, Maurice Macmillan, son of the former prime minister.

Highgrove, a distinguished though comparatively small Georgian house, had nine bedrooms and was set in about 350 acres. It was charming, but hardly befitting the status of a Prince of Wales who might want to raise a dynasty there. Some saw the choice of Highgrove as his future home as a demonstration to the world of his "small is beautiful" philosophy, others saw a natural symmetry in his choosing an area near his sister Anne at Gatcombe Park and his cousin Prince Michael of Kent, thus creating a "royal triangle."

Nothing could be further from the truth. Highgrove—near a main road, and with a worrying public footpath meandering past its door—was a poor choice, but it was there and it was available. Charles plumped for it, later saying: "It was a challenge to create something and I did rather fall in love with it. The big cedar tree in front and the walled garden finally made up my mind."

Possibly. But what is beyond dispute is that the "royal triangle" factor was an irrelevance: Charles at that time saw very little of his sister, who was less than complimentary about his private life and who basked in the love and approbation of their father—something Charles had long ago reconciled himself to live without, but something which galled him nonetheless. No more did he see of the Michaels of Kent—though he was devoted to his cousin Prince Michael, his initial enthusiasm for the prince's wife had turned to a chilly contempt. She was never to be allowed to visit Highgrove—indeed, Charles begged the security services to point out to Prince and Princess Michael that it would be too much of a burden on their resources to have three such obvious terrorist targets living in close proximity.

It was Camilla who made up his mind. The house was a few minutes' drive from Bolehyde Manor, and that was all that mattered. Not for the first time Charles allowed his heart to rule his head. The purchase of the house cost a shade over £800,000 and was made in August 1980, several long months after the affair had gone semipublic. And now that the prince had a house and the heart of "the woman I love," he could concentrate on thinking about marriage.

It was that cold and calculating a step.

★ ★ ★

New Grove, the home of Commander Robert de Pass near Petworth in Sussex, was one of Charles's "safe houses." During the long and lonely years since his first fling with Camilla, he had taken several girlfriends there—though they would be accommodated elsewhere and suffer the indignity of being bused in by a detective, made love to by the prince, then bused out again. One particular girl, wellborn and with high expectations of an evening of courtly love, had been driven away in tears at the brutal reality of Charles's brusque attentions.

It was at New Grove, however, that another young hopeful was first entertained, apparently at the behest of the de Pass's son Philip, one weekend in July 1980. The pair had become acquainted through Rory Scott, a handsome Guards officer who had the distinction of having his shirts ironed by Earl Spencer's daughter and had responded by inviting her for weekends to his parents' home near Petworth. Only as Diana was packing her bags in London to travel south did she discover that a fellow house guest would be the Prince of Wales.

They met, according to legend, on a hay bale. "You're a young blood," Philip de Pass had told her. "You might like him." During that weekend she drove to the nearby Cowdray Park polo ground to watch Charles play with his team, Les Diables Bleus, and at the end of the game the house party drove back to Petworth for a barbecue. The bale of hay was where they first had an opportunity to speak.

Some have painted her opening conversational gambit as a spontaneous message of sympathy which touched the prince's heart to the core. Speaking of his role at the murdered Earl Mountbatten's funeral at Westminster Abbey, Lady Diana Spencer told the prince: "You looked so sad when you walked up the aisle at the funeral. It was the most tragic thing I've ever seen. My heart bled for you when I watched it. I thought, it's wrong, you are lonely, you should be with somebody to look after you."

But James Whitaker, who already knew Diana and in the coming months was to become her confidant, argued that from the time of her sister Sarah's estrangement from the prince, there had been a concerted campaign by all three Spencer sisters—Sarah, Diana, and Jane, wife of the queen's private secretary, Sir Robert Fellowes—to get Diana "in the frame." Thus her conversational gambit can be seen as a guileful ploy to attack Charles's Achilles' heel. If so, there was hardly any need.

Later Diana confessed: "He was all over me and it was very strange. I thought, 'Well, this isn't very cool'—I thought men weren't supposed to be so obvious, I thought this was very odd. The next minute he leapt on me practically and I thought this was very strange, too, and I wasn't quite sure how to cope with this."

The prince left the house party early, insisting that the eighteen-year-old accompany him back to London. Aware from her sister that instant compliance to his wishes tended to downgrade a woman in Charles's eyes, she held out, saying it would be rude to their host and hostess. Charles returned to London alone, to telephone Camilla and discuss his latest move.

The wooing process started, in typically backhanded fashion. At the last minute Charles asked Diana to accompany him to a performance of Verdi's *Requiem* at the Royal Albert Hall. So little advance warning was Diana given that her flatmate Carolyn Bartholemew recalled: "I walked in about six o'clock and Diana went, 'Quick, quick, I've got to meet Charles in twenty minutes.' Well, we had the funniest time ever, getting the hair washed, getting it dried, getting the dress, where's the dress? We did it in twenty minutes flat. But I mean, how dare he ask her so late?"

There was also an urgency about it all, which given the lack of love ("Whatever 'in love' means," delivered by Charles on the day of their engagement, was a phrase that haunted the couple for all their married life) could only mean one thing—Charles had found the solution to the problem.

It would not be long before he would be taking Lady Diana Spencer to be vetted by Mrs. Camilla Parker Bowles, but first came a whirlwind round of backbone-testing royal engagements—Cowes Week aboard the royal yacht *Britannia*, the traditional voyage north to Scotland, then Balmoral. It took less than a month from her first meeting Charles to her being considered, privately at least, to be the future Princess of Wales. "The haste was positively indecent," said one of Diana's friends, while she herself felt "fairly intimidated" by the atmosphere on board the royal yacht. Not only were his friends so much older than herself, but they seemed aware of the royal strategy toward her. Diana found them too friendly and too knowing—"They were all over me like a bad rash," she told her friends.

She added: "I was the youngest there by a long way. Charles used to say, 'Would you like to come for a walk, come for a barbecue?' so I said, 'Yes, please.' I thought this was all wonderful."

Having passed the Balmoral test, Diana headed back to London accompanied by Charles's friend Nicholas Soames. There was one other escort on the flight to Heathrow from Aberdeen—Andrew Parker Bowles. He and Camilla had been part of the Balmoral house party, and Camilla had had her first glimpse of the future princess. Then Andrew headed south with Diana, leaving Camilla and Charles alone together

in Balmoral. The bliss of their lovers' tryst was
unalloyed—Camilla came down with mumps an
off to a hospital.

Whether by now Andrew Parker Bowles cared about his
wife's relationship with Charles is open to debate. Certainly
he had not shaken off his feelings for Lord Soames's daughter, and for some time after it was debated among his friends
whether he would leave Camilla for her—not because of
Camilla's affair with Charles, but because of his own feelings.
In the end his indecision was his undoing: Charlotte Soames
met and married Earl Peel, a Yorkshire landowner, in 1989.

There is no doubt that Diana was aware of Camilla's relationship with the prince from the outset: "I'd been staying at
Bolehyde and (to start with) I couldn't understand why she
kept saying to me, 'Don't push him into doing this, don't do
that.' She knew so much about what he was doing privately,
about what we were doing privately. Eventually I worked it
all out."

Thus the apparent love affair between Charles and Diana
which was played out to the world at large was a sham from
the beginning, a cruel hoax upon those who believed that
even in Britain's new hard-nosed age of Thatcherism, there
was still room for a fairy-tale royal romance.

Charles and Diana both wanted to marry, for entirely
their own reasons. Common to both was a barely veiled ambition—on her side, to become Princess of Wales and ultimately queen; on his, to secure a wife acceptable to both
himself and the populace, who would provide an heir.

Things moved at such a pace between the first meeting
and the first rumors of an engagement that a normally
cynical Fleet Street lost its head and went with the myth. No
single commentator or investigative journalist took heed of
the still, small voice repeating Mrs. Parker Bowles's name in

their ear. The idea of a royal wedding, of the laying to rest of the specter of the previous Prince of Wales, was too seductive.

On the inside, the reality was harsher. Lady Diana found herself pursued by adoring news-hounds, and though she took to the novelty with commendable humor, the wear and tear on her nerves grew increasingly unbearable. In desperation she contacted the press office at Buckingham Palace to seek advice, only to be told in no uncertain terms that she was on her own. Her equilibrium was not improved by Prince Charles telephoning her to discuss at length the enormous stress Camilla was being forced to undergo, with three or four reporters outside her door. Diana, fourteen years her rival's junior and not toughened by worldly experience, habitually had ten times that many.

Nor was her humor improved when, a month later, she and Prince Charles emerged before the public gaze at a race meeting at Ludlow, in the West Midlands. Charles, then attempting to make his mark as an amateur jockey, brought Diana along to admire his prowess in the saddle. Charles finished second on his horse Allibar, but though Diana shouted her support for him there was a marked reticence in her appearance: Only later did people realize that Charles had brought along as chaperon none other than Camilla Parker Bowles. At the end of the day the trio managed to give the pursuing press photographers the slip—whereupon Charles ordered the car to be driven to Bolehyde Manor, where they all spent the weekend. Diana's mood was not improved when she was informed they would be back the next weekend as well.

But there was virtually nothing she could do: Camilla appeared to be holding the reins and Charles was content with that. "Diana had to swallow her feelings," said a friend at the time. "She had to bide her time—she wasn't even his fiancée yet."

Another friend described the courting couple's relationship as being warm enough, but almost master-and-servant: "She had to keep going in the way she did, fitting in with everything that Charles—and Camilla—suggested. The alternative, as she saw it, was that she would be ditched. Can you imagine how awful it was for her?"

It became clear that Diana's mother, aware of the Camilla situation probably through her daughter Jane, was unimpressed by Charles's pursuit of her daughter. She urged caution to Diana without seeking to bring the fledgling relationship to a halt.

There can be no doubt that Diana was completely aware of the situation. She had learned on the grapevine what had happened to her predecessor Anna Wallace, and was privy to the reasons for the breakdown of that relationship. It is even said that Miss Wallace issued a warning to Diana through a third party, alerting her to the Camilla problem.

As September moved into October, Diana dined at Buckingham Palace with Charles; the Parker Bowleses came too. After another weekend at Bolehyde Manor she was told they would spend the following weekend there as well. Charles took her to Highgrove and asked her to decorate it for him: Camilla's helpful comments after this invitation made it all too clear to Diana that the older woman knew the house intimately. It did not take long for the penny to drop: Camilla had helped choose it. "I thought it was very improper [to ask me to decorate the house]," she recalled bitterly some years later.

There were no doubts left in Diana's mind as to the

nature of Charles and Camilla's relationship, but even if there was, they were about to be shattered in a most spectacular way.

On 16 November 1980 the *Sunday Mirror* carried a story which alleged that, ten days earlier, Diana had secretly joined Charles on the royal train, parked for the night in a siding at Staverton in Wiltshire. She was alleged to have stayed on board for several hours—and the implication was clear. There could be no other interpretation than that she had slept with Charles, who was not then betrothed to her.

In Britain, at that time, the story caused a furor. The country was basking in the belief that Charles had found himself a wellborn, good-looking, charming, and fresh young thing for his future bride, a woman who was a virgin and would remain so to the altar. However dated that notion might seem in the present climate, it was what the public wanted.

But the evidence was there. A blond-haired woman had entered the train at night after Charles had finished giving dinner to three Duchy of Cornwall officials. The telephone log subsequently showed that a call had, a little earlier, been made to Bolehyde Manor.

What happened next, some might suppose, was a deception which could only be described as conduct unbecoming a future king. Both Charles and the queen feigned anger at the *Sunday Mirror*'s supposed invention, and the queen's press secretary, Michael Shea, was instructed to write to the newspaper's editor. He protested in the strongest terms about the story which, he said, was "totally false" and a "total fabrication." No doubt in all innocence of the true circumstances— for he was only acting on information supplied to him by the Prince of Wales himself—Shea demanded a printed apology in a prominent position in the newspaper at the earliest opportunity.

The newspaper's editor, a respected journalist called Bob Edwards, was shocked by the vehemence of the palace response. On the one hand he could understand their anger at his printing a story which could derail the much-longed-for royal engagement; on the other it appeared that their complaint stemmed from the utter conviction that Diana had not been on the train.

But the evidence said different—a woman had boarded the train, had stayed for hours, had left clandestinely. What no one could believe, because Fleet Street had fallen in love with Diana and had allowed its guard to drop, was that if there was a woman on board, it was someone else.

Diana herself was caught off guard. Thinking herself to be in grave danger of falling in the public's esteem, and with Charles's proposal of marriage not yet uttered, she hastened to put the record straight. "I am not a liar," she told the *Daily Mirror*'s James Whitaker. "I have never been on that train. I have never ever been near it.

"I stayed in all that evening with my three flatmates, Virginia [Pitman], Carolyn [Pride], and Ann [Bolton]. Please believe me, I am telling the absolute truth. I had some supper and watched television before going to bed early. I had been at Princess Margaret's party at the Ritz the night before, and I was feeling very frail and hungover. I didn't feel like going anywhere and I never moved out of my flat. My flatmates will testify to this."

This was an extraordinary outburst from a girl who had quickly learned, some months before, the virtue of saying nothing to the press. But Diana went further: "These allegations have not put me in a very good light," she told Whitaker. "It is all very upsetting."

In Diana's mind there was no doubt that the woman in question—and by now it was clear that evidence had come from the security services guarding Charles that there was a woman—was Camilla Parker Bowles. It was a shattering thought for Diana that, four months into their relationship, Charles could dance the night away with her at the Ritz, only to sneak away to have sexual relations with his mistress the following night, while she, Diana, bathed in the afterglow of the most romantic evening she had ever experienced in her short life. Worse still was the thought that her own royal ambitions could be thwarted by Charles's foolish infidelity.

The row did not go away. A protest was made to the Press Council; it was clear, said the complainant, that in the light of Buckingham Palace's outright denial, the *Sunday Mirror* should be censured. But by now wise to what had happened, palace officials, in an apparent gesture of magnanimity, said they had no wish to pursue the matter. The *Sunday Mirror*'s editor, still unaware of the true circumstances surrounding his story, met Prince Charles personally; the matter was not alluded to.

Six years later, in recognition of his outstanding services to journalism, Bob Edwards was made a Commander of the Order of the British Empire, only a step away from a knighthood; it appeared he had been forgiven by the palace. Generously, in his memoirs, Edwards had written, "How awful if I had been wrong about the whole silly thing." But he had not. Those privileged to be invited to the editor's home that Christmas could have discovered, among the welter of seasonal cards and greetings, one from a former politician and close friend of the royal family. The card was inscribed with a short message, which simply said: "It was Camilla."

That was in the future. In the aftermath of the Royal Train Scandal, as it became known, Charles flew out to India on a prearranged visit. In New Delhi he made a speech in which he took the opportunity, several thousand miles from home, to have a swipe at those who had questioned his behavior on that fateful night. He hit out at what he described as the "sensationalism" of the British media, and the lack of moral values in reporting. Speaking to members of the Indian Institute of Technology he said: "Honesty and integrity are vital factors in reporting and often get submerged in the general rush for sensationalism." Insofar as personal integrity goes, this was a low-water mark in Charles's life.

In the ensuing rush to see who could capitalize most on the press's discomfiture, Diana's mother, Mrs. Frances Shand Kydd, wrote a letter to *The Times* complaining about the "lies and harassment" Diana was forced to endure. Certainly she was right about the lies, though on this occasion it was not the press who were being economical with the truth. Then sixty members of Parliament took up the cudgels, drafting a motion "deploring the manner in which Lady Diana Spencer is being treated by the media." There was an urgent meeting between Fleet Street editors and the Press Council—and all because the Prince of Wales had telephoned Mrs. Parker Bowles and invited her to come to bed with him.

At this distance Charles's behavior, in particular his New Delhi response, must seem unworthy of his status as future king. But by now he was not acting entirely of his own free will: The nation wanted him to marry, so too did the queen and, especially, his hectoring father. A possible bride had been found, and he was doing his duty—unlike his great-uncle—working his way toward what was required of him. It was tough luck that fate had decreed he should fall in love with a married woman who came quickly to understand his problems, and learned how to comfort him in the way he needed most.

As his need for marriage receded, so he was being pushed into it. He had been caught virtually *in flagrante delicto* and his relationship with a married woman all but uncovered. It was a frustrating and bewildering experience, and he did not respond well to it. Diana did not spend Christmas with him, or New Year's Eve. It was not until New Year's Day 1981 that she was invited to join him at Sandringham.

Whether through compassion for her granddaughter, or the desire not to see the family name besmirched, Ruth, Lady Fermoy, sounded a warning note, cautioning Diana about the difficulties of marrying into the royal family. "You must understand that their sense of humor," she said, "and their lifestyle are very different. I don't think it will suit you."

It made no difference. Having once again consulted Camilla, Charles decided to propose to Diana on his return from a skiing trip to Klosters. Yet his approach was leisurely: Having flown back to London on 3 February, it was not until three days later that Diana was summoned to Windsor Castle. She later recalled: "I went to Windsor and I arrived about five o'clock and he sat me down and said, 'I've missed you so much.' But there was never anything tactile about him. It was extraordinary, but I didn't have anything to go by because I had never had a boyfriend.

"Anyway, so he said, 'Will you marry me?' and I laughed. I remember thinking, this is a joke. And I said, 'Yeah, OK,' and laughed. He was deadly serious. He said, 'You do realize one day you will be queen?' . . . so I said yes. He ran upstairs and rang his mother."

Later the writer Andrew Morton revealed that Diana, in her innocence, believed Charles was in love with her: She noted a besotted look in his eyes which somehow did not ring true. Despite her youth and inexperience she was able to gauge the prince's immaturity when it came to matters of the heart, but she refused to dwell on these perceived imperfections. "For me it was a call of duty, really—to go and work with the people."

How much of the decision to go ahead with this cold-blooded proposal was Charles's, and how much Camilla's, is still a matter for speculation. But having now had plenty of opportunity to size up her protégée, Camilla made a fundamental miscalculation. When asked by friends what she thought of Diana, she replied: "She's like a mouse."

The mouse was not yet ready to roar, and took the silence of her future husband, when she flew to Australia for a ten-day respite, meekly enough. As the days wore on he made no attempt to telephone her, and when she finally plucked up the courage to call Buckingham Palace from New South Wales she was told the prince was not there. He finally returned her call, and upon her arrival back in England she was greeted by a member of Charles's staff with a large bouquet of flowers. There was no card.

Things were moving at an alarming pace. On 28 February 1981, the formal announcement of the royal engagement was made. Charles and Diana made their debut together before the television cameras and were asked the fateful question: "Are you in love?" Was it because he knew Camilla would be watching that all he could stammer was: "Whatever 'in love' means"?

The royal machine took over, and Diana was swept out of her Colherne Court flat forever. She was given a suite of rooms at the queen Mother's London home, Clarence House, and within twenty minutes of arriving she discovered, on her bed, an invitation to lunch from Camilla.

Ironically it was the warmest gesture of welcome she received: No one from the royal family was there to greet her, and she had no idea where her future husband was. Camilla's note had been written several days before the announcement of the engagement, making it clear that she had prior knowledge; but then that came as no great surprise, for in the six months since Diana had entered this extraordinary love triangle, Camilla had been omnipresent. What galled Diana was that Camilla knew where she would be staying—at Clarence House, not Buckingham Palace—whereas Diana herself was only informed a few hours before she left Colherne Court.

The lunch with Camilla was the high point of her first few days in royal custody. With unerring female instinct, she knew what Camilla meant when she asked Diana whether she proposed to hunt when she was at Highgrove. The mouse, compliantly, said no.

Less than a month later Charles flew to Australia for a five-week tour. There was a tearful farewell at Heathrow Airport, but Diana's tears were less sentimental and more of rage and frustration: Earlier that day Charles and Diana were in his Buckingham Palace study when the telephone rang. With no apparent embarrassment, Charles lifted the receiver and launched into his farewells to Camilla while his fiancée was forced into a humiliating retreat from the room.

There can be no doubt that at this stage, three months before the royal wedding, and bearing in mind the humiliation of the royal train incident, Diana had a complete knowledge of the ongoing nature of her husband's relationship with another woman.[1] Equally, she was conscious the moment she walked through the doors of Clarence House that this was

---

[1] Curiously, in her taped conversations with a friend of Andrew Morton, Diana never referred to the royal train incident. Since during these conversations she was in the process of presenting a convincing case for herself, the reader must assume that she chose to ignore an event which, however briefly, had become a national scandal. To have taken it up may have jeopardized the marriage proposal which she instinctively knew was coming.

the point of no return—and yet as the nation prepared to celebrate, the full horror of the price she must pay for her ambition was repeatedly being brought home to her.

It is unsurprising, then, that a girl of her station, subjected to the evils of a broken home and the desertion of a mother, harried by the press, and brought to the steps of the altar in a series of subterfuges, should crack. She did.

Though the outward and visible Diana continued to turn from cygnet into swan, and as the nation opened its heart to her, inside her the deterioration had set in; during the period of her fiancé's absence in Australia she fell victim once again to bulimia nervosa.

With the benefit of hindsight, a helping hand from Camilla at this stage might have strengthened Diana's purpose; but after that initial lunch Camilla had retreated to the country and her family. Day after long day was spent at Buckingham Palace with little to do: Early on, Diana had taken a personal dislike to the courtiers seconded to "educate" her in royal ways, Lady Susan Hussey and Oliver Everett.

The bulimia manifested itself, wrote Ross Benson, in this way: "At lunchtime when she did not have guests, Diana would go into the nursery kitchen. She would take down a large glass bowl engraved with the EIIR cypher which held just over half a packet of breakfast cereal. She would fill it with Kellogg's Frosties and several chopped bananas, strawberries, and sometimes pieces of apple. She would add tablespoons of caster sugar and pour on Windsor cream, a thick double cream from the Jersey herd at the Home Farm at Windsor. She would then sit down on top of the spin dryer and eat her way through the mess, which she then washed down with fresh orange juice. When she had finished, she would go to her lavatory and spew up what she had just forced down. The pattern of gorge and regurgitate would happen twice and sometimes three or four times a day."

Though surrounded by servants, courtiers, and future relations, Diana was alone. Her fiancé returned from his travels, then took off again, often to see Camilla. The pattern was established: He had his duty to go out and press the flesh, she had hers—to stay home and learn how to be a princess. Their meetings during the week were intermittent, haphazard almost. Servants, senses tuned in the hothouse atmosphere of palace life to even the vaguest nuance, declared among themselves that there was nothing physical in the relationship. He would hold her hand, put his arm around her, but as one pronounced, it could have been his sister he was embracing for all the passion there was displayed.

If Diana had doubts, so too did Charles. He felt guilty about the prospect of sharing a bed with another woman, a sacrificial lamb, when the only person he wanted to make love to was Camilla. Equally he felt guilty because Diana was clearly becoming distraught by the pressures that were building inside her. That first spark of attraction, those first carefree summer days, had turned to a dark sense of alienation in both of them—and Charles was the first to balk at what was to come.

"She is exquisitely pretty, a perfect poppet . . . but she is a child," he confided to a friend a month before the marriage. "She does not look old enough to be out of school, much less married." These are not the words of a man in the throes of passionate love, but of one who is racked by guilt and fearful for the future. He spoke to the queen about his doubts, and to Prince Philip; but the explosive end to their meeting depressed him and left him with nowhere to turn.

Nowhere, except Camilla. To her, he plaintively put the case: He did not love Diana, he was not sure she loved him, despite her protestations. If this had been another age, when arranged marriages were commonplace, there could be a perfect understanding between them. But both of them had backed into this marriage in the misguided belief that there was something more to it than mere dynastic considerations. Both were trying to play the love game; but only Diana had her heart in it.

With his sense of duty, Charles realized that there could never be a life for him with Camilla, but equally he would rather stay a bachelor than shackle himself to a woman with whom he had little affinity, sexual, spiritual, or intellectual. All these points he put to Camilla—but again he came up against a brick wall. Diana was "the right bride," said his confidante. He should put all doubt behind him and put his trust in her.

There was a row, almost unprecedented, between the prince and Mrs. Parker Bowles. He insisted he should call a halt to the proceedings before it was too late; she was hurt that he had no apparent faith in her judgment. Indeed, so angry did she become that she refused to see him or accept his telephone calls; and the prince, who had convinced himself that at last he had found his safe haven in her, was disoriented and distraught. He even consulted his sister Anne in the hope of finding an ally in that unlikely quarter. Her response was a flat: "Just close your eyes and think of England."

The dreaded day drew nearer. It was a warm summer and London was beginning to glow in anticipation of the greatest celebration since the queen's coronation in 1953 and, to a lesser extent, her Silver Jubilee in 1977. Charles came back from a trip to the United States, gave his future wife a peck on the cheek, and went up to change for lunch. She burst into hysterical tears at his lack of passion.

Many supposed by now that Charles and Diana, sharing

the roof of Buckingham Palace and within weeks of the royal wedding, were sleeping together. They were not—Diana remained in her small suite on the nursery floor while Charles occupied his own suite literally hundreds of yards away. One night in June, the story is told, there was a violent thunderstorm which sent her scurrying in fright from her bed all the way down to Charles's. It was to be the first night they had ever spent together—"Despite their closeness, it did not turn out to be the momentous night it might have been," one version went. "Charles offered her his protective arm and told her not to be frightened of the thunder. He treated her decorously—more decorously than she would have wished."

With the wedding now three weeks away there was a white-tie-and-tails dinner for a thousand people at Windsor Castle, with a cabaret by Elton John. Charles worked the room, never once dancing with Diana, whom he left to her own devices; later he went to bed, and she danced manically on in the disco until, by five o'clock in the morning, she was the only guest left and the servants had packed up and gone home.

With no one left with whom to share the night, she went back to her room, packed a bag, jumped into her car, and headed for the only place she knew she could be safe— Althorp. Those who greeted her there say she was convinced in her own mind she was not going back—the wedding was off, over, kaput. She would leave the country and Charles could be left to pick up the pieces.

Later that day she had a talk with her father, Earl Spencer, and, the weekend over, she reluctantly agreed to return to London. When she arrived at Buckingham Palace she was treated as though nothing had happened—any aberration in her behavior was put down to last-minute nerves. But the ordeal and humiliation were not over yet: In the final days leading up to the wedding a parcel arrived in the office she shared with Michael Colbourne, the prince's financial secretary. Upon it was inscribed the name of Mrs. Parker Bowles. Despite many protestations, Diana opened up the package to discover a gold chain bracelet with a blue enamel disc and the initials G and F entwined. Charles's pet name for Camilla was Girl Friday. According to Andrew Morton, the prince's office came to a halt while Diana angrily confronted her husband-to-be about the gift before bursting noisily into tears. Colbourne later demurred on this point, but there was no denying that the event itself took place, an indication of the lack of care the prince adopted where Diana's feelings were concerned, even at this late stage.

By the Monday (the wedding was on Wednesday) Diana had once again come to the conclusion that she could not go ahead with it. But by now the television cameras were in place, the crowd-control barriers erected, and thousands of seats, flags, and bunting lined the two-mile route from Buckingham Palace to St. Paul's Cathedral. In the courtyards below, she could hear soldiers from the Royal Mews schooling their horses and shouting orders. The palace itself, like a mausoleum in the months she had been staying there, suddenly sprang to life with the sound of vacuum cleaners, maids singing as they changed bed linen and opened up seldom-used rooms, and the clash and clank of silver and gold plate being polished.

In the July heat, the noise of the Brigade of Guards band was sharper and louder; and whenever she looked out of her window all she could see was a plethora of Union Jacks carried by tourists who had flown in from all over the world to witness the forthcoming spectacle.

Yet despite the fact that millions had prepared themselves to watch her glide down the aisle in true fairy-tale tradition, still she could not reconcile herself to what lay ahead. On that Monday, Charles disappeared, bearing the present he had ordered for Mrs. Parker Bowles. He drove on to Windsor for the ill-timed christening of Princess Anne's second child Zara (Anne's former lover Andrew Parker Bowles made an appearance as a godfather), leaving his future wife to her own devices.

In desperation, Diana called her sisters Jane and Sarah to her side and they had lunch at Buckingham Palace. Suddenly brave after her weeks of depression, she told them she was going to call off the wedding.

"Bad luck, Duch," they said. "Your face is on the tea towels—it's too late to chicken out now."

So the miserable young woman, who a month earlier was still a teenager, slunk away to her rooms to prepare for that evening's ball. It is a tribute to her powers of recovery that by the evening she was in good spirits once more, and reconciled to her fate. Altogether eight hundred guests crowded into Buckingham Palace that night, and Charles and Diana, flanked by liveried footmen, greeted them at the head of the grand staircase. Included in the guests, who ranged from Nancy Reagan to "Acid" Raine Spencer, Diana's ogreish stepmother, was Camilla Parker Bowles.

With mere hours to go before the historic ceremony, with the pop group Hot Chocolate raising a storm in the ballroom, and vintage Krug champagne flowing like the Niagara Falls; with bejeweled women and bemedaled men, the cream of royalty and aristocracy dancing and laughing and drinking in candlelit rooms and halls, there was one last act of betrayal yet to be played out in this historic tragedy.

Chapter Six

"A Little Problem"

———◁◦◦◦▷———

Diana's royal career began in the stately rooms of Clarence House, the Queen Mother's eighteenth-century mansion situated in the Mall, a five-minute walk from Buckingham Palace. It was to Clarence House that she returned in the early hours of Tuesday morning after the nuptial ball, leaving behind Prince Charles—and Camilla Parker Bowles.

It is fair to say that, having first questioned whether he could go on with the marriage—as Diana had done—Charles then committed himself to it, in just the way he committed himself to all aspects of his duty.

If, then, he took Camilla Parker Bowles to bed in those last hours leading up to his wedding, he saw it as no act of betrayal. Rather it was in the belief that he must now dedicate himself to his wife, and to married life. This, he told Camilla, was the last time they would make love.

And they did. Charles's valet Stephen Barry later told James Whitaker: "Sir had always been infatuated with Camilla since they first knew each other in the early 1970s. But when he took her to bed in the very week of his wedding it seemed incredible. Certainly incredibly daring, if not incredibly stupid."

Perhaps. But if this was a passionate farewell, delivered in the dark hours after Buckingham Palace had stilled, and the guests had gone, it was indeed poignant; a full stop to a passion and understanding which had grown and flourished in the past two years, and whose origins stretched back the best part of a decade. The intensity of their relationship was heightened by the constraints imposed upon it, a greater excitement being created by the ever-present knowledge that it was verboten.

But it was an act of betrayal, nonetheless, not only to his future wife but to the queen and the waiting country, all of whom might have expected him to still his ardor on the eve of his wedding vows. Within hours, he would hear the Archbishop of Canterbury, Dr. Robert Runcie, ask a packed and hushed congregation: "If anyone can show cause or just impediment why these two people should not be joined together in holy matrimony, let him now speak, or else here-after forever hold his peace." One person—Stephen Barry—could show such cause, or at the very least open a debate as to the wisdom of Charles's actions; but he wasn't talking.

The night before the wedding Charles sent an emissary to his fiancée with a prenuptial present, a signet ring engraved with the Prince of Wales's feathers. The man had to fight his way through the crowds standing crushed against the Buckingham Palace railings; with voices hoarse with emotion they raised them in song, serenading the prince in his sitting room with "Rule Britannia." "I found myself standing in the window with tears pouring down my face," he recalled; but what were the tears for? In gratitude for the genuine affec-tion of his subjects? In sorrow for the love he must put behind him? In fear of the life to come with a wife he could not love? Or was it because this essentially decent, hard-working, honorable, and dedicated man felt he had let himself and everyone else down?

Meanwhile, over at Clarence House, Diana opened Charles's present and read the accompanying card, which said: "I'm so proud of you and when you come up I'll be there at the altar for you tomorrow. Just look 'em in the eye and knock 'em dead." Diana, for a moment deliriously happy at this uncharacteristically romantic gesture, went down to dinner with her sister Jane, ate everything she could, and was promptly sick.

There was a brief moment of sweet revenge. After the wedding, 120 guests were invited to Buckingham Palace for the wedding breakfast. Camilla Parker Bowles's name was struck off the list, along with that of another of Charles's close friends, Lady "Kanga" Tryon. Camilla responded by hosting a luncheon party herself, content in the knowledge that her wedding present to Charles was packed in his going-away luggage. But, perhaps sensing Charles's determination to put the past behind him—and his acceptance that Camilla and Lady Tryon should not be his guests on that important day was the first step—Diana began to relax. "I had tremendous hope in my heart," she said.

But Camilla never went away. Days into their Mediterranean cruise on the royal yacht *Britannia*, which they had joined at Gibraltar, and after an unhappy consummation, the royal couple were comparing engagements in their respective diaries when two photographs of Mrs. Parker Bowles fell out from the pages of Charles's diary. A tearful row ensued, stoked up by the unreleased tensions from the wedding days before. A cornered Charles, embarrassed at being caught, angry that his new wife so many years his junior should have the moral advantage over him, simply refused to discuss his relationship with the older woman. Diana was distraught.

Several days later the couple entertained the President of Egypt, Anwar Sadat, and his wife, Rhan, to dinner aboard the royal yacht, by now anchored at Port Said. Sadat favored a lounge suit, Charles a form of naval mess kit with bow tie and starched white shirt. Diana, who had been instrumental in rejuvenating Charles's sartorial appearance and who took a close interest in what he wore, noted that in his starched cuffs he was sporting a new-looking pair of gold cuff links.[2] They bore two entwined Cs, deftly symbolizing the bond between Charles and Camilla, and yet again Diana challenged her husband about Mrs. Parker Bowles. He finally admitted they were a gift from her, but rather than admit his boorishness in wearing them in front of his wife, he resorted to a "So what? She's been a friend of mine for years" argument.

Diana's recollection of these early days of marriage demonstrate the hopelessness of the situation: "It was just grim. I just had tremendous hope in me, which was slashed by day two." On board *Britannia* she was surrounded by staff and personnel so that she was never alone with her husband: "By then the bulimia was appalling, absolutely appalling. It was rife, four times a day on the yacht. Anything I could find I would gobble up and be sick two minutes later. I remember crying my eyes out on our honeymoon. I was so tired, for all the wrong reasons totally."

Yet by now, and against all odds, there seemed a determi-

---

[2] After a quantity of jewelry and personal effects were stolen from the Prince of Wales' apartments at St. James's Palace in 1994, inquiries about these cuff links were met with the palace response: "They never existed in the first place." But this statement was made without apparent conviction and not repeated: If there is one instruction above all others the denizens of that office are told to obey, it is that they must not be caught out in a lie.

nation to make things work; after all, in the short term there was nothing else they could do. There may have been mutual suspicion, but both the young ingenue and the older, experienced man knew what they were in. They had seen the expressions on the faces of the crowds, knew what they owed them. And a growing bond of affection, manifested in exchanged letters which touched on the topic of love, demonstrated that there was still hope. "When you are young," Diana said later, "optimism keeps breaking through."

Those who support the Prince of Wales believe there was an absolute determination on both sides, after that last night of love in Buckingham Palace, that Charles and Camilla would go their separate ways. She had a young family and, though she could never be categorized as an "army wife," had certain responsibilities toward her husband in terms of entertaining and being entertained. Charles had a public life and now, at last, a regularized private one.

But, incarcerated with Diana at Balmoral on their return from their honeymoon, Charles found that he was sharing his life with an alien being. Diana was losing weight at a quite alarming rate, though no one—apart from servants who occasionally had to clean up after her—was aware of her bulimic condition. She was isolated at Balmoral, separated from friends and family and the London life she knew, finding herself the most junior member of the royal family who, in any conversation, was the last to be spoken to by members of that xenophobic clan. There were no familiar reference points, no moments of respite, and no escape. She crumbled.

"Inexorably," wrote Andrew Morton, "her thoughts turned to suicide, not because she wanted to die, but because she desperately wanted help."

Diana herself recalled later that she constantly dreamed of

Camilla. Her state of mind so alarmed her husband that, not wishing to acknowledge she was suffering a clinical condition, he called on his friend Sir Laurens Van der Post to come and counsel his wife. To Charles, the writer and philosopher was a visionary—a moral and spiritual guru in whom he could place his trust. But even in this he demonstrated a characteristic lack of judgment: Many felt that Van der Post was not all he seemed, and eventually the myth he created around himself started to crumble. It emerged he had seduced a fourteen-year-old girl whose parents had entrusted him to chaperon on a sea crossing to Britain, then set her up in a one-room apartment in Chelsea for him to visit and indulge his sexual gratification. The girl became pregnant and bore a daughter.

Van der Post's words had little effect on Diana, who, more savvy than her husband, despised the old man. But her problems remained, and in early October she flew to London for professional counseling, seeing doctors and psychologists at Buckingham Palace. Their collective opinion was that she should be put on a course of tranquilizers. This appalled Charles, a man who at best was an innocent unprepared for the buffets of the married state, at worst a man who hardened his heart at any sign of weakness.

In his wife's absence, confused, bewildered, desperately unhappy, and at a loss as to what to do, he broke all the promises he had made to himself and telephoned Camilla.

Whatever her determination at this point to stay away from Charles, there can be no doubt that the call came as a blessed relief. Despite their row over Diana's ability as a future Princess of Wales—and, it must be acknowledged, Charles's reservations were by now seen to be justified—there was a magnetic attraction, forged in secrecy and tempered in adultery, which would not go away. They arranged to meet again.

Thus it was that three days before Buckingham Palace announced to the waiting world that the Princess of Wales was pregnant, her husband was to be found out riding with the Vale of the White Horse Hunt. The hunt was not one with which he had previously been associated, preferring the superior country (and breeding) of the Quorn, the Belvoir, and the Beaufort.

However, on 2 November 1981, four months after his marriage and immediately after his return from his extended Scottish sojourn, this obscure pack of hounds suited the Prince of Wales's purpose. There had been some hopes that he might turn out with the Beaufort, but while he was keen to return to the saddle he chose the remoter charms of Ewen, near Cirencester, where the Vale met that day.

His presence in the field remained undetected for some hours until a fox led hounds out of a wood toward a main road, where about forty people had gathered. The fox went to ground and the prince turned back and rode away as the hunt regrouped, finding his only path was down the empty main street. As he turned the corner, he met the hunt followers and a pack of Fleet Street photographers. Flushing bright red, he bellowed at them: "When are you going to stop making my life a total misery?" His vehemence stunned the witnesses to this scene, but as he spurred his horse back toward the regrouped hunt, a blond woman on horseback joined him and they rode away together. The woman looked suspiciously like Camilla Parker Bowles.

After that encounter, which went unremarked in a press now reaching fever pitch at the prospect of the birth of a future king, Charles and Camilla relaxed. They started to hunt regularly together, often with the Beaufort but sometimes farther afield in Leicestershire where Charles's old friend Ulrike Murray-Smith was to be found. Camilla had hunted from an early age, Charles started when he was older, but both derived the same breathtaking satisfaction from the chase. Royal author Suzy Menkes observed: "I believe that Charles gets a tremendous sexual thrill and charge from hunting, which many people do."

He adored to see Camilla in full flight on horseback—"She's a ruthless horsewoman, aggressive, shouting in the hunting field," said a member of the Beaufort who has ridden with her. "To use the word assertive would be an understatement. You should hear her screaming as you approach a fence. She's shouting, 'Bloody hell, get out of the fucking way!' She steamrollers people and it can be quite frightening."

Compare this red-blooded, sexual, athletic being with the painfully neurotic and bulimic Diana, and it is suddenly easy to see why Charles broke the vows of abstinence he had made himself. For four long months he had nurtured his desperately unhappy wife the best way he could, had been subjected to her temper tantrums, and had heaped even more opprobrium upon himself by showing himself to being a less than competent liar.

Camilla was normal. She was grownup. She was womanly with voluptuous curves, not a bag of bones. She could listen for hours without having to counter Charles's litany of woes with a list of her own troubles. She was sexually adventurous. And she was, in all truth, a very nice, if ambitious, woman.

She had also come to the realization that there was room in her life to cope with the prince and his problems; and the prospect, now that he was married, of truly following in her great-grandmother's footsteps as "La Favorita" was an enticing one.

The couple were pushed closer together by the alarming behavior of Diana, who now had to add the burden of pregnancy to her other miseries. John Bowes-Lyon, a co-godfather with Prince Charles of Camilla's son Thomas, reported: "She had fits which would last just a few minutes, during which she would go crazy and become uncontrollable. Then it was all over as quickly as it began."

Whether, as some claim, Diana's tumble down the stairs at Sandringham that Christmas was a manifestation of this rage, an attempt at suicide (if so, a risible one; the stairs are very shallow), or simply a desire to be noticed, it was depressing for Charles to find himself being called to help pick up his pregnant wife and order a gynecologist to be sent from London.

"At first doctors thought her outbursts might have been epilepsy," John Bowes-Lyon reported. "But that was discounted because she didn't swallow her tongue or have other epileptic symptoms. Apparently what she suffers from can be hereditary and there have been other instances in the Fermoy family, so the royal family have been told."

With—as he saw it—a lifetime's marriage still in front of him, Charles offered an olive branch to Diana. Conscious of her irritation that Highgrove had been chosen in part by Camilla, and her desire to be rid of the house, he suggested they look for an alternative base in the country. Diana took up the suggestion with alacrity, but made the proviso that it should be as far away from Camilla as possible—no more Gloucestershire, no more West Country—and nearer to her own family seat, Althorp.

On 4 March 1982, the *Daily Express*'s unusually well-informed diarist William Hickey recorded under the headline DIANA FALLS OUT OF LOVE WITH HIGHGROVE:

> *The Prince and Princess of Wales are looking for a new home. Despite extensive refurbishments to Highgrove, it is said the princess is "unhappy with the character of the place" and wants to move.*

Having been used to the palatial surroundings of her own family home, Althorp, this is quite understandable. Althorp has 15,000 acres, Highgrove just 348.

The couple have spent very little of their seven-month marriage in the place, and coupled with this comes word from Belton House, the stately home of Lord Brownlow in Lincolnshire, that Charles and Diana are interested in buying.

Belton was, in many ways, ideal. It was grand, unlike Highgrove: An impressive four-square house built originally in the seventeenth century and containing carvings by Grinling Gibbons, it also boasted priceless tapestries and paintings by Titian, Rubens, Raphael, Rembrandt, and Van Dyk, as well as a *Mona Lisa* by Leonardo da Vinci similar to the masterpiece hanging in the Louvre. Equally attractive was the fact that, though situated in prime hunting country, it had no associations with Camilla. Charles had stayed there on many occasions while training as an RAF pilot at nearby Cranwell, and it was within striking distance of Sandringham. It had royal associations—the present incumbent's father, Perry Brownlow, the sixth baron, had been a lord-in-waiting during the brief kingship of Edward VIII and one of the closest friends of the Duke and Duchess of Windsor. And, from Diana's point of view, it was a short drive from her sister Sarah's house.

The royal couple visited Belton on at least three occasions in 1982 and came close to making the decision to move there. Diana, desperate to shake off Highgrove, pressed ever harder. But for Charles two factors weighed against it—the seventeenth-century house, with its nearly five thousand acres, would be costly to run and was too far from Duchy of Cornwall land for resources to be shared; and it would mean abandoning Highgrove. So many of the prince and princess's wedding presents, including the gift of a swimming pool and some ornamental gates, were associated with that particular house that it would be taken as a monumental snub if they walked away from it.

But, as his critics have ever been ready to point out, Prince Charles is indecisive; and he continued to toy with the idea of Belton during the following year. Only in the summer of 1983 was the house finally put on the market; the official reason for Charles and Diana's decision not to move in was that Belton's grandeur was out of keeping with the royal family's new line in frugality. Diana was furious at being forced to stay at Highgrove—even though with the help of interior designer Dudley Poplak she had lavished £100,000 of her husband's money redecorating the place, rubbing out any vestige of Camilla's influence.

The relationship between Charles and Camilla, hinted at and gossiped about in the newspapers since the days of Anna Wallace, now went underground. Even columnists who had kept a close watch on the pair found themselves starved of information, and by May 1982, with Diana's pregnancy nicely on the way, a woefully wide-of-the-mark piece appeared in one tabloid newspaper. It revealed that Camilla, along with her friend Rose Pitman (later to marry Andrew Parker Bowles), was selling secondhand frocks from Bolehyde Manor. Referring to Camilla's exclusion from the wedding breakfast the previous year, the piece concluded: "This step into trade is a far cry from the ways of the royal family, and serves to confirm Camilla's status—on the outside."

If she read it, she must have laughed. But it served her purpose. Fleet Street's article added neatly to the smoke screen which had been laid around the couple: They were finished, a dead letter, if anybody asked. Increasingly, people did not—they were too distracted by the excitement of the forthcoming royal birth.

With the arrival of Prince William of Wales on 21 June 1982, Charles found himself even more alienated from his wife. He attended the long and painful labor and was present when his son was born. It was a rare moment of reunification for the couple, and they shared that sense of pride which all young couples enjoy at the arrival of their first-born.

But Diana was not a well woman when she gave birth: Her body had suffered from the recurrent bouts of bulimia and she was in a weakened state. Once the initial euphoria passed, it was replaced with postnatal depression. This, once again, triggered the bulimia. Charles was aware of the problem; in fact he was not allowed to forget it—Diana's depression evinced itself most often in a series of attacks on him for his continued relationship with Camilla, details of which the princess could not have known yet somehow instinctively felt. There were tears and panic telephone calls when he did not arrive home on time, and nights without sleep when he was away. Charles's telephone calls to Mrs. Parker Bowles became more urgent, and it was only a matter of time before Diana overheard one: The prince was in his bath and talking on the telephone. His words echoed out of the bathroom and ran a dagger through Diana's heart.

The man who, when asked about his feelings for his future wife, had said, "Whatever 'in love' means," raised his voice above the splashing water. "Whatever happens," he said into the telephone to Mrs. Parker Bowles, "I will always love you."

Love, of the physical variety, was not high on the royal couple's agenda after the birth of William. After their move to Kensington Palace a servant confirmed that the couple rarely slept in their four-poster bed together. Often Diana would go to bed early, while Charles preferred to stay up late: "When he had finished what he was doing each night, the prince would creep upstairs and without disturbing his wife slip into his dressing room, which adjoined the master bedroom, from an outside door leading off the corridor. There he would get into the bed which was always made up for him. Whether this was out of consideration for his wife or because he just wanted to be on his own I couldn't say. But it did happen frequently."

The servant could not know but these nights near, but not with, his wife gave considerable ease to Charles's vexed state of mind. He was married—inescapably, it seemed—and there was, even now, a warmth between him and Diana. But Camilla was Charles's greater love: With her he had found peace and serenity, the hope and right of all lovers, and the nights spent in his dressing room allowed her into his dreams. The unbearable life which he and his wife were leading was already doomed, yet he did not know it; and he clung to the belief that as long as he had Camilla in the background he could soldier on.

But it was hard. On the eve of Remembrance Day 1982, the year of the Falklands War, Charles and Diana were due to join the queen at the annual British Legion service of remembrance at the Royal Albert Hall in London. Coupled with the following day's homage at the Cenotaph in Whitehall, this event recalls to the nation those who died in defense of their country, and is considered to be top of the royal family's list of annual public engagements.

"Minutes before the ceremonial was due to begin, a doorman was told that Diana would not be attending: There had been a monumental row, and she was in no state to be seen in public. There was a frantic rearrangement of chairs in the royal box as the queen was informed of her daughter-in-law's intended absence. Fifteen minutes later, with the queen already in her seat, Diana appeared looking "grumpy and fed-up," according to an eyewitness. This latest intransigence was a further embarrassment to Charles, particularly when it was picked up by the newspapers the following day.

"No one is ever late for the queen," wrote the indefatigable James Whitaker, "so I set out to find what was the matter.

"A month or so before, Diana had swept out of Balmoral in a fury, leaving Charles and their three-and-a-half-month-old son behind. She just wanted to get out of Scotland. Most particularly she objected to the way that Charles would always side with his mother in any disagreement. She was also beginning to be extremely irritated with the Queen Mother continually 'helping' her. She had been given no assistance by the Queen Mother on her introduction into royal circles, despite popular myth, and she felt that by now she could cope perfectly adequately without little lectures."

Whitaker also discovered by talking to Diana's press officer, Vic Chapman, that there was, indeed, "a little problem." Chapman vouchsafed that the princess had become obsessive in her behavior, citing as an example a preoccupation with her shoes—when cleaned, they should be put back in precisely the straight lines they were in when taken away. "She is obsessed that everything and everybody around her should be perfect," Chapman explained.

The resulting article by Whitaker suggested, for the first time, that the Princess of Wales was behaving irrationally, and that this could be because of an eating disorder. He described her painfully thin body, and the fact that she would needlessly stress, on meeting members of the public at official functions, that she had to watch her waistline.

The publication of the article created a furor. There was an angry denial from a Buckingham Palace spokesman, who added the desperate rider: "For God's sake, leave her alone." The BBC's top radio presenter, Brian Redhead, criticized Whitaker's article on air as "outrageous"; but the reporter had the information correct, and from the best possible source— Diana's deeply concerned sister, Sarah.

That the media were now publicly discussing his wife's dietary abnormalities was a further humiliation to Charles, who had to answer to his still-critical father every time something damaging about the Waleses appeared in the newspapers. He started taking lunch with Diana "just to make sure she eats properly."

Andrew Parker Bowles had been recently promoted to commanding officer of the Household Cavalry. The regimental headquarters, a high-rise block which blights the south side of Hyde Park, had become home since his duties became increasingly social, as well as military. Camilla was not, as has been noted, an army wife: She was content to live her life at Bolehyde Manor, just a short drive away from Highgrove. Soon the couple were to move to another home, Middlewick House, near Corsham, just twelve miles from Highgrove— even closer. Diana faced this prospect with deep unhappiness, but for form's sake attended the housewarming party without apparent demur.

Charles's enthusiasm for the hunt increased. His official workload had gone down and he was allowing himself more time for personal pursuits—and the fox came high on that list. He would turn out with the Beaufort once, twice, and even three times in a week, which necessitated him staying behind at Highgrove while Diana traveled to London.

Followers of the Beaufort noted that Charles would carefully avoid the meet, then join the field once the chase was under way. Mrs. Parker Bowles, a respected member of the hunt, would at some stage fall back in the field and the couple would walk their horses into the woods, catching up with fellow members much later in the day.

Though she was never present on these hunt days, Diana was only too aware of what was going on. In November 1983, soon after she suffered a miscarriage while staying at Balmoral, a monumental row broke out at Highgrove when Charles left for a day's hunting; Diana was under the impression he had said he would stay behind. There was another screaming match, in front of witnesses, as he left the house to join the Beaufort and Mrs. Parker Bowles. As he drove off, Diana collapsed once again in tears—but by this stage, Charles was immune: He had had enough.

Their conjugal life was not yet quite over, however, and in September 1984 Diana gave birth to Prince Harry. This time the joy of a new life made was savored separately, not together. In his perpetual quest for knowledge Charles had become something of an expert on baby care, so much so that Diana was heard to snarl: "My husband knows so much about rearing children that I've suggested that he has the next one and I'll sit back and give advice."

But there was not to be a next one, for the gap had widened so considerably between the two that now, three years after the wedding, they had ceased sleeping together. Charles had greeted Harry's arrival at St. Mary's Hospital, Paddington, with an airy "Oh, it's a boy" (he had wanted a girl) "and it's even got red hair"—and with that he set off for polo. According to some, this single act signaled the end of the marriage.

But not yet: They continued to attend official engagements together, and between the rows had established a not unendurable truce. Their leisure hours, though, were spent separately: Charles would go to the opera—and Camilla would go too; sometimes bringing along a perfectly content Andrew Parker Bowles who would sit smilingly behind them in the royal box.

For Charles these outings were an oasis of calm in the turbulent domestic life; he would return to find Diana seething with indignation. "Her temper grew worse as the hours passed and by the time Charles arrived home she was often in a towering, door-banging fury," revealed one source. Charles's reaction, more often than not, was non-confrontational; he would simply shake his head and walk away. It drove Diana into even greater paroxysms of rage.

Outwardly, the couple made a great show of togetherness: Public duty was the one point where they saw eye to eye, and indeed Diana's love affair with the public was still extremely hot. Wherever she went she could, on her exit from the official car, create an electric charge through a crowd of thousands. Her early faltering steps on the fashion ladder were gone: She was now a supreme dresser, both daring and modest, and there could be no questioning her success in her public role, both at home and abroad. She possessed in public a heady cocktail of formality and informality which somehow maintained her position as Princess of Wales yet made her accessible to all.

Analysts at that time who detected a certain reserve in Charles's welcome for this success put it down to jealousy. On joint outings he would apologize to the public: "I'm sorry it's me you've got, not my wife." Or: "It's me you've got, I'm afraid. Better ask for your money back." It was an inescapable fact that it was her face which appeared on magazine covers wherever they traveled in the world, not his; that on joint outings the cameras only pointed at her; that when flowers were waved in his direction they were destined for Diana. It was initially confusing, for Charles had devoted his whole life to the idea of service, and thought that his people should be able to sense it and tacitly, by their attention and applause, thank him for it. Even as late as April 1994 he had still not reconciled himself to the impact Diana's arrival on the scene had had on the revival of interest in royalty, and in an interview with former Labor cabinet minister Roy Hattersley repudiated the idea of a "showbiz monarchy." "The media helped create the showbiz idea," he accused. "They invented it, we didn't." But the truth lay somewhere in between, for in the last quarter of the twentieth century the media had been very lukewarm about the House of Windsor until Diana came along. Notwithstanding the inner turmoil she created in that great dynastic house, she helped put it back on the map.

Yet Charles could never voice—except to Camilla—his dismay as to how the public could get it so desperately wrong. Surely they didn't fall that easily for a pretty face? Surely they could sense that there was no substance to her, that indeed there was something wrong with her?

But the adoring public could not. The only person who knew of Diana's instability was Charles. The only person who could share the burden was Camilla. She had found a new house, in the village of Pickwick near Corsham in Wiltshire, called Middlewick House. Built in Cotswold and Bath stone some time in the eighteenth century, the beautiful manor house, complete with ghost, came with five hundred acres— plenty of room to exercise her horses and to escape the unwelcome, though not yet intrusive, attentions of the press. Middlewick was the quintessential English country house and Camilla lost her heart to it: And there was no disadvantage in its being only fifteen minutes' drive from Highgrove. The Parker Bowleses sold Bolehyde for around £500,000 and unexpectedly found the purchase of Middlewick eased by an inheritance, for on 16 August 1986 Sonia Cubitt died.

The daughter of Alice Keppel took with her to the grave the secret of whether she was King Edward VII's illegitimate daughter or not. What she did leave behind, however, was a handsome legacy: Camilla was said to have received over half a million pounds from it. It almost put a rest to the rumors among a certain circle that Middlewick House had been paid for by Prince Charles, but few people wanted to let a good story like that go without examining all the possibilities.

Such rumors were of no consequence to the prince, however, who had greater problems on his mind. The bulimia was still there, an increasing embarrassment to Charles as commentators started, at last, to write about how pitifully thin the princess had become. On a trip to Vancouver to open the Expo exhibition her wasted figure gave cause for excited comment, but the worldwide media went on red alert when she fainted as she reached the California stand. She put her hand on her husband's shoulder and whispered, "Darling, I think I'm going to disappear," and promptly collapsed. She had not eaten for days.

With some justification, Charles was furious. He had a job to do, and she was simply providing a distraction which took away from the purpose of the whole trip. But then, his friends argued, Diana had long discovered how to upstage the family she had come to hate. Attending the state opening of Parliament as a supernumerary to the queen, whose historic role it is to lead her Lords and Commons into the next parliamentary session, she had ordered that her hair be turned up into a chignon. It altered her whole appearance—as she knew it would—and drew all attention away from the queen.

Everyone was furious, including her strongest ally, Princess Margaret, who asked her sister: "How could you let her make such a fool of you?"

In subsequent biographies there was criticism of the prince for neither containing Diana's rages nor investigating their root cause and seeking a solution to them. His refusal, except under extreme provocation, to be drawn into rows with his wife has been dismissed as uncaring and churlish behavior, whereas his friends argue that Charles simply sought to end what he considered to be irrational rantings by defusing the situation. That, to him, meant walking away and giving his partner time to cool down. No great psychologist, he did not realize he was simply making matters worse by refusing Diana her full say. On more than one occasion doctors brought in to deal with the difficulties facing Diana and her relationship with Charles offered advice on this, but the prince was dealing with an irrational being and, it must be borne in mind, was only human himself.

Soon after Charles and Diana had traveled to Althorp, her family home, where they stayed in a specially redecorated suite. On their departure it was left, revealed Earl Spencer, in a "somewhat damaged" state—an antique mirror was smashed, as too was a window, and the leg of a priceless eighteenth-century chair was shattered. Later Lord Spencer, showing others around the house, admitted there had been "an almighty row" between the married couple. Yet Diana, when quizzed by the valet Stephen Barry, vaguely dismissed the devastation. "There was no air in here," she said. "It was an accident."

By 1987 the marriage was over, but no one was yet ready to admit it. From Charles's point of view, he could remain married to Diana for the rest of his life—it did not matter. He had the one person on whom he could rely, Camilla, safely at his elbow and with her undiminished support he was now confident he could withstand most of life's buffets.

From Diana's point of view, she had achieved what she had set out to do—become Princess of Wales. She had borne two children in pursuit of her husband's dynastic ambitions. She had become a world icon, a very important person in her own right. She lacked love—whatever love is—but most other things were in place. For a moment it looked as though the bulimia which had dogged her these many years was on hold.

But then the whole thing started to become unglued. On their skiing holiday at Klosters that year Charles and Diana were accompanied by the newly married Duke and Duchess of York. The Duchess had been asked to bring along a couple of extra men: One was Philip Dunne, a merchant banker, son of the Lord Lieutenant of Herefordshire and godson of Princess Alexandra. One night Diana went to the local disco and spent the evening chatting sociably to Dunne, on another she and Fergie stayed in the chalet and played an idiotic après-ski game which ended up with the princess lying in the bottom of a large chest of drawers pretending to be asleep. One observer reported that she called out that the first person to kiss her would become a prince; Dunne was the one to step forward.

Dunne has always maintained that their relationship was entirely innocent, and there is little evidence to support a contrary view. But what happened next drove a greater wedge between the Waleses than anything that had gone before.

Dunne invited members of the skiing party back to his parents' house, Gatley Park. Soon it emerged that neither Charles nor Dunne's parents were present. When this story appeared in the tabloid press, only one conclusion could be

drawn. The Waleses were having a bumpy patch in their marriage, and Diana had found someone to comfort her. An
almighty scandal looked ready to blow, until Dunne pointed
out—extremely forcefully—that a dozen friends had also
been staying at the house over that weekend.

But Charles, deep in his own adultery, misread the runes.
Certainly he could tell there was an attraction between the
younger man and his wife; maybe for a moment he found
reason to ascribe his own motives and actions to Diana.
Whatever, by the time the marriage of the Duke of Beaufort's son the Marquess of Worcester came around in June
1987, relations between the two were at an all-time low, with
mutual suspicion and disregard the order of the day.

At the wedding reception Charles first danced with the
woman he had once proposed marriage to—Anna Wallace—
then sat down with the woman he had been aching to see,
Camilla. The couple talked to the exclusion of all others for
the rest of the night. Diana, infuriated by what she saw, started
to dance with Philip Dunne. She danced and she danced,
long and hard and frenetically, "pausing only long enough to
wipe her forehead with the hem of her gown," one guest
reported, until at six the next morning the music stopped.
Charles and Camilla had slipped away hours before.

That display, and the publicity surrounding the weekend
at Gatley Park, convinced Charles that his wife had been
unfaithful to him, and it struck a mortal blow to his amour
propre. It does not take a liberated man to identify the dual
standards employed here by the prince, but he was a man
who had grown up bolstered in the belief that as the future
king, all things were his for the asking. And that included a
faithful wife. If she had been to bed with Dunne, writhing on
the dance floor in front of him with this man was simply

rubbing his nose in it—and in front of a wide cross-section of the aristocracy, to boot.

Almost certainly this assumption of Diana's infidelity was based on a false premise, but he did not stop to consider that. Gathering Camilla up, he headed for Scotland and Balmoral, arriving on 22 September.

There began his longest exile, a quite unprecedented gesture which no amount of comment in Parliament and the press could shake him from. He was not to see his wife for the next thirty-seven days, nor did he see his children. No explanation was forthcoming—he seemed not to care what interpretation was put on his actions. He spent long days alone with Camilla, talking his way through the past six disastrous years, reminding her of her prediction that Diana was "a mouse" and would be perfect for the job of princess; he reminded her too of their broken pledge of abstinence, and talked long and hard about the future. He had come to love Tuscany, and saw a future for himself and Camilla there, away from the humiliation and criticism and away from the duty which kept him locked to Diana's side.

Three years later, Charles came close to a nervous breakdown, but it was here, in the purple hills of Balmoral, that the first seeds were sown. Other friends, including Lord and Lady Tryon, came to stay and they passed the days in a mechanical observance of the Balmoral round: fishing, shooting, stalking, painting; but it was here that Charles started to question, possibly for the first time, what it was all for, and whether it was worth it. Even the warmth of Camilla's love did little to stop his downward spiral into depression.

Meanwhile, back in London the newspapers were counting the days the couple were apart, in bigger and bigger type. Diana's relationship with the merchant banker came under the microscope, and another member of that fateful Klosters ski party, Major David Waterhouse, was forced to spring to his defense. "There has been a lot of talk about the princess and Philip," he said. "It is absurd to say they are having an affair. The allegation is totally untrue."

Whether this reached Charles, as it was designed to do, and whether the prince took any comfort from this reassurance, it was difficult to tell. Certainly there was no early reaction from north of the border; no indication that he intended to return home to his wife and children.

Enter, stage left, the most unlikely character in the whole lexicon of British celebrities to propose himself as an honest broker in the Waleses' marriage: Jimmy Savile. A disc jockey whose trademark is fat cigars and a line in death-defying banality which makes all but the lionhearted cringe at its triteness, he had become a TV personality through his can-do TV show for the BBC, *Jim'll Fix It*. This, indeed, was his finest hour—because if he could fix the Waleses' marriage, he would have done the nation a service worthy of the knighthood that was shortly to be his.

Savile suggested to the estranged couple that a way out of their present impasse would be to make a joint appearance in Dyfed in Wales, which had been devastated by flooding. There was a nice symmetry in their coming together again in public on the very soil whose name they both bore. For whatever reason, though probably spurred by Camilla, who saw Charles's credibility ebbing with each day he continued to stay away from his family, both made their way to RAF Northolt for the flight to Swansea.

The trip was a disaster from the very start. Diana arrived first, in an extremely agitated state, but she was clearly unprepared for the naked hostility Charles showed toward her on his arrival—a hostility he took no trouble to conceal from the numerous members of staff forgathered in preparation for their departure.

Unlike Charles, who had been cushioned from world media attention during his exile, Diana had suffered from the spotlight being turned on her during those thirty-seven lonely, and increasingly dramatic, days. Her outward appearance had remained calm as she continued her duties under intense pressure. Some of these matters she tried to explain to her husband on the short flight to Wales, but Charles could barely bring himself to listen. As she described how difficult it was to be in the continued glare of publicity caused by his self-imposed exile, he groaned: "Oh, God, what is the matter?" For much of the flight he completely ignored his wife, and the tour, designed to raise the spirits of the unhappy Welsh, did nothing more than draw attention away from their plight and concentrate on the Waleses'.

The Times, for example, considered this sighting of the estranged couple of such significance that it devoted part of its front page to report: "The prince looked concerned as he heard accounts of the deluge: the princess scowled when she saw photographers, no doubt suspecting that they were there only to record the Waleses' first public appearance together since 16 September."

The brief encounter in Carmarthen lasted six hours, during which time their several duties allowed little time for the couple to speak to each other. They flew back to London, and Charles returned to Balmoral. Meanwhile Diana, realizing that nothing lasting had been achieved beyond a fence-mending public relations job with the people of Wales (despite one flood victim, Mr. Darrel Reynolds, observing: "I would rather have had £2,000 compensation than a royal visit. There is nothing they can do"), gamely set off for a charity auction at Christie's. She was described by one newspaper, whose reporter was not admitted to the proceedings, as "looking happy and relaxed." Jimmy Savile's hoped-for reconciliation had proved a task too Herculean for even this personality with a superabundance of self-confidence.

The pressure on the two participants in this arranged marriage was getting worse. At that stage, friends of Diana and of Charles agree, there was no question but that the marriage was for life: It was a question of both of them knuckling down to agreeing to a formula whereby they lived together, but apart. But neither, psychologically, was up to making that accommodation. After the threat of exposure by her well-meaning former flatmate Carolyn Bartholemew, Diana submitted to the ministrations of Dr. Maurice Lipsedge, a specialist in eating disorders at Guy's Hospital. One of his earliest questions, put directly, was how many times Diana had attempted suicide. The princess, startled, answered: "Four or five times."

Lipsedge's dedication ultimately stilled the bulimia, though there were recurrences whenever Diana was forced to return to Highgrove. Indeed, her hatred of the place had continued to grow since the day when Charles finally announced that they were not to move to Belton in Lincolnshire. But while she fought to contain the bulimia, she found she now had the strength to tackle Camilla.

Early in 1989 there was a party to celebrate the fortieth birthday—on 2 February—of Camilla's sister Annabel Elliott, wife of Dorset landowner Simon Elliott, which was held in a house on Ham Common near Richmond owned by Sir James and Lady Annabel Goldsmith. "There was," recorded Andrew Morton, "an unspoken assumption among the forty guests that Diana would not appear. There was a frisson of surprise among the assembled company when she walked in. After dinner, Diana, who was chatting to guests in an upstairs room, noted the absence of her husband and Camilla Parker Bowles. She went downstairs and found her husband, Camilla, and other guests chatting. The princess asked the others to leave because she had something important to say to Camilla."

Diana recalled this face-out as "one of the bravest moments of my entire ten years. Nobody expected me to turn up but a voice inside me said, 'Go for the hell of it.' So I psyched myself up something awful. I decided I'm not going to kiss her. After dinner we were all upstairs and I was chatting away and suddenly noticed there was no Camilla and no Charles. They tried to stop me from going downstairs—'Oh Diana, don't go down there.' "

She went downstairs to find Charles, Camilla, and another man sitting and happily chatting. The third member of the group, sensing impending disaster despite Diana's apparent calm, suggested they all return upstairs. Charles and the man went, Diana ordered Camilla to stay behind. She recalled: "I said to Camilla, 'Would you like to sit down?' So we sat down and I was terrified and I said, 'Camilla, I would just like you to know that I know exactly what is going on between you and Charles. I wasn't born yesterday. I'm sorry I'm in the way, I obviously am in the way, and it must be hell for both of you, but I do know what is going on. Don't treat me like an idiot.' "

In the car going home, Charles, she said, was over her "like a bad rash" but though there were tears and recriminations, in the end it changed nothing. There was more guilt on all sides, but the die was cast.

Charles succumbed to the pressure. In the autumn of 1990 he was, according to friends, on the verge of a nervous breakdown. Initially it was dismissed as a "midlife crisis," but in private there was concern that he was suffering from clinical depression. "It was the sense of guilt—of having failed his family and himself—with which he found it so difficult to come to terms," wrote his biographer Ross Benson. "It took four months before he was willing to undertake any official engagements, and for some considerable time afterward his friends continued to worry about his mental health."

This mental ailment developed from a physical one—a terrible fall from his pony while playing polo at Cirencester in the summer of that year. The prince's right arm was broken in two places; indeed, so bad were the breaks that the bone could be seen sticking out of the flesh of his arm at the elbow. The injury was a complex one and though originally left to set itself in the normal way, the arm had to be rebroken when it was discovered that the break had failed to heal properly. At the second attempt, a metal pin was inserted and bone from Charles's hip was grafted on to speed the mend— but it was a drawn-out and painful process, added to which it was suggested that, in the initial operation, part of a tendon was caught in the fracture, which then started to heal around it, creating almost permanent pain. The delayed shock from this, it was said, was enough to produce severe depression.

On the prince's exits from these two operations—first from Cirencester General Hospital in July, then from the queen's Medical Center in Nottingham in September—he was accompanied by Diana, who on both occasions escorted him back to Highgrove to recuperate. But she did not stay long. As a royal protection policeman, Police Constable Andy Jacques, was later to reveal, she left almost immediately. "It was a complete sham," he said.

Jacques was to play an important part in providing missing pieces to the marital jigsaw, for by now the nation's suspicions were aroused to the nature of the "close friend- ship" which was the only reference which Fleet Street would make to Charles and Camilla's relationship. It took two years for his eye-witness account to surface, but the police constable's recollection of life at Highgrove in the aftermath of Charles's polo accident was clear and graphic.

"Diana sped off back to London almost as soon as they arrived back at the house," he said. "When she'd gone, Charles sent his detective to collect Camilla Parker Bowles, who lived nearby.

"Later I was patrolling outside the house when I noticed a light on in Princess Diana's private sitting room. There should be no one in there when the princess is not at home.

"The curtains were closed, but through a chink between the drapes, I spied Charles and Camilla dancing cheek-to-cheek. Though the prince had his arm in a sling, they were smooching to very romantic music. Eventually they disappeared down onto the sofa, out of my sight.

"I moved away, but when I returned fifteen minutes later, the light was still on. I saw Camilla emerge from behind the sofa and shake her dress. Then Charles stood up. He looked down and intimated that because one arm was in a sling, he couldn't readjust his clothes."

Another version of this testimony, published in the United States in *Globe* magazine, described his witnessing "a dishevelled Charles and Camilla stand from behind the sofa, doing up their clothes."

This Peeping Tom evidence was said to have shocked Diana on its publication, but as usual it was the press's hyperbole which provided the shock element: Diana was all too conscious of what was going on, even if its increasing visibility appalled her. She enjoyed a particular friendship with the Highgrove butler Paul Burrell and his wife, Maria, and even though no direct information as to Camilla's comings and goings may have emerged from Diana's conversations with Maria, by a process of osmosis the princess was able to construct a fairly accurate picture of what went on while she was in London.

During that long summer the prince allowed only one person to nurse him: Camilla. Diana went to Highgrove from time to time, but the joke among staff was that as she drove in one entrance, Camilla was driving out of another. James Whitaker reported: "Camilla was now regarded by their friends as Charles's official hostess in Gloucestershire. She boasted about the roses she was growing in the Highgrove garden, she threw dinner parties for Charles, and she sunbathed in the grounds in a bikini while Charles pottered in the garden nearby. Set against the standards of most civilized people, this behavior was outrageous. A neighbor told me, 'It was as if neither cared who saw what was going on. They were, to all intents and purposes, living as man and wife.'"

He flew to Balmoral—and Camilla went too. They took with them Patty Palmer-Tomkinson, whose closeness to Charles had deepened after the 1988 Klosters ski accident which killed the equerry Major Hugh Lindsay and seriously injured her. Diana was not invited—indeed, her by now traditional ritual of taking the princes to school neatly precluded her being there. As September moved into October, he showed no signs of returning from Royal Deeside, or of wishing to see his wife and children, even though the boys were said to be missing him. It was a repeat of the 1987 Scottish exile after Charles supposed his wife had been unfaithful; then, his visible exile could be put down to misapplied jealousy and hurt pride. Now, it was because he was suffering a very real depression.

"At this time he underwent a major reappraisal of his life," said a friend of the Parker Bowleses. "In general, he was getting a bad press. He felt tortured by his marriage, and angry at the unqualified adulation his wife attracted wherever she went. Part of this was a selfish jealousy, of course, but mostly he was suffering a tremendously hurt pride: He was doing his damnedest, and nobody really cared. Although he has always had this inner sense of destiny, for the first time in his life he could not see the way forward.

"Wherever he turned it was Diana, Diana, Diana—yet the woman was a nightmare.

"Charles's difficulty then, as now, is his inability to blame himself. But it's hard to avoid the conclusion that he made a mistake not only in his choice of bride and—the choice was his, no one else's—but in the method by which he chose her.

"It was an arranged marriage, no doubt of that, but it was poorly done. It was as if once he'd found Camilla again, he didn't give a damn who the hell he married. He knew he had to get married—his father was perpetually on at him to do something about it—but Charles didn't care. Anyone might have done."

At Birkhall on the Balmoral estate, a decade after plighting his troth to a teenage ingenue, these nightmares came back to haunt him. No one, not the Palmer-Tomkinsons nor the Parker Bowleses (Andrew made fleeting appearances), seemed able to pull Charles out of his depression. On top of the psychological pressure, he was still in great pain from his polo injury. He donned walking boots and tweeds and spent hour upon hour in the open air encouraging his guests to sketch, paint, shoot, and fish: He was digging deep into his spiritual resources to try to find some solution to what seemed an insurmountable problem. For even at this stage, there was no question of separation or divorce all Charles could see ahead was a long, cold, lonely road in a loveless marriage with a woman whose company he could no longer tolerate, even for short periods.

Meanwhile, back in London, Diana was suffering.

Charles's solution to her continued rages was to avoid speaking to her; now that he was five hundred miles away they had no need to talk at all, even by telephone. Diana had no idea what he was doing at Birkhall, how many people were with him or who they were, or how long he intended to stay there. Starved of information, she was trying her hardest to put on a brave face, while knowing that he was with Camilla. She paid an official visit to Edinburgh in mid-October, but lacked the nerve to turn up at Balmoral to ask her husband when he was coming home. Having completed her engagements, she simply turned round and drove south again.

One Kensington Palace servant vouchsafed at the time that Diana had been "desperate with worry" over Charles. She added: "She's normally one of the most pleasant and easygoing people you could ever imagine working for. But this past week she's been a right cow—you can see this situation is getting under her skin. It's like working in a place where a bomb is about to go off."

Toward the end of October, Charles returned briefly for a weekend with his wife and children, but then just as abruptly turned round and flew back to Scotland. It was not until the very end of the month that he finally came south for good, heading for Highgrove and his children. It was no coincidence that Diana was in London on duty when he returned, attending a reception with the president of Italy at an art gallery.

One report of his movements ran thus: "Charles arrived at Highgrove at around 7:00 P.M. on Thursday. He dined alone after working on official papers in his study.

"Around 11:00 P.M. the prince slipped out of the house in a plain Ford estate car. He headed for Camilla's house near Corsham with just one police bodyguard—and did not return until the early hours of Friday morning—while Diana was still in London."

The prince and princess finally met up that night in time for a formal photographic session, the results of which were to be considered, ironically, for the couple's tenth wedding anniversary pictures. But the session, with the newly qualified India Hicks—Lord Mountbatten's granddaughter and a bridesmaid at the royal wedding nearly a decade earlier—behind the camera, was gloomy and fruitless.

Within days Charles found that Highgrove was proving too suffocating: He had become restless, irritated by both the constant pain and his inability to do much more than sit and read. After three months of aches in his arm, he now had the additional burden of pain in the hip from where bone was grafted for the second operation. After consulting surgeons John Webb and Christopher Colton, who pronounced him fit to travel, he flew on Camilla's recommendation to the south of France, where the Baroness Louise de Waldner had offered the use of her Chateau le Barroux at Caromb, near Avignon. He took with him a physiotherapist and a detective and forced himself to start painting again: But despite the restorative powers of sun, the breathtaking landscape, and the regional cherries, peaches, and wine, the mental anguish he was suffering on top of his physical pain did not abate. It was made plain in the haunting photograph which caught the prince, arm in sling, hair disheveled, staring out of a window into the distance. After a week he flew back, in a jet of the Queen's Flight, to Camilla. Diana stayed in London.

As time went on Charles sought less and less to conceal his involvement with Camilla, reasoning that it was demeaning to lie to his wife when she was aware of, if not exactly happy about, the situation. But with it all went a certain cockiness, an "I can have it all" reaction to the stress he felt was being laid on him by Diana. In May 1989 Charles and Camilla pushed their luck by taking a holiday in Turkey.

While Diana carried out official engagements at home, the lovers set out to enjoy a sun-kissed tour of the great archaeological and historic sights around Ephesus as guests of the millionaire businessman Haldun Simavi. Ostensibly in the country on official business—Charles met President Kenan Evren and the prime minister, Turgut Ozal, in Ankara—this was the couple's most daring public adventure to date, having been flagged by at least one newspaper unaware of Camilla's presence as "a cultural trip to Turkey." Charles felt that the country was sufficiently obscure for Fleet Street's royal rat-pack not to want to follow him, simply out of sheer indifference to the dullish venue; but even so his presence did not go unnoticed. Almost immediately he sparked a security row with local police by refusing to reveal where he was going on day trips—and with good reason.

The *Sunday Mirror* sounded a warning note:

> *Prince Charles made waves on a sunshine cruise by keeping his blonde companion Camilla Parker Bowles under wraps. Speculation grew about the mystery beauty in a pink swimsuit who cavorted with him on a millionaire's yacht.*
>
> *The playful pair were pictured swimming, sunbathing and waterskiing off Turkey. Everywhere Charles went on his eight-day trip to see archaeological sights, civic leaders asked: "Where is your wife?"*

The intense interest caused by Charles's visit, not least by a for-once ungagged Turkish press, caused the prince to declare: "I will come to Turkey again—this time with my wife." It was a promise he was unable, and unwilling, to keep.

For on his return he found that nothing had changed in his ill-starred marriage. The imperfections of both partners served, in the end, to provide evidence to each that the other was to blame for its gradual disintegration. Charles's dedication to Camilla, unswerving over a decade, was sufficient for Diana to think him an unworthy spouse: Despite all the talk of Philip Dunne, and later James Gilbey and Captain James Hewitt, few who were close to her were in any doubt that she had remained, at that time, physically faithful to her husband.

Charles's perpetual complaint was that Diana was irrational: She understood the ground rules before he proposed to her, yet was unable to live tolerantly within the framework he had laid down for the marriage. "A contract is a contract," he told friends bewilderedly, but Diana refused to see their marriage as a business arrangement. Her critics argued that, stupidly, she believed what she read in the newspapers and magazines, and sought to turn the hack writers' fantasies of a "fairy-tale marriage" into reality.

As she felt her grip slipping on her husband, Diana made a concerted effort to breathe new life into the failing marriage on a personal and public level. Buttressed by the advice and support of friends outside the palace, she piled on public appearances and wooed the press with a series of svelte new outfits. The irony did not escape her that, while at home she was unwanted and unloved, the moment she set foot outside the portals of Kensington Palace, her personal popularity rating rose higher and higher.

She made attempts to win her husband back: "There was enormous pride at stake. Her sense of rejection, by her husband and the royal system, was apparent," recalled her friend of that time, James Gilbey. Under pressure from her own family and from concerned members of the royal family to rejuvenate the marriage, she agreed that another baby— Charles had always wanted a girl—might help pave the way forward. But that was, of all solutions, the most improbable; for the couple had ceased to enjoy conjugal relations in the summer of 1986, just five years after they had married, on their return from a Balearic holiday with King Juan Carlos of Spain. Charles had quit the holiday two days early to fly to Balmoral where his beloved Camilla was waiting. From now on no attempt would be made to disguise the fact he and Diana slept separately.

In public, Diana held the line. At a reception for journalists in Madrid in 1987, she made an attempt to paper over the cracks: "When we first got married we were everybody's idea of the world's most perfect couple; now they are saying we are leading separate lives. The next thing is I'll start reading that I've got a black lover," she joked, with gallows humor.

She attempted an explanation of why people misunderstood their separate lives. "It's very simple. My husband and I get around two thousand invitations every six months. We can't do them all, but if we split them up, with him doing some and me doing others, we can fulfill twice as many." As she spoke, she was acutely aware that Charles would be flying off to the book fair in Bologna to collect an award for his children's book, *The Old Man of Lochnagar,* which would be followed by a painting tour of Tuscany. He would stay in Florence and Padua: His companion would be Camilla.

It was becoming increasingly obvious that, despite Diana's gallant defense of their marriage, the couple were spending less and less of their free time together. The *Daily Mirror's* James Whitaker calculated that Charles had, in recent months, taken off on seven apparently partnerless jaunts; and the *News of the World* kept a score sheet of how often the couple met. The newspaper's reckoning was that in a ninety-day period the royal couple spent thirty-five apart, and while royal duties were responsible for some of the absences, Charles actually chose to be away from his wife for twenty-six nights. The following April, Charles was back in Italy, again with Camilla by his side. He confessed to Major Ronald Ferguson: "I just want to be with her all the time."

Diana's frustration and anger now became an awesome thing. According to one version: "When he walked out of a room, she would follow him screaming hysterically. She would slam any handy door, then open it and slam it again. She would walk the length of a bookshelf, punching the books and shouting at the top of her voice, 'No, Charles, no, no, I won't, Charles, no, no!' and members of staff remarked that virtually any decision which Charles would make she would seek to countermand. "There was hysteria and tears," recalled one. "Almost everything he wanted to do at that stage, she didn't want to do. She actually seemed to enjoy rowing."

Charles's reaction was, simply, to spend less time with his wife. Prince William was at school at Wetherby's, a £785-a-term preprep school a short drive from Kensington Palace in Notting Hill, which required his and his mother's presence in London all week during term time: Diana would habitually deliver and collect William, giving press photographers an almost daily photo opportunity as she varied her outfits. During this period she appeared a great deal in British newspapers, establishing herself in the national consciousness as a devoted mother, winning the mothers' race at one school sports day while Charles chose deliberately to come last in the fathers." His ploy—to show that he did not have to compete with his wife in public—backfired badly when newspapers ran pictures of the two races, captioning Diana's THE WINNER and Charles's THE LOSER.

The prince increasingly began to base himself at High-grove, but even when Diana came down at weekends he would rarely see her. Verbal communication had all but broken down and Charles, always one to avoid demeaning himself by an outright confrontation, would devote his Saturdays to polo or hunting. Diana would return with the princes to London on Sundays, having barely spoken to her husband—"He couldn't bear to sit with Diana anymore," said one member of staff—and as Diana left, Charles would go to see Camilla, whose husband also had to return to London on duty.

But Charles's sanguine behavior, his unstated attempt to establish in his marriage what the French would term an "arrangement," all served to drive Diana into further parox-ysms of rage. In the years from 1987 to 1990 these rages, according to those who witnessed them, were frightening: "Her face turned bright, bright red."

According to Andrew Morton, one particularly ferocious exchange ended with Diana telling her husband that unless he altered his attitude toward her and acknowledged her virtues, she would have to "reconsider her position." With this, she ran upstairs in tears to the bathroom; while she regained her composure, Prince William pushed a handful of paper tissues under the bathroom door. "I hate to see you sad," he said.

She learned to hit back where it hurt. In May 1988 Charles was on another visit to Italy; Camilla was said by friends to be accompanying him. On his way to Paris he was informed that Prince Harry, then not quite four, had been taken into the hospital for an emergency hernia operation. He immediately offered to fly home, but was told it would not be necessary. It did not take him long to learn that Diana had refused to go home after the operation at the Great

Ormond Street Hospital, and had instead spent the night curled up in a chair watching over her little boy. The following day's headlines labeled her a saint; Charles was furious. She made a speech on AIDS on the day he made one on education: She stole the headlines again. She had mastered the art of upstaging him, and she began to enjoy it. On a trip to Australia they paid a visit to a music college where Charles was persuaded to play the cello, an instrument which was part of his history but which, in truth, he had barely mastered all those years ago. He made some faltering passes at its strings, but as he did so Diana walked across the room, sat down at the piano, and struck up the opening theme of a Rachmaninov piano concerto. All eyes—and cameras—swung round to witness this great event, and Charles's photo opportunity was quickly and brutally brought to a close.

Inevitably the atmosphere of mutual suspicion increased between man and wife, with Charles constantly complaining to Camilla that Diana's was a "rowdy act"—lots of noise and not much substance. One of Diana's closest friends complained: "It's time he started seeing her as an asset, not as a threat, and accepted her as an equal partner. At the moment her position within the organization is a very lonely one."

This perceived inequality was a fact which evaded Charles, enlightened freethinker though he claimed to be. With the support of Camilla, now ferociously anti-Diana, he viewed his wife as nothing more than a royal aberration; a low-class music-hall turn by comparison with his own intellectually superior stage act. By virtue of the splendid isolation in which he had lived for most of his life, he failed to recognize that his wife had forged a historically unique and powerful bond with the nation, and had done so without his help.

His own attempts at popularity could be staggering in their banality: As he made a self-conscious return to public life after breaking his arm, he proposed that he should make a statement regarding the speculation which had attended his injury and his subsequent state of mind. According to Diana's friends, he ordered that a stage-prop false arm with a hook on the end should be found, so he could appear like Captain Hook while delivering his statement. What he hoped to say, how he hoped to deliver it, no one will ever know. The arm and hook were found, then "lost" on Diana's instructions in order to preserve the prince's dignity.

With the battle between them now as disconcertingly visible as the broken bones a year before, Charles wilted before his steely wife, and Diana was able to take the upper hand from time to time. When Prince William was hit on the head with a golf club by a fellow pupil at Ludgrove, his prep school, Charles was in Gloucestershire with Camilla while Diana was in London. The royal couple hurriedly arranged to meet at the Royal Berkshire Hospital in Reading, but it was Diana who took control as Charles dithered about sending his son on to the Nottingham Hospital where his own arm had been operated on the previous year; the consultants recommended the Great Ormond Street Hospital in London. "You heard what was said," she barked at her husband. "Fix it!"

The day ended with another propaganda coup for Diana, for Charles left her at the hospital while William was undergoing surgery, so that he could fulfill a longstanding engagement at the Royal Opera House. The headlines next morning trumpeted: WHAT SORT OF DAD ARE YOU?

And yet Charles had learned how to hurt back. Their rows were no longer conducted behind closed doors, and all personnel in the prince's and princess's offices were witness to the venomous attacks they would launch on each other. According to people who worked for the Waleses, Charles now responded in kind to Diana's onslaughts: One Kensington Palace employee reported that he would spit at Diana, "You stupid woman" or "You silly young girl," over and over again. He added: "It was awful. I felt so sorry for Diana. But it was obvious that the two hated each other and I knew they were bound to separate—I could tell by the way they talked to each other."

Another employee witnessed arguments which would culminate in Diana telling Charles to "shut up," to which he would reply: "I can't stand living with you." The employee added: "He told her he didn't like the way the children were being brought up—that she was far too casual with them and didn't respect their positions in life. And he said that he thought her encouragement of the boys to go go-carting all the time was stupid."

But at the root of all these arguments lay the stumbling block of Camilla Parker Bowles. In April 1991 Diana was forced to take the two young princes skiing by herself; Charles had cried off at the last moment and was heavily criticized for having done so. Palace officials and members of his household agreed that a public split of this nature would cause adverse press comment, and so it proved: But Charles was in no mood to compromise, or spend leisure time with his wife. The excuse that was offered up to the public was that Charles had to go to Scotland that weekend, and had some important speeches to write.

Indeed Charles did to go Scotland—where Camilla was already waiting for him; Diana knew, and secretly cursed the fact that the world's royal press photographers were all on the slopes photographing her, while not a single one was on the River Dee, where they would have found an altogether more intriguing shot.

From having a walk-on part in Diana's life, Camilla

Parker Bowles was now moving center stage and beginning to mop up the limelight. Diana professed to be deeply wounded by her husband's suggestion that Camilla attended the memorial service for Leonora Knatchbull at St. James's Palace. The six-year-old daughter of Lord and Lady Romsey had battled bravely against cancer and lost. The nation had taken the little girl to its heart when, in June, she had been seen on the balcony of Buckingham Palace watching the annual Trooping the Colour ceremony. Though there was delight in her eyes, she was soon to succumb to the fatal illness; in December, a family memorial service was held in her name. As she left the service, Diana, who had held Leonora close on the palace balcony, was photographed in tears—but they were tears of rage.

"Diana was upset that Camilla Parker Bowles, who had only known the Romseys for a short time, was also present at such an intimate family service," wrote her biographer Andrew Morton, though in truth Lord Romsey's home, Broadlands, had been a welcome retreat for the couple.

"It was a point she made vigorously to her husband as they traveled back to Kensington Palace in their chauffeur-driven limousine. When they arrived at Kensington Palace the princess felt so distressed that she ignored the staff Christmas party, which was then in full swing, and went to her sitting room to recover her composure. Diplomatically, Peter Westmacott, the Waleses' deputy private secretary, sent her avuncular detective Ken Wharfe to help calm her."

The real significance of this event was that, among a broader group of friends and family, Charles was going public with his relationship. That may have been in defensive response to his wife's hysteria, as a reaction against her much-vaunted relationship with James Hewitt, or simply because he believed that with more space in his ailing marriage, nobody

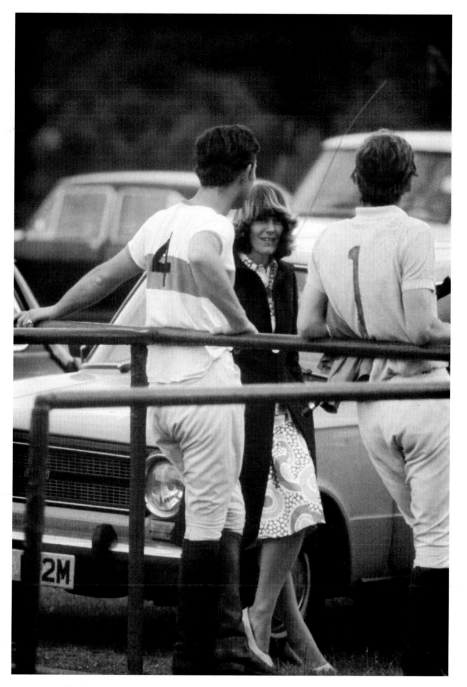

In their element. . . . Prince Charles and Camilla Parker Bowles
chat at a polo match in 1975.
(© Hulton-Deutsch Collection/Corbis/Serge Lemoine)

Prince Charles and Lady Diana Spencer pose for photographers at Buckingham
Palace after the announcement of their engagement. When a reporter asked,
"Are you in love?" all Charles could stammer in response was "Whatever 'in love'
means." Was it because he knew Camilla would be watching?

(© Hulton-Deutsch Collection/Corbis)

Lady Diana being put through the "Balmoral test" three months after the engagement. The strain was beginning to show in this rare unguarded moment at a photo opportunity. It can't have helped matters that the Parker Bowleses were part of the house party. *(Bryn Colton/Assignments Photographers/Corbis)*

The Prince and new Princess of Wales kiss on the balcony of Buckingham Palace after their wedding at St. Paul's Cathedral on July 29, 1981. How could onlookers ever have guessed at the reality behind the fairy-tale facade?

(© Hulton-Deutsch Collection/Corbis)

The Prince and new Princess of Wales in Gibraltar at the beginning
of their seemingly idyllic summer honeymoon. . . . But in Charles's wallet
were pictures of Camilla, and that night at dinner he wore Camilla's cufflinks.
(Bryn Colton/Assignments Photographers/Corbis)

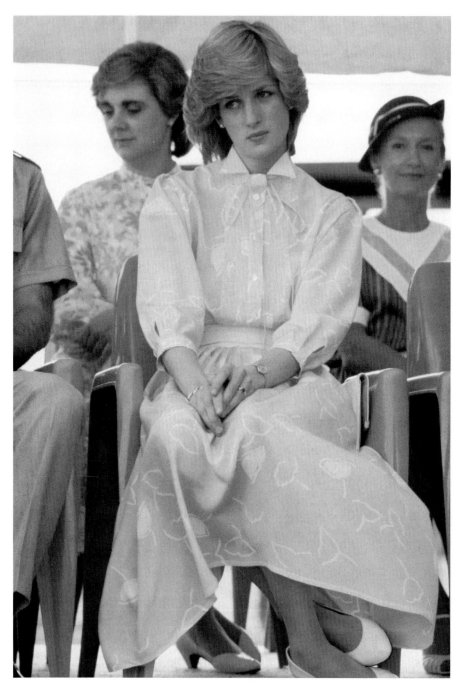

A glimpse, perhaps, of how the newly married, yet forlorn, princess really felt on a tour of Australia with Prince Charles in 1983.

(© Bryn Colton/Assignments Photographers/Corbis)

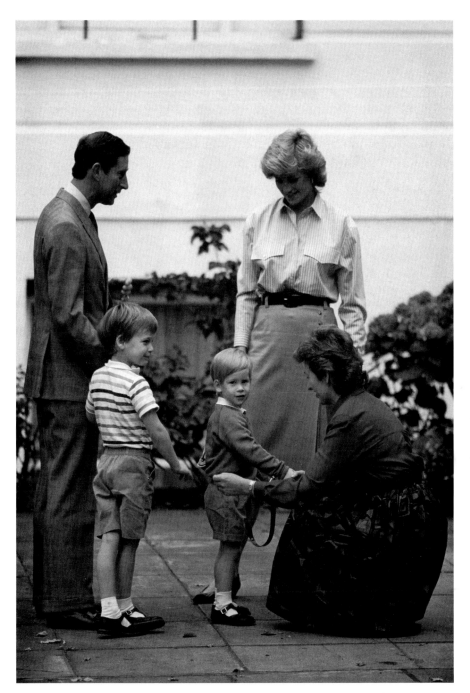

The Waleses and Prince William accompany Prince Harry to his first day
at Mrs. Mynor's Nursery School on September 16, 1987. But the marriage
was already dead and the portrait of togetherness a sham. *(Tim Graham/Corbis)*

A pre-Valentine's Day snub in front of the world's media as Diana deliberately turns her face away from her husband's kiss after a polo match in Jaipur, India, on February 13, 1992. This very public humiliation is said to have enraged Charles when he viewed the next day's newspapers.

(Reuters/Newsmedia Inc./Corbis)

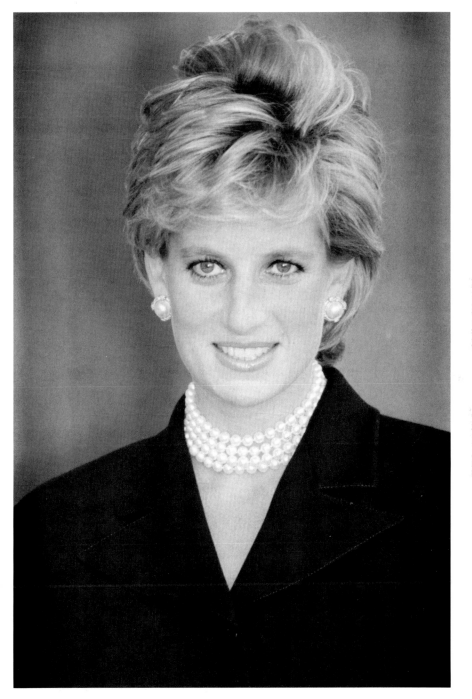

Princess Diana looking very chic in Paris, 1995.
(© B.D.V./Corbis/Laszlo Veres)

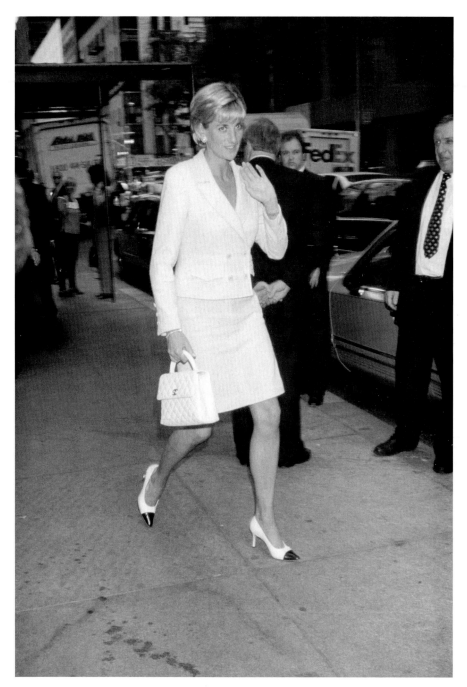

An independent and confident-looking Diana on a visit to New York in 1997.
It's hard to believe that she only had months to live.
(© Mitchell Gerber/Corbis)

Seven days after Diana and her companion Dodi Fayed were killed
in an automobile accident in Paris, her funeral cortege passes in front of her sons,
Princes William and Harry; her younger brother, Earl Spencer;
and her former husband, Prince Charles. *(© David & Peter Turnley/Corbis)*

Camillla Parker Bowles and Prince Charles leaving the Ritz Hotel in London on January 28, 1999. It was the first time they'd appeared in public together in over two decades. *(© AFP/Corbis)*

Prince Charles and Prince William arrive at the Press Complaints Commission's
10th anniversary party. Camilla arrived a short time afterward,
making it the first time that the three attended the same official function.
(Reuters/Newsmedia Inc./Corbis/Jonathan Evans)

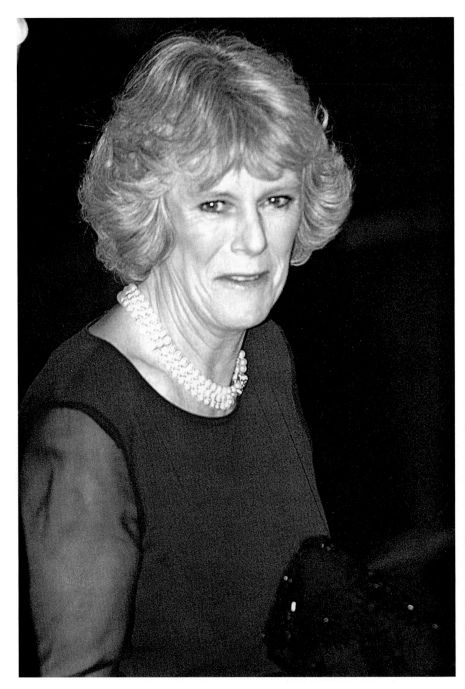

Camilla at the Press Complaints Commission's 10th anniversary party
at Somerset House in London on February 7, 2001.
(© *AFP/Corbis/Adrian Dennis*)

Charles and Camilla patently enjoying themselves at the
It's Fashion charity gala dinner at Waddesdon Manor, Buckinghamshire,
on June 11, 2001. Hiding from the cameras is now a thing of the past.
(© Reuters/Newsmedia Inc./Corbis/John Stillwell-Pool)

No more subterfuge. . . . A smiling kiss for all the world to see
at the National Osteoporosis Society's 15th birthday celebration
at Somerset House, London, on June 26, 2001.
(© *Reuters/Newsmedia Inc./Corbis/Stephen Hird*)

would much mind. Diana's outburst came as a huge surprise: After all, she knew about the trips to Italy and Turkey, she knew about Camilla's visits to Balmoral and Sandringham, and she knew that on their much-hyped "family" summer holiday aboard Greek tycoon John Latsis's yacht, Charles had spent hours on the telephone to Camilla. In fact, on that particularly barren piece of failed public relations, Diana had insisted on having her own quarters, had eaten with the children, and had convinced herself that Charles had exchanged more words with his mistress than with her.

Friends also noted Diana's "morbid game" at social events, where all three were unavoidably present, of eyeing Camilla, then avoiding her, or watching to see the eye contact between Charles and Camilla. In the days before a concert to raise money for the Salisbury Cathedral spire, Diana learned that her rival would also be present, and was furious. But by the time all three attended she was able to watch the eye contact with something approaching amusement.

Sometimes Diana's frustration at this ménage à trois reached breaking point. Pedestrians around Marble Arch witnessed an extraordinary scene one night as the royal couple passed by in their official car; a clearly vicious exchange of words culminating with Diana trying to force open the door of the moving car to throw herself out. One witness, a road sweeper, recalled that the princess was hysterical and crying. He said, "She was clearly saying something like 'I've had enough of this' and then I watched as a man in front, who I presumed was a detective, held her back."

But by this time, Charles's adulterous relationship with Camilla stretched back in an unbroken line for well over a decade. The Queen Mother knew, and accepted it, encouraging the couple to stay at Birkhall, her house on the Balmoral estate. The House of Windsor's view, from the other side of the ramparts, is remarkably different from the one enjoyed by the public: their raison d'être is to strengthen the dynasty, not weaken it—and as soon as Diana showed signs of recalcitrance, they closed ranks around their favorite son, though the queen had long ago issued instructions that she was, under no circumstances, ever to enter in the same room as his wife's lover. While others in her family took a more pragmatic stance, she herself would never condone adultery.

However, observed one of Diana's friends, "There is one rule for the royals, another for the rest of us. Unfortunately they don't see her as royal—they see her as one of the rest." No matter that she was wife and mother of future kings—her role ended after the birth of her second son, and if she refused to be compliant over the matter of Charles's greater love, then, argued senior courtiers, she must be sidelined.

The queen, agreed observers, was sympathetic to Diana's isolation; but only up to a point. A powerful Buckingham Palace machinery existed to preserve the monarchy at the top of Britain's totem pole, and she would do nothing to interfere with its workings. Camilla understood what was required of royal women—silence, compliance, devotion—and earned the respect of all for her discretion.

The same could never be said of the Princess of Wales.

Chapter Seven

Prolonging the Agony

From the very beginning of 1992, there was a whiff of impending disaster in the air. Charles rode out with the Meynell Hunt only to be faced by a crowd of angry hunt saboteurs, to whom he bellowed with unusual fury: "Shut up!"—possibly because he felt that among these subversives one of them might spot the figure of Mrs. Parker Bowles on horseback.

The prince and princess were committed to a tour of India—"yet another foreign minefield for the Waleses to traverse," observed the seasoned royal watcher James Whitaker—and Charles started out as he meant to go on. Although it was Diana who had "adopted" Mother Teresa of Calcutta, the prince insisted to his private office that when a bouquet of flowers was sent to the celebrated nun in Rome, where she was recovering from a heart operation, it should bear his name alone.

Bidding farewell to Camilla, Charles set out on what was to be the first of two disastrous tours with Diana, which would signal more clearly than anything else the end of their marriage. Charles ducked his promise to the Indian nation, made several years before, that one day he would bring his wife back to stand in front of the Taj Mahal, the exquisite edifice built by the seventeenth-century emperor Shah Jelian. Diana alone posed for pictures in front of its ornate facade, while Charles was in Delhi unromantically addressing a group of business leaders—once again misunderstanding the need of the world's media to see a couple reunited in the shadow of one of the world's most romantic buildings.

Reporters took Charles's absence from his wife's side, a symbolic if historically unimportant picture opportunity, as a snub to Diana—the loss of a lasting image for the tour. "Instead," wrote Whitaker, "the image that is retained is of the Prince of Wales looking a complete idiot."

On the eve of St. Valentine's Day, Charles played polo at Jaipur. At the end of the match, he stood in line with his teammates to receive a trophy from his wife. The world's media were waiting for the couple to exchange kisses—as once they had done habitually in such circumstances—simply because they all, to a man, did not want to see an end to the fairy-tale marriage. Would they kiss, or wouldn't they?

"The answer was not slow in coming as I watched one of the cruelest, most public put-downs of any man by his wife, executed in front of a hundred professional cameramen and five thousand laughing Indians. With triumph in her eyes, Diana waited until her husband's lips were almost on hers; then she turned her head away. Not so fast that Charles would be able to pull back—no, it was much more calculating than that. Instead, she moved her head to the left, slowly.

"Charles, who knew the world would see what happened next—television was there too—politely and gallantly tried to follow Diana's turning head. He chased it all the way round until he could reach no farther without falling over. He ended up kissing Diana half in midair, half on her gold earring." Seeing the results in the next day's newspapers, Charles was overcome with humiliation and rage: Once again, Diana had upstaged him. But it would be the last time, he told Camilla on his return home.

In March, Diana took the children to Lech in Austria for their traditional spring skiing week. But unlike the previous year, when Charles stayed in Scotland with Camilla, the prince warned that he would be flying in at the weekend from Milan, where he (and secretly, Camilla) had spent the week. William and Harry were to be paraded outside the Arlberg Hotel to await their father's arrival, along with the assembled cameras of the world's paparazzi. Diana, who had been hogging the cameras for the past few days, was to stay out of sight.

It was organized, it was efficient, and it got on the front pages. It was the start of a "no more Mr. Nice Guy" routine for Charles: The next morning he rammed the point home by organizing more happy-family shots with his sons, and gradually, following the public-relations disaster in Jaipur the month before, seasoned hands could detect that some radical thinking had been going on in Charles's camp—for the first time in his life, he was coming out on the PR offensive.

Indeed it was this modest start, and its relative success, which gave Charles and his protector and private secretary, Commander Richard Aylard, a clue to the way forward which was, in due course, to turn into Charles's so-called "charm offensive" to win back the hearts and minds of the British nation ahead of the twenty-fifth anniversary of his investiture as Prince of Wales. But a return to popularity was not that easily won, as Charles discovered when the news came through that Diana's father, Earl Spencer, had died in the hospital.

The royal couple flew out of Austria on a BAe 146 of the

Queen's Flight next morning: The cameras were waiting for the grieving Diana on the tarmac at RAF Northolt. Whatever good Charles had achieved in Lech was suddenly shattered, however, as he stood chatting at the foot of the stairs with Commander Aylard. Suddenly, at the top of the steps appeared a gaunt-faced Diana struggling with a heavy bag. In this hour of grief, the freeze-frame photographs of that moment seemed to say, no one could be bothered to help the world's most famous woman with her luggage. In the snakes-and-ladders game of royal one-upmanship, Charles had just landed on a snake.

The couple headed for Kensington Palace, where Diana was left with the boys. Charles headed west for Highgrove and Camilla. He told her of the massive row which had taken place in Lech while the couple had been waiting for transport arrangements to be finalized: that he had naturally wanted to fly back with Diana, but that she had wanted to come home alone. "The standoff lasted several hours before his private secretary called the queen at Windsor, explained the situation, and requested her to intercede," reported Nigel Dempster. "Only then did Diana agree to travel home with her husband." It was a further humiliation for the prince, who—despite being forty-three years old—had to rely on his mother to settle a domestic squabble, albeit of major proportions.

The relationship had reached the breaking point, Charles and Camilla agreed. All that remained was to devise a method of unraveling the marriage, with tact and decorum. Clearly the future of the boys had to be taken into account—as well as what to do with Diana, the woman Camilla had dubbed, not so long ago, the Mouse.

Warmed by the succor and comfort from Camilla, Charles prepared himself for Earl Spencer's funeral. A Wessex helicopter of the Queen's Flight was sent down to Gloucestershire to pick him up and take him straight to Northamptonshire: Diana, in disgrace for having embroiled the queen in her travel arrangements back from Lech, was left to make her own way to the family seat. Charles insisted that there should not be a joint wreath from them, but separate ones: Buckingham Palace officials endured a sticky few minutes trying to explain that one away.

Charles briefly returned to Althorp and, with a troubled look in his eye, caught the attention of the new earl, Diana's brother Charles. Upset at his father's death—the two were estranged at the time and the younger man had yearned for a reconciliation—Diana's brother had some difficulty in focusing on what the prince was saying to him. "He did not seem to appreciate how I felt at my loss," he said later. "We had just buried my father and he kept telling me how lucky I was to have inherited so young!"

"I wish I had inherited so young," Prince Charles had said. "My parents don't trust me with anything."

If this was a low point in old Earl Spencer's sendoff, it was not the only one. An apparent reconciliation in church between Diana and her stepmother, "Acid" Raine Spencer, left Raine's personal assistant Sue Ingram decidedly underwhelmed. "The graveside note about missing her "darling Daddy" just did not make sense. She hardly ever saw him. She hadn't been to Althorp since her brother's wedding in 1989 and she made very little effort to see him in London," she dryly observed. Indeed, others remember a mournful Spencer arriving at Kensington Palace to see his daughter, only to be told she was too busy. On one occasion, they recall, he was turned away; on another he was allowed in to play with his grandsons but did not get to see his daughter.

Charles helicoptered away from this dismal interment

before the proceedings were over, claiming a prior engagement; before long he was in Gloucestershire reporting back to Mrs. Parker Bowles. Once again Diana was left to find her way home: Even her father's death failed to forge a truce between her and Charles.

The Princess of Wales, in not a happy state of mind, paused in her return only to agree to having her stepmother evicted from the house and her luggage rifled: At least Charles had the decency to send Raine a five-page, handwritten letter offering his condolences.

A month later Charles was holidaying in Turkey without Diana, who had undertaken a solo engagement in Egypt. In Cairo, she let slip her vision of the future in a strange, rather spooky set of asides made at a dinner hosted by Britain's ambassador to Egypt, Christopher Long. In answer to a question, and speaking just as a lull occurred in the conversation, she said: "I still see myself as Lady Diana Spencer."

One of the guests, Mohamed Salmawy, a playwright and former Ministry of Culture official, pointed out that she had been Princess of Wales for more than a decade. "What about when your husband is crowned?" he asked.

"Oh," said the princess, toying with her coffee cup, "I think I will still be Lady Di." This effectively stopped all conversation in its tracks—for all were aware of the implications of what Diana was saying, even though the momentous announcement of the end of her marriage was still seven months away. But then she knew where her husband and Camilla Parker Bowles were while she made this official trip, and she was blind with rage.

Older and wiser after his untimely discovery in that country in 1989, Charles, in Turkey, gave floundering pressmen no opportunity to catch him with Mrs. Parker Bowles, though later a photograph did emerge of the couple, complete with a grinning and complaisant Andrew Parker Bowles, enjoying a picnic out of the back of a Range Rover. Yet the trip was not without incident, since an aircraft of the Queen's Flight was used to carry Charles and Diana back individually from their separate, but simultaneous, trips. One newspaper reported that Diana's jet would not stop to pick up Charles, even though it flew directly over Ankara: Buckingham Palace officials said the twenty-seater airplane was "too full" to carry Charles as well as his wife, and the plane was forced to make a return journey the following day to pick up the prince. It only fueled speculation that Charles had, indeed, managed to take Camilla on holiday with him once again and was not prepared to share the plane back to Britain with his wife.

On their return to London, Charles and Diana set out together for Seville in Spain for the Expo World Fair, their marital ship heading surely and swiftly for the rocks, for within days the royal couple's reputation, and their eleven-year marriage, was to be irreparably holed below the water-line.

In retrospect, the Princess of Wales deeply regretted the publication of Andrew Morton's *Diana: Her True Story*. As the polemicist and popular historian Paul Johnson observed in his book *Wake Up Britain:* "Morton's book was the most grievous blow inflicted on the British monarchy since Edward VIII's abdication. It is important to grasp that the damage was essentially self-inflicted."

Indeed it was through interviews she gave to a go-between, Dr. James Colthurst, who relayed the information on to Morton, that Diana was able to relieve herself of the massive burden she had carried since first encountering Charles on that fateful hay bale in Sussex. The perpetual shadow of Camilla Parker Bowles; the emotional helter-skelter which drew her onward toward bulimia; the ever-increasing demands by press and public who had made her a goddess and now wanted to own her; the pressures of parenting children in a natural way, in contradiction of her husband's atavistic instincts; the bullshit brigade who make up Buckingham Palace's inner guard and made her life hell; and the sheer bloody loneliness of it all—all came tumbling out in a jumble of confused and sometimes contradictory complaints which, in print, constituted the angriest, saddest, and most damaging wound ever inflicted on the House of Windsor. For a woman who was avowedly proroyal and devoted to the idea of monarchy, to sanction the dissemination of so much ammunition against the very establishment she sought to uphold was, said her critics, an ill-considered, vain, and utterly stupid act.

If there was one virtue to be found in it all, it was that ordinary people were at last given a glimpse behind the heavy veil which camouflages the royal house: something to which, given the Civil List monies they contribute toward the royal upkeep, they may feel themselves entitled.

Diana: Her True Story was perforce an incomplete portrait, since it dwelled much on her husband's relationship with Camilla Parker Bowles, and rather less on Diana's own questionable relationships with the car salesman James Gilbey and the soon-to-be redundant army officer James Hewitt.

Her grievances were legitimate enough, but the means by which Diana aired them effectively wrecked the work she had done over the past eleven years in adding luster to an outmoded, stuffy, and self-obsessed institution, in turning world attention from more mundane matters and back toward the antique delights of the British monarchy.

Ironically, Diana's star shone for roughly the same period as that of Mrs. Margaret Thatcher. In the eyes of the world, these two women exemplified what was best about Britain: glamour, compassion, magic on the one hand; verve, courage, steadfast resolve on the other. Neither picture was an exact representation of the woman in question, but these images did serve to bolster Britain's standing around the world, and gave the nation cause to pat itself on the back for being so clever as to be British.

In the end the Thatcher dream—wealth at pernicious cost—and the Diana dream—flawless caring beauty—both turned sour, and for the same reason: Both lost control of their destiny by succumbing to *folie de grandeur*. All the time Diana remained in private conflict with her erring husband, she had the moral advantage: He had cheated on her all his married life. But in believing that the nation would back her against him, she made a grave miscalculation. Her friends had persuaded her that she was more popular than Charles—and after all, the opinion polls said so, in spades—and predicted that she would win the battle, whatever the battle was, once the whole thing came out in the open. It was ineffable nonsense.

For Diana's objectives, beyond venting publicly a justifiable anger at Charles's self-contained life—a life which effectively excluded her—were woolly. While her instincts had never let her down in all her years as Princess of Wales—she embraced AIDS victims and took the nation's sympathy along with her; she could spot wheelchair-bound pensioners at forty feet and, in greeting them, make their day—her decision to sanction a book which exposed her private life merely served to demonstrate an inability to sustain a line of thought through to its logical conclusion.

Diana: Her True Story did more than punish her husband for his transgressions. It brought the British royal family to its knees.

Each royal biographer has recourse to Walter Bagehot's well-worn decree: "We must not let in daylight upon magic." Nowhere can it be employed to greater effect than here; for Charles's love for Camilla Parker Bowles—or, perhaps more accurately, the way that it was divulged in Morton's book—doused overnight the nation's love for royalty. Suddenly people felt silly for believing in an institution so palpably misleading and corrupt; they eloquently wreaked their revenge in the subsequent opinion polls.

Those who know Diana claim that this was not her intention: She simply wished to expose the humbug surrounding her marriage, assert her equality within that marriage, and shrug off the growing accusations of her unacceptable behavior. But with *Diana: Her True Story* the whole house of cards collapsed around her, and in the end it is she who must take the blame for the House of Windsor's drastic loss of credibility.

The kindest interpretation to be put on it is that she did not know what she was doing. No intellectual, Diana lacked the solid backing of the great-and-good who surrounded her husband and mother-in-law. Her friends were to be found exclusively among the upperclass underachievers of this world— the wife of a man who ran a disco; a used-car salesman; an army officer who failed his promotion exams; and an immigrant restaurateur. However marvelous as human beings these people might have been, they lacked the education and the historical vision to be able to launch a successful attack on a thousand-year-old institution. Largely ill-equipped in their own lives, their succor and advice was worthless, and ruinous.

On 7 June the first extracts of Morton's book were seri-

alized in the London *Sunday Times*. The press camped on
Camilla Parker Bowles's doorstep as the extent of Charles's
relationship with her was revealed. There was a world of difference between veiled hints of a "confidante" and the raw
facts of adultery with which the public were now being
entertained. But those who hoped for a sight of the woman
now officially branded the prince's mistress were out of luck:
Two nights before, she had decamped with her sister Annabel
Elliott, her bags in the back of the car. Breathlessly, the tabloid
press reported that she had "vanished." One added:

> *When asked about Andrew Morton's book shortly before
> she vanished, Camilla said: "I haven't read it, but I will
> with interest when the time comes."*
>
> *The book claims that Camilla spends days and nights
> at Highgrove whenever Charles is there. She hosts dinners
> and lunches for him, sits beside him at the table, organizes
> his personal life, checks the menus and the guest lists—and
> even organizes the staff kitchen and chefs.*
>
> *Former royal bodyguard Andrew Jacques said: "Camilla
> steps right into Di's shoes. Charles is closer to her than
> anyone else in the world and she is the only person who is
> allowed into his precious walled garden."*

Brigadier Parker Bowles was sought out at his Kensington
house and the facts, such as were known, were put to him.
"It's fiction, fiction. I've nothing to say," was his measured but
disingenuous response. But if he had nothing to say, plenty of
others did. Even the Archbishop of Canterbury felt obliged
to offer his opinion: "The current speculation about intimate
personal matters has exceeded the boundaries which should
be observed in a society claiming to respect basic human
values."

Yet what emerged in those early days of revelation was only a partial picture; for Morton's book, based on his briefings from the princess's friends, skirted neatly around a pivotal question: Why, since Diana knew from the very first of Charles's all-consuming love for Camilla Parker Bowles, did she ever accept his hand in marriage?

That question has never satisfactorily been answered. But at the time, so many thunderbolts were crashing down upon the House of Windsor that there was no time for cool analysis. All hell had broken loose; the public uproar was unprecedented.

In private, in the royal corridors from Windsor to Balmoral, from Sandringham to Buckingham Palace, the atmosphere was grim. From time to time, servants had sold their stories to newspapers and magazines for large sums of money—they were considered to be lower than scum. It was unthinkable that a princess would give away family secrets and jeopardize the entire royal family. Strangely, it was the anger among the servants and retainers which made itself most felt: The courtiers and members of the royal family, too stunned by the magnitude of what had occurred, and the long-term implications of it, said little.

But there could be only one person to blame—Diana. Her protestations of innocence cut no ice, and very soon her early feelings of triumph at having redressed the balance, as she saw it, turned to alarm and panic as she realized just how grave the effect of her revenge had been—not on her husband, but on the whole royal family and its loyal staff. Suddenly, within the royal compound, she was friendless.

The same could not be said of Camilla. Bravely—some would say foolhardily—she ran the gauntlet of public reaction on the very day the serialization of Morton's book commenced. She arrived at Windsor Great Park for the Queen's Cup polo tournament, though reports that she was greeted with a warm and friendly smile by the sovereign—at one stage they were in the same building at the same time and reporters put two and two together to make five—were wide of the mark.

If the denizens of the royal enclosure were staggered at her sudden appearance, they were even more staggered by what she wore—a gray suit in Prince of Wales check. "No one knew whether this was a deliberate statement, or whether it was the only clean thing in her wardrobe"—said a friend in reference to Camilla's lighthearted attitude toward her personal turnout.

It was clear to observers by this stage that Diana was not entirely in control of her actions. That week most newspapers carried pictures of the princess making an off-duty visit to the home of her friend Carolyn Bartholemew, in apparent support and approval of Mrs. Bartholemew's assistance with the damaging book. Tipped off by a well-spoken woman who called five newspapers half an hour before Diana was due at the house in West London, cameramen were waiting for her when she arrived.

Mrs. Bartholemew, who as Carolyn Pride had been a flatmate of Diana's in the Colherne Court days, said she had "no idea" how the press had learned of the visit. But whoever made the calls, behind them was Diana at her Machiavellian best—"Never before had the world's media been manipulated in such a way," said the *Sunday Times*—though it was difficult to see her purpose. Yes, she wanted to show solidarity with her old friend, but by now she needed to put as much distance as possible between herself and *Diana: Her True Story*.

Reacting, as always, like a supertanker desperately trying

to crash into reverse, the royal machine took an uncon-
scionable time to decide what to do. As is usual in such cases,
courtiers opted for doing nothing in haste—just carry on as
normal, was their advice. Five days later a guilt-stricken
Diana, faced with the enormity of what she had done in
sanctioning Andrew Morton's book—she had not seen the
finished text before publication—was on Merseyside visiting
a hospice at Southport.

As she arrived, she noticed that a group of well-wishers
had unfurled a banner which said: DIANA, WE LOVE
YOU. The princess shook hands with people in the crowd,
then suddenly covered her face with her hands and wept. An
eyewitness, Mr. Bob Bird, said: "She was sobbing. She had her
face in her hands and was weeping. Her mascara was all over
the place. She looked terribly upset." A detective told another
onlooker: "It's all been too much for her."

The princess was hastily ushered into an official car and
driven to RAF Woodvale, where in the bar of the aero club
she asked for a glass of water and to be left alone. The area
was cleared and Diana sat with her head in her hands for
twenty minutes while her sister, Lady Sarah McCorquodale,
doubling as her lady-in-waiting, comforted her. She arrived
at her next official destination several minutes late, a police
officer explaining that a car in the royal fleet had suffered a
"mechanical fault."

The standard "do nothing" policy, once in place, was not
about to be altered. And so it was that, days after delivering
this mortal blow, its perpetrator—Diana, Princess of Wales—
rode down the course at Royal Ascot along with the rest of
the House of Windsor, to the cheers of tens of thousands, just
as if nothing had happened.

In preparation for this major televised event Charles and

Diana appeared at the more low-key ceremony of the Order of the Garter at St. George's Chapel, Windsor. Afterward Charles decorously helped Diana into an open carriage, but the couple did not exchange a glance on the five-minute ride back to the castle. The princess was said to be in emotional turmoil and spending many hours in the company of a personal counselor, Stephen Twigg, who had been treating her for three and a half years.

Charles and Diana appeared together at Royal Ascot simply because no one knew what else to do; they left together, to the confusion of race-goers who the Sunday before had learned even more lurid facts about the royal marriage split. The only open animosity described by anybody was when Diana walked into the royal box overlooking the course, having just descended from her open carriage—to be brutally snubbed by Prince Philip, the royal family chief executive. Underneath the outward harmony, there was tremendous rage at what she had done.

Charles, during this crisis, had spent much time on the telephone at Highgrove discussing with Camilla what was to happen next. Her house was under siege from the press, and she learned then what Diana had discovered years before: that it is permissible, in the mother of all democracies, to be put under house arrest by the Fourth Estate.

Suddenly, she became accustomed to what Diana had been living this past decade. In addition, she was deluged with hate mail. One tabloid newspaper reported:

> Camilla . . . is distraught at the hundreds of letters arriving at her home. A close friend said: "The letters are all blaming her for damaging the royal marriage. It seems very unfair. Some of the letters have been disgusting and very

rude. They basically say that Princess Diana is a goddess and how dare Camilla do anything to upset or hurt her or damage her happiness."

In the end the Parker Bowleses were forced to change their telephone numbers and quit the house to seek refuge with friends. Andrew returned to his army work, and Camilla went to stay with her former brother-in-law, Nick Paravicini, in Breconshire. Later she was to travel to Venice in an attempt to shake off the dogged attentions of pressmen.

Meanwhile Prince Charles drove to Windsor for a crisis meeting with the queen and his wife during which, it was reported, Diana said firmly: "I know my duty." The implication was that she would not walk out on the marriage; she had had her say, and that would be an end to it. This infuriated Charles, but recognizing the crisis for what it was, he agreed that they would turn out as a couple for a state banquet at the end of June when the queen was due to celebrate forty years on the throne: It might just calm the feverish debate now raging outside the castle walls.

Again Charles returned to Gloucestershire while frantic attempts were made by Buckingham Palace to paper over the cracks. So concerned were Charles's friends at the very palpable damage being done to him, on a daily basis, that Lord and Lady Romsey tried to encourage him to organize a letter-writing campaign to The *Times*. The idea fizzled out rapidly, and support for the prince continued to hemorrhage at an alarming rate.

Though the couple had already endured a Greek cruise on a luxury ship provided by John Latsis, and promised themselves it was an experiment they would not repeat, it was suddenly decided that a reprise might assuage the ever-thirsty press and convince them that the marriage was still a going concern. The palace's sudden volte-face on the holiday idea surprised some of the Greek tycoon's staff, who had been told that, however desirous he might be for a prestigious rerun of the previous year's cruise, he could forget it. It was billed, to the delight of palace officials, as a "second honeymoon': Invited along as extras in the dismal drama were Princess Alexandra and her husband, Sir Angus Ogilvy, and Lord and Lady Romsey.

The cruise had the benefit of being on a sufficiently large yacht that the couple did not have to speak. Diana spent her time waterskiing and topping up her tan, Charles spent his time sketching and telephoning Camilla. They ate and slept apart.

Camilla, meanwhile, had flown to Guidance in the center of Venice's panoramic lagoon with her sister Annabel and their parents. Fellow diners at the Cipriani Hotel noted how tired and pale she looked as she sat beneath a parasol sketching the Venetian scene. At the same time it emerged that Charles had been to visit Camilla at Middlewick House in July, arriving by helicopter.

Back at home, public opinion had swung so far against Charles that the efforts to present a united front alongside Diana—and there were some—came largely from his side: Diana was in pole position, both from the moral standpoint and also in the opinion polls: Charles's popularity rating had sunk to an all-time low. But all that was about to change.

Much has been made of the comical figure of Cyril Reenan, a retired bank manager with a penchant for listening in to late-night telephone calls, who accidentally found himself at the center of an even greater scandal than Diana's confessions to Andrew Morton.

But to Charles and Camilla, closer now than they had ever been, Reenan was an unlikely knight in shining armor, who listened in to a private telephone conversation, recorded it, listened to it again, then sold it to the *Sun* newspaper for a large sum of money. Not everybody's idea of knightly behavior, perhaps, but to Charles and Camilla it was the next best thing.

For Reenan delivered to a public thirsty for new information the Squidgy Tapes, a record of a conversation between the Princess of Wales and her car-dealer friend, James Gilbey. More than anything the conversation exposed Diana's frailty of mind at the time of the recording—on New Year's Eve, 1989—and the car dealer's overweening ambition. The *Sun*, with commendable enterprise, broadcast the tapes on a pay-as-you-listen telephone line and those with the stomach to eavesdrop on these sad exchanges were able to judge for themselves how far from normal life Diana, their goddess, had strayed.

For Charles and Camilla the publication of the Squidgy Tapes was a godsend. In the days which followed there was a merciless pursuit of all those associated with Diana, and in the heat of the moment, the prince and his love were forgotten. Their turn would come, and the damage caused would be infinitely greater, when one of their own private conversations was finally aired; but for the moment they were safe.

In among the scores of lurid headlines about Diana's relationships with James Gilbey, her in-laws, and her husband, there were one or two—but not very many—questions put as to the original source of the tapes. In the end, investigators were drawn to the inescapable conclusion that rogue elements within the British security services had been bugging the royal family; but at the time the content of the tapes was so explosive that, once they had been authenticated, no one paid too much attention to where they had come from.

In the meantime, moves had started at the palace to draw up the terms of an official separation. The queen's private secretary, Sir Robert Fellowes, and the palace press officer, Charles Anson, were heard in conversation discussing the end of the marriage during the summer of 1992, even though the announcement was some months off and attempts were still being made to fool the outside world that no permanent damage had been done to the royal union. The reasons why this charade was kept up were inexplicable, beyond an innate secretiveness among courtiers who do not like to share even the time of day with the outside world; and possibly—but only possibly—a last-ditch determination by Charles to breathe life into something that was, in all truth, long dead.

Still they tried to hold it all together. In October the nation gave thanks for victory against the German army at El Alamein, the most significant land battle of the Second World War, which had been won fifty years before. One of the many combatants to attend was Major Bruce Shand, and with justification. In the days leading up to the historic battle, Shand had been in the Libyan desert when he was suddenly pounced upon by Winston Churchill. The wartime leader was on a surprise visit to the troops, and his eyes had lighted on the ribbons on Shand's chest—which denoted not one Military Cross, but two.

Camilla's father later recalled the encounter thus:

"My hand was being vigorously shaken.

" 'You're a very young man. How old are you?'

" 'Twenty-five, sir.'

" 'Well, well—and a major and you've got two of them.' He prodded vigorously at my medal ribbon. 'How splendid. But you look so thin.' "

Shand was destined to become thinner. On the night of 3 November, as the battle raged and the British troops advanced, he was leading his squadron forward through an unexpected downpour of rain when suddenly he saw vehicles ahead. In his own self-deprecatory way he describes what happened next:

"Some of them came nearer, and before I knew what had happened my own [armored] car was being heavily engaged with fire. Something like a whiplash stung my cheek, and Sergeant Francis beside me slumped to the bottom of the car with a large hole in his chest, killed instantly. I could hear all the other cars firing away hard. My mouth was full of blood but I managed to tell Corporal Plant, my imperturbable driver, to turn the car around. I also tried to talk on the wireless but it had become dislocated.

"The car started to move but something hit it a tremendous blow, and I saw poor Plant subside over his wheel. A second later the car began to burn. Crawling forward I found that Plant was dead and I prepared to leave the vehicle. I got through the top, jumped down, and sheltered under the leeward side. Firing was still going on around me.

"I think I must have had a few minutes' blackout as I next remember Edward's car approaching, with him shouting 'Jump on.' I managed to clamber on and hung rather precariously on to his hand as we began to move. It was then that I was hit in the knee, and in the sudden shock I let go, although he tried to hold me. I do not remember hitting the ground. A buzz of German voices greeted my return to consciousness."

Shand spent the rest of the war in Spangenburg, making light of his internment just as he did of his injuries. Fifty years on, he stood in Westminster Abbey with his daughter by his side remembering those brothers in arms who had died while he lived—"I suffered appalling remorse," he admitted—while statesmen and royalty, who had not endured the hardships of war, occupied the best seats.

Among those wearing medals and finery were the Prince and Princess of Wales. By now their joint public engagements were a rarity, but according to the master plan laid down by the faceless men at the palace, it was incumbent upon them to turn out together from time to time. But this was one occasion when, in retrospect, all wished they hadn't.

For the El Alamein service represented much more than just a single battle victory: It was the land forces' celebration, if that could ever be the word, of their triumphs throughout the Second World War. It was a national moment for reflection, for thanks, and for sorrow at the loss of so many lives in the cause of liberty. But the next morning the headlines said something else. MEMORIAL DAY WRECKED BY CAMILLA, proclaimed the *Sun*. PRINCESS SNUBS RIVAL AFTER SHOCK AT MEMORIAL SERVICE. The newspaper reported:

> *A rare public show of togetherness by Charles and Diana was wrecked yesterday—by the unexpected appearance of the prince's ex-girlfriend.*
>
> *The troubled pair had to walk right past Camilla Parker Bowles as she sat in Westminster Abbey for a memorial service.*
>
> *Charles politely acknowledged her with a knowing nod and a smile as he walked past. But his unforgiving wife looked the other way. Throughout the service of thanksgiving the two women did not exchange glances.*
>
> *They are known to loathe each other. And the princess even stayed behind after the memorial to avoid walking past Camilla again.*

This was, arguably, the lowest point of the whole affair: a national memorial which affected thousands of people besmirched by a petty marital squabble and the distortive media attention to the close proximity, in church, of the three key players. It was a bungle on an amazing scale, demonstrating more than anything how warped the judgment of the participants and their advisers had become in the past few months. Charles was said to have known that Camilla would be there; in fact she took the place of her unwell mother at the last minute, but her presence as her father's escort was entirely justified. Whether, by this late stage, the Princess of Wales should have attended is a matter for debate. Palace officials, pushing the togetherness line, wanted to see Charles and Diana side by side at a national event, no matter the cost to the many other participants. And so she came, adding luster to an occasion, about the origins of which she will have known little, in a brand-new Catherine Walker outfit with a broad-brimmed hat and gloves. "Camilla," wrote the *Sun*, somewhat missing the point, "wore a dowdy blue suit with long skirt."

But that was not the end of it. Somehow in the inverted, pro-Diana world, it was deemed that the cuckoo in the nest on this occasion was Camilla. A friend was quoted as saying: "Given the events of the summer, this represents a clear slap in the face for the princess. Everyone knows of Charles's friendship with Camilla and how deeply it has hurt Diana."

The reportage demeaned everyone. The *Daily Mail* proclaimed:

> *They were like the twin faces of war—the dullness of defeat and the radiance of victory. As a piece of theater it was compelling. The Princess of Wales, her eyes wide, bright, and*

open, wearing a jacket of shimmering silvery grey and tight-fitting white skirt. Camilla Parker Bowles, a funereal figure, pale, thin, and hair flecked with grey, in shapeless, somber blue.

The burden of this report was that Camilla was a shriveled shell "who looked so much more than her forty-three years as she shuffled out of the abbey"; and that she had no particular reason to be at Westminster Abbey, getting in the way of the more glamorous players. Diana, on the other hand, looked wonderful and therefore her presence was entirely justified.

Bearing in mind Bruce Shand's own preoccupations that day—of his own life nearly lost, of others who never returned—his response to the grappling paparazzi outside Westminster Abbey who threatened to rob the occasion of its last shreds of dignity was remarkable in its restraint: "It was very good of her to accompany me to the service and she couldn't have been better company," he said. "But I think she found it off-putting to be confronted by thirty-odd photographers outside Westminster Abbey." As to her health, he had no doubts. "As far as I am concerned, she is very well and remains in good spirits. The constant press scrutiny does not seem to have taken its toll on her."

It was bravely spoken, and with decorum. If there had to be a public showdown between the two women in Charles's life, no worse place could be conceived than a memorial for the war dead. But contrary to the reports of the day, it was the Shands who came out with heads held high.

Three weeks later, the ubiquitous Andrew Morton came out with a paperback version of his book. It stated that Diana could not bring herself to speak Camilla's name and instead called her "the rottweiler." The Mediterranean trip aboard John Latsis's yacht earlier in the summer—the so-called "second honeymoon"—had been a disaster, made worse by Diana stumbling across her husband making furtive telephone calls via a satellite link to Camilla's Wiltshire home.

Somewhere along the line, desperate men thought they could do a patch-and-mend job on Charles and Diana with "The Togetherness Tour." It was a shambles.

Billed as a "business as usual" enterprise by Commander Richard Aylard, it was supposed to be a kiss-and-make-up tour of South Korea. Aylard madly pulled strings on the eve of departure, in November 1992, to ensure it had a good sendoff. Headlines such as WHY CHARLES AND DIANA ARE BACK TOGETHER in the *Daily Express* and FROM DIANA, THE LOOK—AS HOPES RISE OF A MARRIAGE ON THE MEND in the *Daily Mail* may have raised the expectations of royalists the world over, but did no more than raise a smile from the journalists who had been instructed to write them. It was common knowledge in Fleet Street that the marriage was all over, bar the shouting—but the Fourth Estate was allowing Charles and Diana to do whatever they had to do, in their own time.

They did not have to wait long. From the moment the royal jet touched down in Seoul, royal watchers knew the worst. With minutes to go before landing, the couple had engaged in a massive row: They emerged angry and red-faced, and stayed that way for the next five days. Observing this unedifying spectacle, one journalist who accompanied the royal tour wrote: "It was a very public, and very humiliating, end to the love story of the century." So it came as no great surprise to those who had followed the couple closely over the past few months when John Major, the prime minister, rose in the House of Commons on 9 December 1992 and declared:

"It is announced from Buckingham Palace that, with regret, the Prince and Princess of Wales have decided to separate.

"Their Royal Highnesses have no plans to divorce and their constitutional positions are unaffected. The decision has been reached amicably, and they will both continue to participate fully in the upbringing of their children. Their Royal Highnesses will continue to carry out full and separate programs of public engagements and will, from time to time, attend family occasions and national events together.

"The queen and the Duke of Edinburgh, though saddened, understand and sympathize with the difficulties that have led to this decision. Her Majesty and His Royal Highness particularly hope that the intrusions into the privacy of the prince and princess may now cease. They believe that a degree of privacy and understanding is essential if Their Royal Highnesses are to provide a happy and secure upbringing for their children while continuing to give a wholehearted commitment to their public duties."

The royal watchers had known, but the House was shocked. Privy councilors, among them Camilla Parker Bowles's uncle Lord Howe, the former Chancellor of the Exchequer, had been forewarned. Clearly some of them, including Howe, had been instrumental in guiding the prime minister's hand that day. But when it came, John Major's statement, though brief, made history.

There was not the slightest hint of triumph in Camilla Parker Bowles's public statement, eagerly sought by the newsmen gathered around her Wiltshire home. "Obviously if something has gone wrong I'm very sorry for them," she said.

She added, without the merest trace of a smile: "But I know nothing more than the average person in the street. I only know what I see on television."

Then she swept from her home in regal style, driving into the night with her sister Annabel Elliott in a Mercedes, and followed by a police escort. They headed for Bowood, the home of the Earl of Shelburne, a twenty-minute drive away— a home which was to achieve greater prominence within the space of a few short weeks.

Chapter Eight

Lies in the Wind

———————⊰◦∘◦⊱———————

While Charles was born to expect the attentions of the press, and Diana had come to enjoy and manipulate them, Camilla found their dogged pursuit disturbing and disorientating.

To the woman with a backbone of steel who had endured the spartan regime of Dumbrells, and a fearless horsewoman who would take the most terrifying fences with barely a blink, this new psychological torment—of being perpetually on the run, like so many of the foxes she had chased—was undoubtedly the low point of her life.

But there was yet more agony to endure. With world interest in her affair with Charles showing no signs of abating, suddenly in January came rumblings from half a world away which were to thrust her entirely private life even more before the public consciousness.

In the second week of January 1993 the Australian women's weekly magazine *New Idea* published a full transcript of the so-called Camillagate Tapes. Almost simultaneously the text of the conversation was published in the *Sun* in Britain, and other newspapers worldwide.

By the time the tapes were published, the conversation

was three years old, and whatever intimacies had passed between Camilla and her lover might properly be expected to have been lost in the mists of time. But the night before publication in Britain, extracts were read to Camilla over the telephone. Her reaction was one of incredulity and mounting horror: To the reporter delegated the ugly task of refreshing her memory of the exchanges, she suddenly blurted: "I can't believe it, I can't believe it. I must speak to my husband. He is on his way home."

That instant reaction gives yet another clue as to the lasting nature of her relationship with Andrew Parker Bowles. Other women, caught in a similar deceit, would instantly turn to their lover for protection; but the mention of "my husband" foxed some editors, who were finding it hard enough to come to terms with the evidence which had been laid before them.

The conversation took place on the night of Sunday, 17 December 1989. Charles was staying at the Cheshire home of his old friend Anne, Duchess of Westminster (referred to on the tape as Nancy), after a heavy week of duties which included attending a reception at Kensington Palace for his Prince's Trust, acting as a counselor of state in receiving diplomats, meeting the foreign secretary, and hosting a dinner for the Royal Opera House Trust as well as attending receptions for various other organizations with which he was involved. He ended the week with a tour of Wales, which included visits to Greenfield, Mold, and Wrexham; meanwhile Camilla had hunted with the Beaufort and made her preparations for Christmas.

The fragment of conversation, which lasts eleven minutes, goes as follows:

Charles: . . . he thought he might have gone a bit far.
Camilla: Ah, well.

Charles: Anyway, you know, that's the sort of thing one has to beware of. And sort of feel one's way along with, if you know what I mean.

Camilla: Hmmmm. You're awfully good at feeling your way along.

Charles: Oh, stop! I want to feel my way along you, all over you and up and down you and in and out.

Camilla: Oh!

Charles: . . . particularly in and out.

Camilla: Oh, that's just what I need at the moment.

Charles: Is it?

Camilla: I know it would revive me. I can't bear a Sunday night without you.

Charles: Oh, God.

Camilla: It's like that program *Start the Week*. I can't start the week without you.

Charles: I fill up your tank!

Camilla: Yes, you do!

Charles: Then you can cope.

Camilla: Then I'm all right.

Charles: What about me? The trouble is, I need you several times a week.

Camilla: Mmmmm. So do I. I need you all the week, all the time.

Charles: Oh, God, I'll just live inside your trousers or something. It would be much easier!

Camilla: *[Laughs]* What are you going to turn into? A pair of knickers? *[Both laugh]* Oh, you're going to come back as a pair of knickers.

Charles: Or, God forbid, a Tampax, just my luck! *[Laughs]*

Camilla: You are a complete idiot! *[Laughs]* Oh, what a wonderful idea!

Charles: My luck to be chucked down the lavatory and go on and on for ever swirling round on the top, never going down!

Camilla: [*Laughing*] Oh, darling!

Charles: Until the next one comes through.

Camilla: Or perhaps you could just come back as a box.

Charles: What sort of box?

Camilla: A box of Tampax, so you could just keep going.

Charles: That's true.

Camilla: Repeating yourself. [*Laughing*] Oh, darling, I just want you now.

Charles: Do you?

Camilla: Mmmmmm.

Charles: So do I.

Camilla: Desperately, desperately, desperately. Oh, I thought of you so much at Garrowby.[3]

Charles: Did you?

Camilla: Simply mean we couldn't be there together.

Charles: Desperate. If you could be here—I long to ask Nancy sometimes.

Camilla: Why don't you?

Charles: I daren't.

Camilla: Because I think she's so in love with you.

Charles: Mmm.

Camilla: She'd do anything you asked.

Charles: She'd tell all sorts of people.

Camilla: No, she wouldn't, because she'd be much too frightened of what you might say to her. I think you've got . . . I'm afraid it's a terrible thing to

[3] The home of Earl of Halifax, friend of Prince Charles and once tipped as a future husband for Princess Anne; married to the ex-wife of Andrew Parker Bowles's younger brother Rick.

say, but I think, you know, those sort of people feel very strongly about you. You've got such a great hold over her.

Charles: Really?

Camilla: And you're ... I think as usual you're underestimating yourself.

Charles: But she might be terribly jealous or something.

Camilla: Oh! *[Laughs]* Now that is a point! I wonder, she might be, I suppose.

Charles: You never know, do you?

Camilla: No, the little green-eyed monster may be lurking inside her. No, but I mean, the thing is you're so good when people are so flattered to be taken into your confidence. But I don't know they'd betray you. You know, real friends.

Charles: Really?

Camilla: I don't ... *[Pause]* Gone to sleep?

Charles: No, I'm here.

Camilla: Darling, listen. I talked to David[4] tonight again. It might not be any good.

Charles: Oh, no!

Camilla: I'll tell you why. He's got these children of one of those Crawley girls and their nanny staying.[5] He's going, I'm going, to ring him again tomor-

---

[4] Lord Willoughby de Broke, a close friend of both Charles and Camilla, who had a Gloustershire farm near both Highgrove and the Parker Bowleses' house.

[5] The children of either Andrew Crawley, who died in the Turin air crash of 1988. Sarah is the daughter of a former chairman of Lloyd's, Murray Lawrence, and has a son; but it is more likely that it is Marita's two children, Aidan and Cosima, who are being referred to. Marita is the sister of the present Duchess of Westminster.

row. He's going, I'm going, to ring him again tomorrow. He's going to try to put them off till Friday. But I thought as an alternative perhaps I might ring up Charlie.[6]

Charles: Yes.

Camilla: And see if we could do it there. I know he's back on Thursday.

Charles: It's quite a lot further away.

Camilla: Oh, is it?

Charles: Well, I'm just trying to think. Coming from Newmarket.

Camilla: Coming from Newmarket to me at that time of night, you could probably do it in two and three-quarters. It takes me three.

Charles: What, to go to, um, Bowood?[7]

Camilla: Northmore.[8]

Charles: To go to Bowood?

Camilla: To go to Bowood would be the same as me really, wouldn't it?

Charles: I mean to say, you would suggest going to Bowood, uh?

Camilla: No, not at all.

Charles: Which Charlie then?

Camilla: What Charlie did you think I was talking about?

Charles: I didn't know, because I thought you meant . . .

Camilla: I've got lots!

[6] The Earl of Shelburne, who was Page of Honor to the queen in 1956.
[7] Family home of the Earl of Shelburne.
[8] A stud farm near Newmarket in Suffolk. At the time it was owned by Hugh van Cutsem. a longtime friend of the prince, and son of the racehorse trainer Bernard van Cutsem.

Charles: Somebody else.

Camilla: I've got lots of friends called Charlie.

Charles: The other one. Patti's.[9]

Camilla: Oh! Oh, there! Oh, that is further away. They're not . . .

Charles: They've gone.

Camilla: I don't know, it's just, you know, just a thought I had if it fell through, the other place.

Charles: Oh, right. What do you do, go on the M-twenty-five, then down the M-four, is it?

Camilla: Yes, you go, um, and sort of Royston or M-one, at that time of night.

Charles: Yes, well, that'll be just after, it will be after shooting anyway.

Camilla: So it would be, um, you'd miss the worst of the traffic, because I'll, er, you see the problem is I've got to be in London tomorrow night.

Charles: Yes.

Camilla: And Tuesday night A's coming home.[10]

Charles: No!

Camilla: Would you believe it? Because, I don't know what he is doing, he's shooting down here or something. But, darling, you wouldn't be able to ring me anyway, would you?

Charles: I might just. I mean tomorrow night I could have done.

Camilla: Oh, darling, I can't bear it. How could you have done tomorrow night?

[9] Patti and Charles Palmer-Tomkinson. Patti was seriously injured in the 1988 Klosters skiing accident which killed royal equerry Major Hugh Lindsay.

[10] Andrew Parker Bowles

Charles: Because I'll be *[Yawns]* working on the next speech.

Camilla: Oh, no, what's the next one?

Charles: A Business in the Community one, rebuilding communities.

Camilla: Oh, no, when's that for?

Charles: A rather important one for Wednesday.

Camilla: Well, at least I'll be behind you.

Charles: I know.

Camilla: Can I have a copy of the one you've just done?

Charles: Yes.

Camilla: Can I? Um. I would like it.

Charles: OK, I'll try and organize it.

Camilla: Darling . . .

Charles: But I, oh, God, when am I going to speak to you?

Camilla: I can't bear it, um . . .

Charles: Wednesday night?

Camilla: Oh, certainly Wednesday night. I'll be alone, um, Wednesday, you know, the evening. Or Tuesday. While you're rushing round doing things I'll be, you know, alone until it reappears. And early Wednesday morning, I mean, he'll be leaving at half past eight, quarter past eight. He won't be here Thursday, pray God. Um, that ambulance strike, it's a terrible thing to say this, I suppose it won't have come to an end by Thursday?

Charles: It will have done.

Camilla: Well, I mean for everybody's sake it will have done, but I hope for our sakes it's still going on.

Charles: Why?

Camilla: Well, because if it stops he'll come down here on Thursday night.

Charles: Oh, no.

Camilla: Yes, but I don't think it will stop, do you?

Charles: No, neither do I. Just our luck.

Camilla: It would be our luck, I know.

Charles: Then it's bound to.

Camilla: No, it won't. You mustn't think like that. You must think positive.

Charles: I'm not very good at that.

Camilla: Well, I'm going to. Because if I don't, I'll despair. *[Pause]* Hmmm . . . gone to sleep?

Charles: No. How maddening.

Camilla: I know. Anyway, I mean, he's doing his best to change it, David, but I just thought, you know, I might ask Charlie.

Charles: Did you say anything?

Camilla: No, I haven't talked to him.

Charles: You haven't?

Camilla: Well, I talked to him briefly, but you know, I just thought I—I just don't know whether he's got any children home, that's the worry.

Charles: Right.

Camilla: Oh . . . darling, I think I'll . . .

Charles: Pray, just pray.

Camilla: It would be so wonderful to have just one night to set us on our way, wouldn't it?

Charles: Wouldn't it? To wish you happy Christmas.

Camilla: *[Indistinct]* Happy, oh, don't let's think about Christmas. I can't bear it. *[Pause]* . . . Going to sleep? I think you'd better, don't you, darling?

Charles: *[Sleepily]* Yes, darling.

Camilla: I think you've exhausted yourself by all that hard work. You must go to sleep now, darling.

Charles: *[Sleepily]* Yes, darling.

Camilla: Will you ring me when you wake up?

Charles: Yes, I will.

Camilla: Before I have those rampaging children around. It's Tom's birthday tomorrow.[11] *[Pause]* You all right?

Charles: Mmmm, I'm all right.

Camilla: Can I talk to you, I hope, before those rampaging children . . .

Charles: What time do they come in?

Camilla: Well, usually Tom never wakes up at all, but as it's his birthday tomorrow he might just stagger out of bed. It won't be before half past eight. *[Pause]* Night-night, my darling.

Charles: Darling . . .

Camilla: I do love you.

Charles: *[Sleepily]* Before . . .

Camilla: Before half past eight.

Charles: Try and ring?

Camilla: Yeah, if you can. Love you, darling.

Charles: Night, darling.

Camilla: I love you.

Charles: I love you too. I don't want to say good-bye.

Camilla: Well done for doing that. You're a clever old thing. An awfully good brain lurking there, isn't there? Oh, darling, I think you ought to give the brain a rest now. Night-night.

Charles: Night, darling, God bless.

Camilla: I do love you and I'm so proud of you.

---

[11] It was Tom Parker Bowles's fifteenth birthday.

Charles: Oh, I'm so proud of you.

Camilla: Don't be silly, I've never achieved anything.

Charles: Yes, you have.

Camilla: No, I haven't.

Charles: Your great achievement is to love me.

Camilla: Oh, darling, easier than falling off a chair.

Charles: You suffer all those indignities and tortures and calumnies.

Camilla: Oh, darling, don't be silly. I'd suffer anything for you. That's love. It's the strength of love. Night-night.

Charles: Night, darling. Sounds as though you're dragging an enormous piece of string behind you with hundreds of tin pots and cans attached to it. Must be your telephone. Night-night, before the battery goes. *[Blows kisses]* Night.

Camilla: I love you.

Charles: I don't want to say good-bye.

Camilla: Neither do I, but you must get some sleep. 'Bye.

Charles: 'Bye, darling.

Camilla: I love you.

Charles: 'Bye.

Camilla: Hopefully talk to you in the morning.

Charles: Please.

Camilla: 'Bye, I love you.

Charles: Night.

Camilla: Night.

Charles: Night.

Camilla: Love you forever.

Charles: Night.

Camilla: G'bye, 'bye, my darling.

Charles: Night.

Camilla: Night-night.

Charles: Night.

Camilla: 'Bye-bye.

Charles: Going.

Camilla: 'Bye.

Charles: Going . . .

Camilla: Gone.

Charles: Night.

Camilla: Press the button.

Charles: Going to press the tit.

Camilla: All right, darling, I wish you were pressing mine.

Charles: God, I wish I was. Harder and harder.

Camilla: Oh, darling.

Charles: Night.

Camilla: Night.

Charles: I love you.

Camilla: *[Yawning]* Love you, press the tit.

Charles: Adore you. Night.

Camilla: Night.

Charles: Night

[Camilla blows a kiss]

Charles: Night.

Camilla: G'night my darling . . . love you . . .

[Charles hangs up]

The effect on Camilla of the publication of this conversation was shattering. One picture tragically captures her state of mind at the time, as she returned from the news-agent's carrying newspapers plastered with banner headlines revealing even more lurid details of her secret life. With a scarf wrapped around her head to shield her from the flashes of the photographers' cameras, her face is a picture of uncontrolled anguish and despair.

Hate mail arrived by the sackload. And though it was not revealed until much later, Camilla, who had spent much of her life shielded from the directness of the less privileged classes, suddenly found herself face-to-face with their contempt and derision. She was spotted walking through the car park of Sainsbury's supermarket in Chippenham, four miles from her home, by a group of women who, upon recognizing her, jeered and hurled abuse. Then they dipped into their carrier bags and brought out bread rolls and buns, which they threw at her as she attempted to flee. A neighbor, Jessica Webb, said of this extraordinary sight: "Camilla was apparently very upset. The women who did it apparently disapproved of her friendship with Charles."

Buckingham Palace officials, never at their best in an emergency, were caught on the back foot both by the revelations and by public reaction to them. Typically, they said and did nothing while the storm raged on: The *Sun*, the newspaper with the biggest roar, proclaimed: 6-MINUTE LOVE TAPE COULD COST CHARLES THRONE and, in the heat of the moment, probably spoke for nearly every one of its millions of readers.

The *Mail on Sunday*, in no less forgiving mood, ran a story headlined: CABINET MINISTER'S PLEA TO CHARLES: NEVER SEE HER AGAIN. The newspaper, on harmonious terms with virtually all of John Major's cabinet, did not specify which minister they had spoken to at length, but the message was clear and stark:

> *While Prince Charles is believed to be reluctant to end the long friendship, one senior cabinet minister said last night: "He would be well advised to break all connections with Mrs. Parker Bowles and start off with a clean slate."*

The cabinet, said the paper, believed that the British public was "in danger" of becoming deeply disillusioned with the royal family, which could have long-term consequences for the monarchy.

This was a not particularly coded message from the Tory government to the Prince of Wales that he was in deep trouble, and that the next step would be a more public breach between Crown and State—unless something was done to show that Charles was remorseful and intended to mend his ways.

The attack, which sounded like anything but an attack but carried a very heavy threat behind it, came in response to Charles's leaked reaction to the publication of the Camilla-gate Tapes. He let it be known that he thought it was the "low point in the crisis."

"This was the Sword of Damocles hanging over him," one friend said emotionally. "The worst is over now. Things can only get better."

This impossibly naive view merely served to fan the flames of anger in the cabinet. Ministers felt that, given the huge deception that had been perpetrated on the British public over the nature of Charles's relationship with Camilla, some small sign of remorse was the very least that could be expected. Instead the message from Charles's side was fool-hardy and upbeat—he would "ride out the storm."

The way he chose to ride it did little credit to someone who could manage to stay in the saddle so ably when playing polo: Certainly, it hardly encouraged an increasingly ill-tempered cabinet. The prince's plan involved repairing to Balmoral with Lord and Lady Romsey and Charles and Patti Palmer-Tomkinson, his skiing friends, for a council of war; officially it was described as a sporting weekend.

Bludgeoned by bad headlines, Charles was unable to tell

a drama from a crisis. On hearing what steps he had taken, privy councilors could do no more than look down their noses at the woeful inexperience of the people upon whom the Prince of Wales was calling in his hour of need: It compared most unfavorably with his predecessor's choice of chums, sniffed one, and look what happened to *him*.

But, as the world's media turned its spotlights beyond Charles and Camilla, it was suddenly the turn of the bit-part players in this most extraordinary of dramas. Those suddenly unmasked as coconspirators in the Machiavellian plot to mislead the nation found their doors being hammered on, and their telephone lines jammed, by those who took it upon themselves to ask on behalf of the nation just exactly what was going on.

Some escaped their notice, like Camilla's former brother-in-law, Nick Paravicini, a polo-playing friend from the days of the couple's fledgling romance in the early 1970s, whose spacious Breconshire home had welcomed Camilla and Charles on more than one occasion; and Camilla's sister Annabel Elliott, whose house at Stourpaine, near Blandford Forum in Dorset, had accommodated the lovers on a number of occasions. Also on the list was the Marchioness of Douro, a Prussian princess in her own right, who was married to the Duke of Wellington's heir. A devoted friend of the prince, she had lent Charles a country cottage and was rewarded by learning that the Princess of Wales would never speak to her again.

Others were wrongly accused of harboring the lovers, including the Canadian billionaire Galen Weston, whose multinational food-to-retailing conglomerate includes among its smaller outlets the queen's grocer, Fortnum and Mason.

Weston, a close friend of Charles and a man who dines with the queen and named his Vero Beach, Florida, seaside resort community after her Berkshire castle, was someone the press very much wanted to get close to. His British home is Fort Belvedere, an eighteenth-century Gothic Revival folly whose best-known former occupant was Charles's great-uncle and predecessor. The idea that two princes of Wales should, in succession, make love to their mistresses under the same roof was almost too much to bear. Given Charles's fondness for Weston and the prince was known to visit the fort anyway—it *had* to be true, didn't it?

Weston and his Irish-born wife, Hilary, found themselves beleaguered, and turned to Buckingham Palace advisers to ask what should be done. Weston was secure in handling the press when it came to his own multinational empire, but he did not want to say anything which might cause offence or distress to an already hard hit Prince of Wales. Already he, and Charles, had endured embarrassment the previous summer from an article in an American newspaper saying that Weston had bought Fort Belvedere from the Crown Estates (he has it on a long lease) and was handing it over as a gift to Charles and Camilla.

"They were appalled by the response they got from Buckingham Palace," a friend recalled.

And Hilary Weston revealed: "Galen rang up the press office at Buckingham Palace, which gave him the most ridiculous advice, that he write a letter [to newspaper editors] saying, 'To the best of my knowledge . . .'—can you imagine anything so stupid? So Galen wrote the only letter you can write: 'Mrs. Parker Bowles has never been in Fort Belvedere in her life.' "

It put paid to that particular line of inquiry. Other news-papers, anxious now that the relationship was revealed to put a location to these secret and historic assignations, sometimes got it wrong in their haste. A couple of them came across pic-tures of the Queenwood Golf Lodge on the Earl of Shelburne's Bowood estate, put two and two together . . . and had to offer an apology. Shelburne rightly said that Charles and Camilla had never stayed there; he saw no reason, as he extracted the newspapers' corrective paragraphs, to specify where exactly the couple *had* spent time on his estate.

Once the commentators had had their say on the sexual content of the Camillagate conversation, it was largely forgotten. What remained was a deep sense of unease that people had been fooled by the royal family—even though, as yet, they had only the merest notion of the length of the relationship, and the extent of the knowledge and forbearance of the "injured" parties.

Some of their anger manifested itself in attacks on Commander Richard Aylard, who was accused of manipulating the press, stifling stories, and offering misleading information. The "Togetherness Tour" was cited—when two midmarket and largely pro-royal newspapers had been fed a completely misleading line; and then the *Sun*, the most forceful voice in Britain if not the most influential, with a circulation close to four million, weighed in.

They instanced a story they had written the previous summer—at the time of publication of Andrew Morton's book—which Charles, through "a friend," had asked not to be published. In the story the Princess of Wales was described as a "megalomaniac" and a "scheming woman." The friend elaborated: "She has become a megalomaniac. Her behavior is endangering her marriage, the country, and the monarchy. The book paints the princess as whiter than white, but people must question her motives. Can she really claim to be a loving mother and caring person if she goes to these lengths to damage her husband?"

Another "friend" added: "Diana wants to be the Princess of Wales without the prince. She is convinced she is the one thing propping up the monarchy. It is no coincidence that we see lovely family photographs of the princess with her boys at Alton Towers and Thorpe Park. How do they happen to be taken? It is common knowledge that many of the tipoffs to photographers come from those closest to the princess."

These comments had the ring of authenticity about them. Whoever made them, it was Commander Richard Aylard who realized suddenly that they were over the top, and negotiated for their excision from the newspaper.

Much anger was generated by the release of the Camillagate Tapes, but in the eye of the storm the eponymous Mrs. Parker Bowles was trying to put her life to rights. Shattered by guilt for the effect all this was having on her husband—he was now forced to run a daily gauntlet of press photographers, and despite taking a large dose of sangfroid before walking out of the door of their London home, his legendary charm was beginning to wear a trifle thin—and worried about the effect of the publicity on her children, she began to lose weight rapidly. Within two months it was said she had lost nearly two stones, and her face had aged visibly. Bewildered, caught in the headlights, not daring to see her lover, she stayed indoors—under house arrest for the second time in a year. As before—indeed, as always in time of crisis—she called on her father. Bruce Shand, by now seventy-six, and ever the gentleman, turned out for the press. "I think we'd better keep our traps shut," was his deathless line, though earlier he had opined: "I shouldn't imagine they [Andrew and Camilla] will ever get divorced. Nothing is a hundred percent certain in this world, but that is the position as of now." The serried ranks of photographers parted in respect as he walked through them.

Indeed, old-fashioned family ties were the thing which kept Camilla going during the early weeks of 1993. Charles, whom she loved as much as when she spoke those fatal words on the night of 17 December, was on the rack: Friends say that Camilla felt as much guilt for him as she did for her husband, her children, and her aging parents. But not for her the ministrations of New Age therapists: Diana might go in for holistics and acupuncture and astrological guidance and the whole bag of tricks, but Camilla just lit up a cigarette, poured herself a stiff drink, and got on with the rest of her life as best she could.

"For a time she thought she was the most hated woman in the country," says a friend. "She had the hate mail, she had crank calls, and though Andrew did his best to support her, his patience was wearing thin. She went through agonies about what all this was doing to her children: Tom, particularly, had had a bad time of it at Eton from boys who'd picked up the papers and read extracts from the Camillagate Tapes in silly voices.

"On top of all that, what really spooked her was the idea that she was being spied on."

She was not the only person to worry on that score. It seemed that there was only one conclusion to be drawn from the fact that the Squidgy and Camillagate Tapes had been recorded within the space of fourteen days of each other— and that a third tape, eavesdropping on a conversation between the Duke and Duchess of York while Prince Andrew was aboard his ship HMS *Campbeltown*, had been recorded as well.

The royal family had been bugged. The *Sunday Mirror* reported:

> *Britain's spy bosses recorded a total of 28 intimate telephone calls between Prince Charles and Camilla Parker Bowles.*

Now MI5 chiefs who ordered the Camillagate bugging are desperate to stop more of the sensational tapes leaking out.

The other recordings are said to be just as intimate [as the first].

MI5 boss Stella Rimington has set up a team of agents to hunt the mole who leaked the Camillagate Tape—and stop any more coming out. She believes the mole is inside Britain's main spy center, GCHQ in Cheltenham, where the "professional recordings" were made. Some used a spy satellite.

This story did nothing to still the alarm and despondency felt by Camilla, since, if true, the mental turmoil she had been through was nothing by comparison with what was to come. Each telephone conversation with Charles—they could not see each other—filled her with fear.

But despite the threat of renewed revelations, nothing more emerged, and though members of Parliament demanded to know what was going on—were the security services bugging the royal family, and if so, on whose orders?—no answers were forthcoming. Fleet Street instigated its own inquiry, and came up with nothing.

The most plausible theory put forward was that rogue cells of navy or army intelligence—answerable to neither MI5 nor MI6—had utilized ultrasophisticated scanning devices to plot the exact position of the Prince of Wales via his cellular telephone. A further theory was that their operatives analyzed the content of royal conversations "in defense of the realm"—a self-serving, catchall excuse for justifying all levels of espionage.

These were theories, but there were no hard facts. One MP, Geoffrey Dickens, the Conservative member for

Littleborough and Saddleworth, tabled a parliamentary question demanding an inquiry into the bugging. His request was disallowed, the Speaker of the House of Commons citing the Birkett Report which prevented too close a scrutiny of the undercover work of the security services.

The government was in a quandary—to witch-hunt or not to witch-hunt?—but on the advice of their security advisers they fell back on that time-honored device for getting around a problem—have an inquiry. At the end of March 1993 the prime minister, John Major, published two official reports which cleared MI5 and other intelligence agencies of spying on the royal family. The findings were greeted with almost universal derision by members on all sides of the House.

The prime minister published one report on phone tapping and another on the security services generally. In the first, the Master of the Rolls, Sir Thomas Bingham, said a tribunal had found no evidence of breaches. In the second, Lord Justice Stuart-Smith said he could see no reason why the security services would shoot themselves in the foot by bugging the royal family.

These findings simply made MPs even angrier, since it was clear to them that the very inquiries themselves were off-target. The Conservative, Richard Shepherd, summed up the general discontent when he stated: "All we have here is two old buffers saying that in their opinion the security services act with integrity."

One year on, in the summer of 1994, the MP Geoffrey Dickens knew as little as when he tabled his original question: "I never got a satisfactory answer—I was told that questions of national security are protected under the terms of the Birkett Report," he said. "At the time I was particularly unsettled by the quality of the tapes—I mean, some of them were boat-to-shore, some country-to-city. That quality could not have been achieved by amateurs. It had to have been taped by someone with access to first-class equipment, and that is why I felt it should be investigated.

"The subject matter of the royal tapes was so explosive that I don't believe that it could have just been some amateur tuning in. It must have taken thousands of hours of recording, which made me think that it must have been recorded on a permanent basis. I think in the end it was perhaps a mole in the security services—the whole thing was quite disgraceful.

"The ironic thing is that under the terms of the Birkett Report, even scoundrels in the security services get protected."

In the aftermath of the Camillagate Tapes, Prince Charles swapped his cellular phone for a portable with an in-built scrambling device. He was by now conscious of the fact that the telephone call between his wife and the car dealer James Gilbey—the Squidgy Tape—overheard by the ever-vigilant Cyril Reenan, was a compilation of two telephone calls, tapes of which had been patched together and rebroadcast by persons unknown with the specific intention of being picked up by an amateur. There was a danger of it happening again.

This knowledge did nothing to calm the fears of Camilla Parker Bowles; indeed the cavalier way in which the relevant government agencies misdirected their inquiries left her with only one conclusion: that she, along with Prince Charles, was bugged by Britain's security services on a round-the-clock basis. And nobody was going to do a thing to change that state of affairs.

But the Camillagate Tapes are just as valuable to those with an interest in the future of Britain's royal family as to those, including rogue elements in the spy network, with an interest in its destabilization. They give the clearest possible picture of the nature of Charles and Camilla's relationship, nearly two decades after that fateful night in Annabel's.

That two people should still love each other as passionately after so many years is remarkable in itself. The endearments, when daylight is shed upon them, are of course an embarrassment—but no more so than for any other loving couple who have had their most private moments exposed to the public gaze. Beyond that first hurdle, there emerges a picture of a woman who cares deeply for her man—tenderly concerned for his happiness and spiritual well-being, happily indulgent when he dwells too much upon his own problems.

She is deferential: The conversational confusion over where they meet next is all Charles's, but she does not hasten to correct him. Charles meanwhile is generous in his praise of her—"Your great achievement is to love me"—and though this seems a backhanded compliment, centering as it does on himself, it comes from a man whose life has been forged on a path toward his own destiny. Unlike most people, Charles is aware that he is part of history in everything he does—and that, in time, history will also mark with greater kindness the role that Camilla played in his life. Fifty years from now people in supermarket car parks would not feel inclined to throw bread rolls at her.

The conversation highlights the number of friends who are prepared to offer the loving couple sanctuary in their homes, but equally it demonstrates the high level of subterfuge required in arranging these love trysts. Clearly as few people as possible must know they are sharing the same roof, and that includes small children as young as six. Additionally, the couple appear to be exercising a very rudimentary form of self-censorship in not directly naming friends or houses.

The speech to which Charles refers was delivered at the Guildhall in the City of London the following Wednesday morning. As president of Business in the Community, he relaunched the Dragon Awards for Community Involvement, then walked to the Brewers' Hall to attend the Community Trust Conference. Not a single one of the hundreds involved in such a high-minded scheme that day could have realized that, as he wrote the words intended to spur them on to greater good, his mind had been occupied with Camilla and when he would be able to bed her next.

There was, as one commentator pointed out, a moment of dereliction when the conversation came around to Andrew Parker Bowles. The ambulance strike of 1989 was one of the ugliest industrial confrontations in Britain since the miners' strike. It lasted six months and cost the nation more than £35 million. The police and army hurriedly had to work out a cover system which would provide the same kind of service—and though this was finally achieved, the public inevitably suffered. It was suggested that people had died needlessly because the professionals were out on strike. By the time the strike was resolved in 1990 the police had dedicated an extra 1.1 million hours to ambulance-related duties, which had necessarily taken them away from their core role of crime prevention and detection.

When Charles and Camilla's conversation took place the dispute was three months old and at its height. Andrew Parker Bowles had a key role to play in providing army-ambulance backup, and the job proved demanding and time-consuming. Interestingly, it is Camilla who is apologetic about wishing the strike would carry on so as to keep her husband in London. No such regrets are uttered by the prince—"Just our luck," he says at the thought that he might have to miss his next assignation with Camilla. As a privy councillor and future king he would argue publicly that the restitution of order to the ambulance service was paramount to the health of the nation. But not, it would appear, if it was to interfere with his private life.

Andrew Parker Bowles's response to these ugly intrusions on his life was to maintain a heroically stiff upper lip, not allowing himself even the satisfaction of a sharp word with inquisitive reporters. Part of the reason may have been that, since Princess Anne's separation from Captain Mark Phillips, he had been seeing a great deal of the woman he had once wooed, taking her to the cinema, the theater and out to dinner at a number of restaurants. She visited his home when Camilla was away, and saw much of him while he was still at Knightsbridge Barracks. In addition he spent some time in the company of Charlotte Hambro, whom he had met and fallen in love with a decade earlier when her father, Lord Soames, was governor of Rhodesia.

Interestingly, considering her own extramural involvements, Camilla was less than sanguine about Andrew's romantic life. "Camilla hated the intensity of the relationship with Charlotte. But even if it did go on for quite a long time, she was really in no position to complain," said a friend.

And indeed, whatever accommodation they had reached in their marriage remained unchanged. Andrew Parker Bowles, whose father, Derek, had been, according to some, the Queen Mother's closest male friend after the death of King George VI, remained a favorite of hers. A tradition had sprung up that he and Camilla would stay at Royal Lodge, Windsor, each spring and travel down to Cheltenham for the National Hunt Festival, that uproarious week of equine excellence. This year was to be no exception: Though the Queen Mother was acutely aware of what the newspapers had written, she saw this as no bar to her friendship with either Andrew or

Camilla. The couple, however they were feeling about each other at that particular juncture, were ready to face the world at Cheltenham. For too long now, they told friends, they had been trapped in their own home.

About this time, a very strange story started to circulate about Camilla's father, Bruce Shand. It was said that Major Shand could take no more and had demanded a meeting with the Prince of Wales at Buckingham Palace. When the two men met, he told the prince that his wife was an invalid and that his daughter's life had been ruined; Charles must leave his daughter alone, for ever. The prince, it was said, responded by bursting into tears.

When quizzed about this tale, Major Shand did nothing to rebut it: But it was his "trap shut" policy which stilled his tongue, rather than a reluctance to tell the truth. The reality was that the meeting never occurred, it was simply the product of fevered imaginations in an overheated atmosphere of intrigue and drama.

One rumor which was confirmed, however, was the very existence of Charles and Camilla's longstanding relationship at a time when newspapers still fought shy of describing Camilla as anything other than Charles's "confidante." Astonishingly, the confirmation came from Buckingham Palace itself. A member of the press bureau, Dickie Arbiter, interviewed by the *Daily Mirror*, admitted as much.

"So what?" he said. "So the prince has had an affair with this woman—it happens in France all the time. Politicians and famous men in all walks of life in France have mistresses and nobody turns a hair."

After all the years of intrigue and subterfuge it was a staggering admission, a princely own-goal which showed just how out of control the situation had become.

Indeed, by mid-1993, royal advisers had lost the will to

try to control events. Punch-drunk with the seemingly end-less barrage of revelations, and with no way of knowing what might yet come spilling out of the woodwork, they simply gave up. No move was made to pacify the renegade Princess of Wales, who was now considered to be an outlaw; this policy in itself was ill-advised since, in her anger and frustra-tion at the way she had been treated—"after all I've done for that ******* family" was her catchphrase—she posed a very grave threat to the House of Windsor in a number of ways.

First, and most dangerous, was the influence she had over her children, and most particularly Prince William. No matter how often the little princes were to be seen at Sandringham Church, treading in their father's footsteps, she saw more of them than did Charles—and if she so chose—was in a posi-tion to exercise a malign influence over them, whether it be in relation to their father, their grandmother the queen, or the whole royal apparatus. Given her overexcited state it would have been reasonable to take precautions, to "keep her sweet"—but instead she was treated like an enemy.

Second, she had the capacity to upstage the entire House of Windsor at virtually any event: A carefully staged shopping expedition while Charles made a keynote speech on the environment would drive him off the front pages; a change of hairstyle or the choice of a hat at the annual Service of Remembrance would take all eyes from the queen; a speech on virtually any subject—but especially one which dwelt obliquely on her problems—would absorb the nation's atten-tions, it would seem, for days.

And then there was the ever-present threat that she had not yet finished telling home truths. In the summer of 1994, after her so-called withdrawal from public life, the princess was observed in lengthy discussion with the journalist Richard Kay. It was said that Mr. Kay was planning a book:

Was this to be a further, and even more damaging, version of *Diana: Her True Story*? The havoc she could wreak on the House of Windsor's national and international standing was incalculable.

Yet nothing, it seemed, was being done by the palace *apparatchiks* to accommodate her—within the household, she was simply viewed as someone who had let the side down, someone who had pulled the plug from the bottom of the boat in which they all sailed. There was a great sense of satisfaction when she finally moved out of Highgrove, getting her sister Lady Jane Fellowes to help her pack personal belongings so she could quit the house she had always felt belonged to Camilla.

In March 1993, Charles, spurred on by Camilla, set to work eradicating all traces of Diana from the house. One of the first targets was the princess's sitting room, a sanctuary close to the pink-and-green master bedroom with its four-poster which was used mainly by Diana from the early days of their marriage.

In 1981 the room had been decorated in shades of yellow by interior designer Dudley Poplak, who was recommended by Diana's mother, Mrs. Frances Shand Kydd. But now the Wiltshire-based designer Robert Kime was brought in on Camilla's advice to strip the walls, pull out built-in bookshelves from the alcoves, and give the room a "more masculine" feel. The changes, unannounced by Charles, gave Diana a considerable shock when she revisited the house in May to spend two nights under its roof, in an abortive attempt to give the little princes a taste once again of home life with both parents. Once she saw the changes wrought in the Highgrove garden by Camilla, she decided it was an experiment which was not to be repeated.

Camilla's stamp would also be placed on Charles's new

apartments in St. James's Palace, where he had moved from Kensington Palace in the wake of the separation. And Diana, too, was ready to quit the London marital home for somewhere nonroyal: She saw Kensington Palace as "secure, but a gilded cage." She encountered more difficulty in relocating.

Meanwhile, Andrew and Camilla Parker Bowles put a brave face on the deluge of damaging revelations. The Queen Mother, for one, was not about to dump them simply on the basis of what she would perceive as pernicious gossip. Indeed it was the Queen Mother's influence—she had, after all, signed the register as principal witness to the couple's wedding twenty years earlier—which governed the queen's own reaction to the scandal of the tapes. Unsure now what her relationship should be with the man who had been her Silver Stick in Waiting, the woman who was the daughter of a trusted member of the Queen's Body Guard, and her own son, she adopted the attitude of her mother, who blithely saw the whole issue as a blip on the dynastic horizon.

But while at the heart of the royal family there seemed a determination to overcome any embarrassment Charles's love for Camilla may have caused, there was no letup outside in the real world. In April 1993 Andrew and Camilla allowed themselves to be photographed ostensibly giving a luncheon party at Middlewick House for a dozen friends: But this display of marital solidarity was rudely shattered by the too-close attentions of the press, who not unreasonably demanded some clarification of this historic ménage à trois. Andrew slammed the door shut on them.

His own relations with the press had recently taken a dip. Unsure what they could justifiably say about a man whose wife was having an affair with the Prince of Wales, they had skirted decorously around the soldier. He, in turn, had treated even the more rapacious representatives of the Fourth Estate with an uncommon courtesy, with the result that, while Camilla came in for wholesale criticism, from her looks to her clothes to her morals, he remained exempt.

However, the brigadier's highly successful army career had recently hit a rocky patch. Having headed the Household Cavalry, he was now given a new command, as director of the Royal Army Veterinary Corps. For the 200-year-old corps, this came as a heavy and demoralizing blow—for never before in its history had anyone who was not a qualified vet led them.

It prompted the instant resignation of the corps' colonel commandant, Brigadier Robert Clifford, who had served for more than thirty years with the RAVC. He wrote to the Ministry of Defense: "I have just been notified by the director that his successor is to be Colonel A.H. Parker Bowles, OBE, late Blues and Royals.

"As Officer Commanding Household Cavalry, Silver Stick in Waiting to RM the Queen and Steward of the Jockey Club, he is no doubt eminently qualified for the promotion, but he is not a veterinary surgeon." This rather sour tally of Parker Bowles's achievements constituted an unprecedented attack on a brother officer, and led to accusations that the protest had less to do with the brigadier's want of professional qualifications and more to do with his extramural activities and friendships. Moreover he was accused—though not by Clifford—of having ducked foreign postings which would have carried brigadier rank, preferring to remain in London: "The army had to look round for a suitable position and that was the only brigadier's job available, so they gave it to Andrew," said a friend. "It caused a lot of resentment."

Indeed Brigadier Clifford was not alone—he was joined by other retired brigadiers from the corps who launched an attack via the Royal College of Veterinary Surgeons, claiming the appointment of a nonvet was unethical. "They were very upset and demanded some immediate action," said a member of the college.

The Ministry of Defense climbed down. It decreed that when Brigadier Parker Bowles took up his controversial appointment he would limit his orders to management, and keep out of the clinical field. This meant, inevitably, that the veterinary workload of other senior officers would increase. But it also meant that this last command before retiring from the army in December 1994 would be a bed of nails; he would be surrounded by brother officers who would continue to mutter, with little justification, that he got the job because of his contacts, not on merit. For a man who, in Rhodesia, persuaded a group of guerrillas to lay down their weapons while he himself was unarmed, this was a bitter pill to swallow: Veterinary surgeons were hardly front-line troops.

The tensions at work and at home took their toll on Andrew and Camilla, and for the first time friends started to discuss quite seriously the possibility that the couple might part after twenty years of marriage. The *Daily Express* columnist Ross Benson observed: "Despite an almost superhuman effort to come to terms with the revelations of the past few months, the tension generated has pushed them to breaking point." Camilla was now rarely to be seen at home; she had made a visit to Italy in the wake of the Camillagate scandal, and was now spending considerable amounts of time in London. What the article did not say, but the implication was clear, was that she was seeing Charles: It was easier to be anonymous in London than risk his visiting her house, or her going to Highgrove. Their carefully constructed network of "safe houses" had been blown, at least for the time being— and both Camilla and Charles desperately needed to see each other.

Soon the talk of divorce became a roar, but such defeatism from friends drew a sharp rebuttal from Andrew's cousin Lord Beaverbrook, a former lord-in-waiting to the queen, who protested: "This is totally preposterous. Anyone who knows Andrew will understand that he will stand by his wife in these difficult times."

Andrew's younger brother Simon—who had introduced the couple all those years ago—said: "Both Andrew and Camilla have said they will never divorce and, while the relationship is rather eccentric, it appears to work. They get on well."

Maybe the pill was sugared somewhat by the publication of a racy novel on one of Andrew's favorite sports, *Polo*, by Jilly Cooper. The narrative was enlivened by a character called Drew Benedict, a dashing captain whose name—and possibly his exploits—was inspired by the brigadier. The fictional captain's Christian name is a diminutive of Andrew, and Benedict is a neat reference to his Roman Catholicism. Parker Bowles was said to be highly amused by this canonization in print.

It was a brief moment of levity in an otherwise grim drama. Fearful of being bugged, desperate that their continuing relationship should not be further uncovered, Charles and Camilla were at pains to put distance between each other. Camilla's by-now traditional spring sojourn at Birkhall on the Balmoral estate was canceled and she and Andrew made sure that they were seen together publicly—as much for the sake of their children as anything else.

In May the couple turned out for the wedding of twenty-five-year-old Sarah Ward at the village church of Chilton Foliat in Wiltshire. But as the bride was given away by her father, Gerald Ward, Camilla's thoughts must have strayed back to the night in 1972 when he, and she, and Prince

Charles and Princess Anne danced the night away at Annabel's, and to what might have been if things had worked out differently.

During this period, in the summer of 1993, Charles and Camilla's relationship intensified under the immense pressure both were facing. Charles, attacked on all sides, had lost the confidence of the nation. Opinion poll after opinion poll offered alternative solutions to his acceding to the throne, mostly involving his passing the kingship straight on to Prince William; his popularity sank to an all-time low, way beneath the errant Duchess of York.

"Despite all the talk about him having no real job, Charles has always had a clear-cut picture of his own destiny," one royal source observed. "Though he could be frustrated by the wait for kingship, he had created what he considered a worthwhile role for himself, championing the common man against the bureaucrats and taking a swipe at political correctness where it prevailed over traditional values." All fine and dandy, except that it was now rendered worthless by the publication of a telephone call.

The royal disinformation machine kicked in. In June the *Daily Express* ran the headline: CHARLES GAVE UP CAMILLA 2 YEARS AGO, and underneath, its royal correspondent wrote:

> *Friends close to the prince, who is beginning to grow in confidence as he puts the controversy of his marriage behind him, are anxious to play down this latest outburst. One said: "There is nothing more that can come out about the prince's relationship with Camilla. As far as we are concerned, it is all old hat."*
>
> *It was also claimed that the prince's relationship with Camilla has been over for more than two years, a full twelve*

months before Andrew Morton's book Diana: Her True Story *was published.*

"It was all so unnecessary," said the friend. "All the humiliation, pain and heartache that followed could have been avoided. The prince ended his relationship with Camilla two years ago in the spring of 1991. He knew he had to give her up and he did."

This was one of the most outrageous pieces yet planted in a journalist's ear. The source was sufficiently highly placed for the reporter to believe what he was hearing—it was, after all, a carbon copy of Commander Richard Aylard's briefing to selected newspapers, months before, about the "Togetherness Tour." But now, as then, the information was misleading. The source went on to vouchsafe that Charles had made a concerted effort to save his marriage but Diana had rejected all his approaches; and that it was on the ill-fated tour of Korea—the last Charles and Diana would ever undertake—that the princess had flatly refused to consider a reconciliation.

The source continued: "After that trip he knew his marriage was finished, but suggestions that he again turned to Camilla are just not true. The prince feared that if he was ever seen with Camilla again it would finally wreck his chances of becoming king. The people would not accept him."

So in "an emotional meeting" Charles said he wanted to end the friendship so he could make a final effort to save his troubled marriage, and since then, he had "stuck to his word" and not pursued Camilla.

The report concluded:

In fact, it was forty-five-year-old Camilla, now beginning to lose her looks, who could not cope with being dumped

*by the man she cherished. She pursued him. In January, after
the Camillagate scandal hit the monarchy even further, the
prince made a gentleman's agreement with Brigadier Parker
Bowles never to see his wife again.*

The report was arrant nonsense, but the Machiavellian
men who purveyed it were by now desperate. The twenty-
fifth anniversary of Charles's investiture as Prince of Wales
was now just a year away, and the task of eradicating the
damage of the Tampax conversation was proving considerably
more difficult than had at first been envisaged.

Meanwhile the strain on Camilla was becoming ever
more visible. By June, friends were expressing alarm at the
state of her health and talked about the "intolerable pressure"
she was under: "I am genuinely worried about her. The spark
has gone out of her life and she looks haunted and hunted,"
said one. As her forty-sixth birthday approached she was said
to be looking older than her years; friends conceded that she
was "in touch" with Charles, though maintained the fiction
that she had not seen him for six months. This not wholly
credible version nonetheless put paid to the claims of Charles's
"friend" who averred they had not met for two years.

But the stakes were high in the game to win back the
affections of the British public in time for Charles's first great
anniversary, and the end justified the means.

In the early autumn Camilla's spirits had revived sufficiently for her to embark on a tour of India with Gerald
Ward's wife Amanda, and with Emilie van Cutsem, whose
house Northmore had featured in the Camillagate Tapes.
Fears that she had undergone a nervous breakdown during
the summer were quashed by Andrew Parker Bowles, who
declared: "She is perfectly all right. She has gone away on
holiday with another couple of girls, that's all." He added

with uncharacteristic frankness that the couple were working hard to make their marriage work: "Everything is all right between us."

Days later, on her return, Camilla neatly avoided Diana at a memorial service for the Earl of Westmorland, the former Master of the queen's Horse. Unlike the E11 Alamein service a year before, there was no confrontation between the two women but observers were able to assess the comparative damage that events had inflicted on each of them: Diana, the nervous, self-obsessed bulimic who had made theatrical attempts at suicide, sparkled radiantly in black. Camilla, the steely horsewoman whose resolve had stiffened Charles's backbone, looked shattered and almost old enough to be Diana's mother. Though she had regained some of the curves which her prince found so appealing, it was an ironic twist to see such a difference between the two women.

At this point, disbelievers who still clung to the hope that the events of the past few months had been simply a weird and distressing nightmare were finally disabused when Andrew's sister-in-law Carolyn gave an interview to an Australian women's magazine. The Parker Bowles marriage, she said, was a "convenient and unusual" one.

"Everyone knows Camilla and Andrew have an arranged marriage," she said. "Ever since they married they have had a fairly free life together." However, she dismissed the suggestion that the couple might divorce: "Why would they? They get on very well and what they do suits them both quite well."

The effect of the Camillagate Tapes' publication had changed their subject's life: "She just doesn't go out, except to private parties. Can you blame her? Imagine going to the supermarket after you have had those tapes quoted at you in all the newspapers and magazines."

The public, by now almost as battle-fatigued as the players in this drama, took this admission from a member of the Parker Bowles family—that Charles and Camilla had had an affair—with remarkable calm. Christmas was coming, and after nearly a year of scandal and intrigue, they felt they'd heard the worst.

Two or three days later Camilla made a brief appearance in front of the cameras to demonstrate how unmoved she was by her sister-in-law's comments. Indeed, she looked remarkably healthy and confident as her brother-in-law Simon confirmed that she was feeling much better. Close friends had helped her through a bad patch, he said, and added: "Things have really picked up for her. She's been out much more than before. I don't know what her relationship is with Prince Charles at the moment, but she seems happy."

He added that royal circles were still what he described as a "no-go area" for Camilla: "The one thing she would never do is embarrass the royal family," he said. As if to underline this, Camilla authorized friends to let it be known that there would be no divorce between her and Andrew: Discussions had taken place over their respective positions which had managed to resolve whatever problems existed in their highly unusual marriage. A two-sentence statement, issued jointly but unofficially, proclaimed: "We will never divorce. It is not something that has been considered."

Into this flurry of feel-good communication with the outside world suddenly stepped the surprising figure of Bruce Shand. He declared that he had never given an interview before, but suddenly he was ready to do so, and one must surmise that, since he had nothing in particular to sell, this was to be his own small contribution to his daughter's rehabilitation.

In the event, the interview was remarkable for what it did

not say, rather than what it did. His feelings on sexual permissiveness: "It's a pity that the ties of marriage have been so destroyed by it." Has the country gone to the dogs? "There's been a tremendous deterioration of conduct and respect." He revealed a potentially embarrassing encounter with the queen—not over his daughter and her son, but in his role as a member of the queen's Body Guard ("always dressed for the Battle of Waterloo").

His most arduous duty, he said, was to carry the queen's standard on State occasions. Once, cramped for room when he was required to lower the standard to the queen as she passed through the royal gallery, he managed to hook the handbag of a French visitor on its butt end. "That was dramatic, what? The queen was very amused by the whole thing."

It was a deft and charming display, without giving a thing away.

When the Princess of Wales wrested away the initiative from her husband with the publication of *Diana: Her True Story*, she must have known it was only a matter of time before she lost the advantage she had gained. From the moment in June 1992 when it hit the bookshops, courtiers and royals alike were searching for a solution. And, it must be said, their judgment was tinged with more than a hint of revenge.

It took eighteen months. But by December 1993 the die had been cast—and the princess was forced into a humbling withdrawal from public life, which left politicians, churchmen, and the public gasping in amazement.

The statement was so effectively stage-managed that no one grasped that her withdrawal was involuntary. In the unlikely surroundings of the Park Lane Hilton hotel in

London, the princess announced: "I will be reducing the extent of the public life I have led so far. Over the next few months I will be seeking more suitable ways of combining a meaningful public role with, hopefully, a more private life."

Should anyone, in the heat of the moment, suddenly remember to ask why the princess was making this astonishing announcement, a barely veiled reason was contained in the section which read: "When I started my public life twelve years ago, I understood that the media might be interested in what I did. I realized then that their attention would inevitably focus on both our public and private lives. But I was not aware of how overwhelming that attention would become; nor the extent to which it would affect both my public duties and my personal life, in a manner that has been hard to bear."

This part of her statement touched the hearts of her audience, drawn from supporters of the Headway National Head Injuries Association, for within the previous month sneak photographs of the princess working out in a West London gymnasium had been published by the Mirror Group, to universal disgust. But still, her declaration stopped just about short of humbug, for the present crisis, which had kept the House of Windsor's name in the headlines on a daily basis for the past eighteen months, was entirely of Diana's making.

Blaming the message bearers is an old trick, much beloved by politicians, and here Diana used it to great effect; but one academic, Dr. David Starkey, of the London School of Economics, was unimpressed: "She wanted not only to protect her privacy, but to have all the indulgence and pleasure of the private life of a rich young woman," he said. "But you can't do it, especially when you've paraded your private life before the public when it suits you. She is now complaining of media intrusion, but who was it who spilled the beans on every detail of her married life to the press via Andrew Morton's book?"

But upon closer scrutiny the message she gave out was riddled with inconsistencies. In June 1992, at the time of the Morton book, the message she delivered via intermediaries to the *Sunday Times* was interpreted to mean that she had a greater understanding of herself and a surer sense of purpose. In her work with the sick, the dying, and the distressed, she had found a calling. In December that year, at the time of the separation announcement, she delivered a public message which went, in part: "I want you to be certain of this—our work together will continue unchanged."

But even as she spoke, the machinery was in motion to put Diana on the back burner—and off the hob altogether in due course. For, in the aftermath of the separation she perceived a globe-trotting role for herself where she would become a figure on the world stage. Friends of the princess revealed that she would return to a scaled-down public life in the spring. "She will no longer be the Princess of Wales but a princess for the world," said one, somewhat grandiosely. "She will concentrate on the international side of her charity work, while the royal side of her life will diminish."

Another version, authorized to be leaked by the princess, continued the "dynamic new role on the international stage" theme. Plans were under way for her to head a charitable foundation, working as an executive and decision maker rather than simply a photogenic figurehead, it was hinted. This independent organization would be dedicated to offering help and encouragement to the disadvantaged around the world, with Diana concentrating her efforts on overseas issues, leaving her husband to work on projects in Britain without the inevitable clashes. Whatever, reports of her going into exile were "grossly exaggerated," she said.

But Charles was having none of it—his advisers warned him that his own role would continue to be diminished all the time Diana stayed on the public stage. A squabble arose over separate trips to Russia: Both wanted to go, neither was prepared to back down.

In a meeting with the prime minister, Charles made it clear that he had to stand alone on the royal stage, and that if he was to become an effective king, there must be no distractions from his center-stage position. While the premier remained immobile with indifference over this royal push-me-pull-you, his foreign secretary, Douglas Hurd, wasted no time in coming to Charles's aid.

Hurd, the Old Etonian son of an obscure peer, had distinguished himself in the diplomatic service before carving an equally successful career in politics. He was, most people thought, sufficiently "Establishment" not to be dazzled by royalty: Yet the encomium he delivered on Charles's behalf was positively embarrassing, coming as it did from the man holding the country's second highest political office. Charles, he claimed joyfully, was "a star. . . . I have seen him in action in many different circumstances and he is a star," he said. "He would be a star even if he were not the Prince of Wales.

"We must use his particular gifts, which go beyond the ordinary matters of royalty into the interests which he has developed, sometimes business, sometimes social, sometimes environmental.

"Thank heavens," he proclaimed, that Charles would one day be king. It was difficult to imagine that the rest of the cabinet felt quite as Douglas Hurd did: Maybe, said some observers, he was overcompensating for the indifference or downright hostility some ministers felt toward someone who had let the side down.

In October, Diana, too, had a meeting with John Major in which she outlined her plans for the future, to include more trips like her recent successful tour in Tibet. Even at that late stage, she harbored the belief that she would have a future as a roving ambassador—she and the Overseas Development Minister Baroness Chalker had reached an understanding and mutual respect, and saw much fruitful work ahead together in the underdeveloped countries of the world. At that stage it seemed possible that she might attract the support of John Major, who was not slow to recognize her international appeal: "He has always taken an interest in the royal marriage, and took the unusual step of announcing the separation himself when it was widely regarded that the palace should have done it," said a government source. "He believes she is a very important figure as she is the mother of the future King, so he feels it is his business to make sure she is given a suitable role."

Diana even drafted in Sir Gordon Reece, a deft and dapper image-burnisher, to help in her attempts to set up her own secretariat and her own agenda. But it all came to nothing, for in the end Charles, as future king, pulled rank. Sir Gordon told Diana she was fighting a losing battle, and with few other big hitters behind her to support her cause— she had, after all, no constitutional position even though she was wife and mother of future kings—the bid for her own platform collapsed.

It would not be entirely misleading to suggest that palace sources, briefing the press and thereby the world, did not contradict anyone who suggested that Diana's decision to quit was hers, and hers alone. Was it hasty? Possibly. Emotional? No comment.

One seasoned observer, looking at Diana's plight, commented: "It was a classic mistake, and a classic ploy used by the royal family. Whenever they want a problem to disappear they manipulate that person into a corner so that they inevitably go abroad or disappear from sight. You have only to look at the way they dealt with the Duke of Windsor or the Duchess of York: They believe 'out of sight, out of mind' and by the look of it, Diana has fallen for their plan hook—line, and sinker."

Even so, one other figure—as bizarre in his way as Sir Jimmy Savile, who all those months ago had tried to broker a reconciliation after Charles's self-imposed exile at Balmoral—emerged as a supporter at this time: Lord Archer.

The former deputy chairman of the Conservative Party, best-selling novelist, and future jailbird was summoned to Kensington Palace the day before Diana's speech and invited to read it and offer suggestions. Archer later commented: "I was very sad when I read it. We discussed how and when she would speak, and the best way to do it with dignity."

A measure of decorum was achieved that day, but Diana's next outing was anything but dignified: On the following Monday she turned out at Heathrow Airport to name a new Virgin Atlantic jet. She was subjected to a humiliating ordeal at the hands of the effervescent head of Virgin, Richard Branson, who popped champagne corks, put his arm round her, and treated her like an actress from a television soap opera.

It was a demoralizing rout, and she headed for anonymity with her head down and the tears once again welling in her eyes. Her husband, meanwhile, spent two hours that night in the company of Camilla Parker Bowles.

This was something which would not have found favor with the Reverend Tony Higton, a vociferous member of the Church of England synod and the longstanding vicar of Hawkwell in Essex. "It is with great sadness," he began, "that I have reached the conclusion that Prince Charles is not fit to be the next King of England.

"I believe that Charles can only become king if he totally denies he committed adultery with Camilla Parker Bowles. Alternatively he should make a public expression of remorse and penitence. And if he really said that he was sorry, and confirmed that any romance was over, then I think that he could still be king.

"But in the absence of either of these options, I have to say I think he is unfit to be king, and I think it would be better if the crown passed straight to Prince William—provided he maintained the highest standards in his private life."

Mr. Higton was, perhaps, one of the most clamorous of the clergy, but he nonetheless spoke for a still significant Establishment body—the Church of England. Charles's road to respectability was barred by their surpliced figures: He needed their sanction before he could be fully rehabilitated in the eyes of the populace.

"We require even higher standards from people in public places today than we did in the past," continued Mr. Higton. "We must take a firm stand on adultery—I think it is very unfortunate if people in such high places as Prince Charles cannot behave morally.

"This country has one of the highest divorce rates of any country in the world and I believe that we have all got to start pulling together to put right this moral decay. We should have strong leadership from our royals."

And Arthur Leggatt, secretary of the five-thousand-strong Church Union, said: "It would compromise the teachings of the scripture which say clearly that a person taken in divorce has committed adultery. An adulterer should not be head of the Church of England."

The Church, silent all these years, had suddenly found its voice.

Chapter Nine

An All Time Low

The words "constitutional crisis" strike terror into the hearts of the royal family and their supporters. There has already been one within living memory, and the healing process after the abdication was perforce a long and slow one, jerkily started by King George VI but more smoothly developed by his daughter.

Ever conscious of the waxing and waning appeal of monarchy worldwide—the rise of King Juan Carlos of Spain had been matched by the final deroyalization in 1994 of King Constantine of Greece—the House of Windsor remains sensitive to its critics. Though during the royal marriage crisis no active republican movement emerged, it became perfectly clear that the royal family's greatest enemy was the nation's contempt. Britain stood back and watched with indifference as its first family dug their own grave.

Certainly in the early stages, it seemed that others were more alive to the growing crisis than were the royals themselves. Following the announcement in the House of Commons by the prime minister that Charles and Diana were to separate, a jittery Church of England moved swiftly to dispel any idea that the prince's future position as supreme governor could be jeopardized. The Archbishop of Canterbury, Dr. George Carey, instructed the Archbishop of York to go to the House of Lords to deliver the Church's own deliberations on the crisis.

On 9 December 1992, the same day as the prime minister's historic statement, the archbishop told a thunderstruck upper chamber: "We urge the public to react with compassion and understanding and not to add unnecessarily to the pain already suffered by those involved. The interests and feelings of Prince Henry and Prince William should be borne constantly in mind."

He went on: "Questions will inevitably be raised about the implications of the separation for His Royal Highness's position as future supreme governor of the Church of England.

"From a legal viewpoint, marital status does not affect the succession to the throne and hence to the title of Supreme Governor. The monarch is supreme governor of the Church by virtue of being the sovereign: There is no other legal requirement. Under the Act of Settlement of 1701 the sovereign must be a communicant member of the Church of England.

"In the case of unsuccessful marriages, the Church of England accepts that there are sometimes circumstances, however sad, where separation is the lesser evil and hence the best way forward. To undergo such an experience and take such a decision does not in itself in any sense disqualify a person from holding the title of Supreme Governor."

Six weeks later, the archbishop's position appeared to have altered somewhat. Appearing on the BBC television show *Heart of the Matter,* he said that while he did not agree that recent exposure in the media of the Prince of Wales's relationship with Camilla Parker Bowles had made it difficult for him to become supreme governor of the Church of England, "all tolerance has its limits."

Thus, the Church's position was set out in clear and unequivocal terms—Charles would be supreme governor when he became king. But things were far from being that simple. And within a year discussions would have taken place, the purpose of which was to prevent Charles from ever becoming the Church's figurehead.

Many in a nonreligious age might ask what it matters in Great Britain if the established Church and the royal family should part company. Though Anglicanism is the nation's official religion, only a small percentage of the population now attends church regularly: Since the coronation of 1953 an increasingly multiracial society has evolved, with more and more Britons belonging to other religions. If Charles is to reign as king, he will be these people's sovereign too, and—his supporters argue—the backing of the established Church is far less crucial to successful kingship than at any time since the reign of King Henry VIII.

Having pledged to investigate these minorities—Sikhs, Muslims, Hindus—in his travels up and down the country, and having familiarized himself with their lives and cultures, Charles had come to a somewhat diluted view of the importance of the Church of England. But he had underestimated the reaction against him: The seismic rumblings among a powerful minority within the Church finally erupted on 5 December 1993 when the Archdeacon of York, the Venerable George Austin, spoke up for many disaffected fellow clerics when he launched an outright attack.

"Does he have the right to be trusted with the role of king, if his attitude to matrimony is so cavalier?" he asked.

"Prince Charles made solemn vows before God in church about his marriage, and it seems he began to break them almost immediately. He has broken the trust on one thing, and broken vows on another. How can he then go into church, into Westminster Abbey, and take the coronation vows?"

He concluded, to devastating effect: "Are we to believe him that he will keep those? It brings into question the whole attitude of Charles to vows, trust, and so on. The Church forgives of course; if I as Archdeacon of York fiddled the books or cheated on my wife or broke my ordination vows, God would forgive me if I repented. But I might be totally unsuitable at the end of it to be Archdeacon of York."

The response was instantaneous, and dramatic. Though Austin's position in the Church was acknowledged as that of a dedicated antiliberal and was thus discounted by many of his senior colleagues, his statements echoed the notorious speech made by the Bishop of Bradford in December 1936 to an annual diocesan conference.

Spoken in the dying days of Edward VIII's brief reign, it had the effect of opening the floodgates of criticism which for too long had been held back. Ingenuously, Blunt later claimed he had meant something else when he commended the king to God's grace "which he will so abundantly need— for the king is a man like any other—if he is to do his duty properly. We hope that he was aware of this need. Some of us wish that he gave more positive signs of such awareness." Many took this to be a reference to the king's all-consuming and destructive love for Mrs. Simpson.

Whatever their original purpose, Blunt's words had the effect of finally releasing a nation's newspapers from the yoke of degrading self-censorship. While the whole American nation was able to read daily of the deteriorating situation, in

Britain all but a few had been kept in the dark. Now at last—
when the abdication crisis was almost over—Fleet Street felt
free to reveal to its readers the appalling truth of what had
been going on for many months in Buckingham Palace and
the corridors of power.

Almost fifty-seven years later, to the day, in December
1993, the more superstitious courtiers in Buckingham Palace
sensed a similar disaster in the offing. Though the bush telegraph had given them warning of earlier shocks in the press,
they could not be certain that other embarrassments which
for many months had been held back—just as the Squidgy
Tapes had been—were not about to be released.

This new assault from the Church, at the very heart of the
Establishment, would give Fleet Street the justification it had
long been seeking to reveal even more damaging material.
Nothing happened immediately. But three days later the
Archdeacon of York returned to the attack, in the *Times*.

Half a century earlier, the country's most respected newspaper had held the line, along with the rest of Fleet Street, in
its silence over Edward and Mrs. Simpson; though, in its
bookish way, it managed to convey to the cognoscenti a whiff
of the hushed-up scandal by publishing a letter which
included these lines from Racine's *Berenice:*

> . . . so vile a thing,
> Tied to thy train—a hopeless, throneless King,
> Loathsome to men below, to gods above,
> A sad example of the sleights of Love.

But now it was the *Times* which, this time more forth-
rightly, was to spur a nationwide debate. In his article of 8
December, Dr. Austin wrote of his conviction that Prince
Charles began to break his marriage vows soon after promis-

ing lifelong faithfulness to the Princess of Wales. In this, he was unwittingly close to the truth.

Referring to the vows Charles would make at his coronation as king, he observed: "If his attitude to his vows of matrimony was so cavalier, has he the right to be trusted in this second solemnity?" He repeated what he had said on BBC radio—that he himself would feel duty-bound to resign if he cheated on his wife because he would have betrayed the trust placed in him. "It may be that Prince Charles has gone too far for that same trust to be restored," he concluded.

To the dismay of the prince and his advisers, it was learned that several senior bishops were also privately expressing their reservations about Charles's fitness to succeed to the throne.

The Bishop of Sodor and Man went one step further by going public on the issue. He declared that the breaking of the marriage vows was "an indication of a moral flaw which would be worrying. It is scriptural to think that of those to whom much is given, much should be expected." He added: "I think marriage vows are vows and I do not happily accept the remarriage of divorcees in church."

He concluded: "It would he right for us to say that anyone who aspires to a position of real high office must also have really high morals. If you cannot take that on, you should not actually do it. If I had a future monarch who was divorced I would find it very difficult to say I was giving allegiance to that person."

Next it was the turn of the Bishop of Kensington, who delivered an equally devastating analysis: "The Church might well remind him [Charles] that the royal family is fighting for its credibility. Some attempt to repair his family life would be the best example he could give to the nation. He ought to be looking in a positive way at the restoration of the family.

"To marry a divorcee would render his position untenable. If he were to marry a divorcee he would have to renounce the crown."

The many pro-Establishment figures within the Church wishing to preserve unaltered the relationship between Sovereign and Church kept their own counsel. Others, however, felt strongly that the ties were loosening. The Right Reverend Peter Coleman, Suffragen Bishop to the Diocese of Exeter, stated ominously: "If Charles were divorced, depending on the reason, this would be a matter of serious anxiety vis-a-vis his coronation. Most of us will be realizing that there are real difficulties ahead."

The implication was quite clear: Could an utterly discredited king summon sufficient bishops to crown him? These anxieties were echoed by the Archdeacon of Canterbury, the Venerable Michael Till. "There may come a point where the credibility has disappeared," he said. "People are holding their breath about it. There is a question mark. Whether that fades into silence or is consolidated depends upon the next weeks, years, and months." He added that the prince's position would be undermined by divorce and would worsen still further if he remarried a divorcee. "The Church would find it difficult, as would the congregations. All those people who have kept their marriages going would find it very hard to handle."

These comments rained like hammer blows upon the prince and his advisers. It is not unusual for members of the royal family to suffer criticism by politicians, the press, and pressure groups. But such a concerted display of displeasure from within the ranks of the religious establishment could do nothing but cause acute alarm.

The prince's friend Nicholas Soames, long ago his equerry but now a government minister and bound into the affair by his sister Charlotte's relationship with Andrew Parker Bowles, could remain silent no longer. As the *Times* printed the Archdeacon of York's attack on the prince, Soames insisted that Austin spoke for no one but himself. He declaimed: "What he has said is a disgrace. The suggestion that being heir to the throne is a lottery is completely inappropriate. To be heir to the throne is not an ambition, but is a duty and an obligation which will befall the Prince of Wales at a sad moment later in his life.

"The archbishop [of Canterbury] has made it plain that the archdeacon speaks entirely for himself and not for the Church of England. What was said today was utterly outrageous. I am very surprised by what this man has said—it is disgraceful, wounding, ignorant, and hurtful."

Some interpreted this vigorous and unscripted defense of his best friend as an indication of the panic which had set in at St. James's Palace. But Mr. Soames had not finished. "The archdeacon shows a remarkable ignorance of the true feelings of most people in Britain who want to see the happiness of the Prince of Wales and the stability of the throne with everything that implies for British life. I do not think the vaporings of a completely unrepresentative archdeacon will make any difference. But it was still quite, quite disgraceful."

If Soames felt this quixotic attack was sufficient to turn the tide, others did not. Clerics rarely drawn into public controversy were suddenly determined to be heard. That so many voices, despite Soames's belief, sang in unison against the prince impressed itself upon the nation—and in the absence of any real indicators, official or otherwise, of what was to happen next, most came to the conclusion that the publication of the Camillagate Tapes must result in divorce for the Parker Bowleses. That in turn led many to believe that Charles would marry Camilla. His expressions of devotion on the tapes made it plain that he had been distracted from the course of duty by her: Who was to say what would happen next?

Within the space of days, a survey was taken of a hundred members of the 574-strong Synod, which is divided into three houses of bishops, clergy, and laity. Of this sample, 47 percent thought the Prince of Wales should not become supreme governor upon accession, while 27 percent thought he should not become king if it were shown to be true that he had had an affair with Camilla Parker Bowles.

A day after these findings were published, *Today* newspaper reported that a worried prime minister had ordered his ministers to come out in Charles's defense. This was an unprecedented step in twentieth-century politics and cannot have been done without full consultation with the queen's private secretary, Sir Robert Fellowes, and the prince himself, since for one political party to deviate from a neutral line on the royal family invites the opposition to take the contrary view; and bringing the royal family down into the cockpit of domestic politics is something successive monarchs and their advisers have tried hard to avoid.

Nevertheless John Major's instructions resulted in Foreign Secretary Douglas Hurd's description of Charles as a "star." Other ministers also offered their opinions—consistently favorable—on the heir to the throne. Lord Wakeham, the Lord Privy Seal, added that there were grave dangers "if churchmen vandalize our monarchy," deftly omitting from his attack the fact that the churchmen's voiced opinions had only been triggered by Charles's own dual standards of morality.

In addition an irritating, but inescapable, point was raised by the former Bishop of Birmingham, the Right Reverend Hugh Montefiore. What, he asked, would happen if the queen dropped dead tomorrow? There was no way you could have Diana—officially separated from Charles as she was—crowned as queen. His comments exposed a massive flaw in the leisurely distancing process going on between the princely husband and wife; and more importantly they dealt a death knell to the optimistic claims by Buckingham Palace and Downing Street that Charles and Diana's separation had "no constitutional implications."

Dr. Montefiore said: "The separated Princess of Wales cannot be crowned queen. It would be abhorrent to a large proportion of the English people. The question is bound to arise whether the archbishop [of Canterbury] would in good conscience be able to crown her."

Just at that moment, this debate on the succession seemed an arbitrary one—yet within weeks the queen, now sixty-seven, had fallen heavily from her horse while wearing no protective headgear. If the accident had taken place on a metaled road, or the horse had rolled on her, the argument would not seem quite so abstruse after all. There would be the coronation of a new king: By then it would be too late to ask the question—what to do with Diana, still married to the king, still mother of the next King?

None of this was lost on courtiers at St. James's Palace, who felt on the one hand a very real anger that their attempts to reestablish Prince Charles's credibility were seen to be built on shifting sands, yet on the other hand no means of venting their frustration on those they felt were truly to blame for the present impasse—the press, the Church, and inevitably Diana herself. Theirs was truly a no-win situation.

At that point, in late 1993, there was a very real danger that the issue could turn from an ugly row into something permanently damaging. Privy Council sources leaked their grave concern that Charles's relationship with Camilla showed no signs of abating and, more importantly, that Mrs. Parker Bowles now appeared to be wielding considerable influence over him—to the extent that she was said to have put her foot down over an attempt during the summer to create a new working relationship between Charles and Diana.

This, if true, put Camilla Parker Bowles in a new and far more sinister position. It was one thing for her to be the prince's mistress, tending to his every need and soothing his fevered brow—that, to some, was bad enough. Far worse was the idea that she should now step between the Prince and Princess of Wales and ordain what Charles should, and should not, do. This, if true, really was the exercise of power without responsibility.

By now even privy councilors, let alone senior clergymen and other leading public figures, were feeling jumpy. No one had anything to gain by a major constitutional crisis breaking just now, but the difficulty was that no one knew what Charles's next move was going to be. Would he divorce? Would he marry Camilla after she had obtained a divorce? Would he do what he had secretly threatened to do—quit the country of his birth and set up home with Camilla in Florence, where Alice Keppel ended her days? There were many questions, but no answers. Charles, striving to maintain his equilibrium, had decided on the policy of "least said, soonest mended." It was hard to put over to him the highly anxious state of others who had rather more vestigial roles in this drama.

One political source, referring to the alarming lack of information over Charles's intentions, revealed: "Some of the most senior palace and Anglican figures believe that Charles will face enough difficulties if he insists on going ahead with a divorce from Diana, without any further complications.

"They feel that if Mrs. Parker Bowles comes back into the picture, Charles would be publicly signaling his intention to renounce the throne at a future date and step aside in favor of Prince William. That would be contrasted unfavorably with the position of his aunt, Princess Margaret, who put duty before love when she agreed to break with Group Captain Peter Townsend." The not particularly coded message—tell us what you plan to do, Charles, before the entire Establishment turns against you.

Suddenly, and to some shockingly, it was hinted in the *Times* that senior bishops had been discussing a range of options with the queen at Buckingham Palace over a change to the 460-year relationship between the sovereign and the Church. This crucial reexamination resulted in a general conclusion that future legislation should be introduced shortly before or after the next coronation (though not within the queen's lifetime) to amend the sovereign's position.

It would take a fly on the wall at Buckingham Palace to tell whether this was a plot by a mother against her erring son, but the proposed amendment would weaken the traditional links by abolishing the sovereign's position as supreme governor, while maintaining the title of Defender of the Faith.

Of one thing most senior clerics were certain: Prince Charles was now an unwelcome figure in the Church of England. One observer commented: "In the eyes of many within the Church, the prince's image is in need of drastic improvement if he is to win back confidence and take on the role as figurehead.

"At present, in the queen as supreme governor, they have an exemplary role model. To have someone with a quite frankly sleazy reputation such as Prince Charles in this position is a completely different matter. He has a difficult task ahead of him, and it is unlikely that he realizes just how far he will have to go to win back general favor within the Church.

"His image must be improved immeasurably, and that improvement can only be done by diligent work. There has to be an indication that he is attempting to do deeds for the good of society, and there is a need for years of celibacy."

To a society whose mores have changed incalculably within the space of a generation, a pledge of celibacy may seem an excessive penalty. Outside the Roman Catholic church, few people in Britain are prepared to listen to lectures on their sex lives, and the Prince of Wales was likely to be no exception. He was faced with the frustrating example of his ancestors—some near, some far—few of whom were beset by such moral strictures, and many of whom enjoyed their sexual *droit de seigneur* unhindered by nagging clerics.

Indeed, it might seem to the rationalist, in an age where the Church has an increasingly weak grip over morality, that in seeking to impose their rules not upon the whole nation but upon one man, the bishops had completely lost the plot.

Nonetheless the hard-liners were backed up against Charles. One insider explained: "The major problem is Charles's inability to realize the importance of his role, and the consequence of his behavior. He felt he could carry on in the adulterous manner he had seen his father and great-uncle behave in; but he had reckoned without the combined forces of his wife, the Church and the tabloid press. He is under scrutiny in a way no other future monarch has been, and he doesn't seem to be able to understand that the rules have changed."

Such was the determination within the Establishment to play down any hint of a constitutional crisis at this time, there appeared to be a general agreement that the standoff between Charles and the Church of England would only come when the queen died. But then, at his coronation, the new king might well find that the wording of the monarch's ceremonial vows had changed.

In the traditional coronation oath, the Archbishop of Canterbury asks the new sovereign to solemnly swear to govern the peoples of Great Britain according to the law, then asks: "Will you to the utmost of your power maintain the laws of God and the true profession of the Gospel? Will you to the utmost of your power maintain in the United Kingdom the Protestant Reformed Religion established by law? And will you maintain and preserve inviolably the settlement of the Church of England, and the doctrine, worship, discipline, and government thereof? And will you preserve unto the bishops and clergy. . . . all such rights and privileges as by law shall appertain to them?"

The sovereign answers: "All this I promise to do"—but can only do so if the question is put. At the time of writing there was a growing belief that this section of the coronation ceremony will be rewritten, with or without Charles's consent, and that he might find himself without the title Supreme Governor.

Any sovereign may take himself out of this historic linkage, or be taken out, and survive. But if Prince Charles were to lose the support of the supposed bedrock of the Establishment, if he were to find that the Church was disputing his fitness for kingship, there would indeed be a crisis of epic proportions—one which would make his great-uncle's abdication seem piffling by comparison. Disentangling state from church, crown from miter, would fundamentally weaken them both and dissolve the glue which binds together the nation's fabric.

As Sir Douglas Lovelock, the first Church Estates Commissioner, argued, one or all of the main pillars of the

Establishment may be changed—"but history shows that once one aspect of a structure is altered, people quickly start asking if the whole thing is worth retaining."

Charles had courted the support of a wider spectrum than merely the Church of England, but only the established Church could assist him in his attempts to surmount the constitutional hurdles he faced. Catholic loyalties will always lie first with Rome, Muslim with Mecca, and the support he needed most—from a purely pragmatic standpoint—was from the religion which felt the greatest unease about his personal behavior.

Given the content of the Camillagate Tapes, and the real sense of shock felt throughout the Church of England after their publication, it surprised many churchmen that the prince made no special effort to recapture their support. Successive public statements from palace aides hinted at irritation, anger, and depression at the furor that had been created in the wake of Camillagate. Never once was there a hint of contrition.

To the Church, once the monarchy's greatest supporter, it seemed almost as if Prince Charles believed that when his time came, like Henry VII half a millennium ago, he could pick up a crown from some wayside bush and, settling it on his head, pronounce himself king.

Chapter Ten

Ditch the Bitch

———————⟫◦◦◦⟪———————

The Prince of Wales's 1994 tour of Australia began amid a welter of new opinion polls, in both Britain and the host country, which showed his popularity had sunk to an all-time low.

In Britain, one poll showed that only the Duchess of York, still stumbling in the dark after the public humiliation of her toe-sucking activities in the South of France with her Texan lover John Bryan two summers before, had a lower popularity rating.

In another Charles found that, infuriatingly, only 3 percent of people polled blamed Diana for the breakdown of their marriage, though there was some small consolation to be found in the fact that 57 percent in a nationwide poll did not think that his relationship with Camilla Parker Bowles made him unfit to rule.

Nevertheless he was swimming against the tide in this, his twenty-fifth year as Prince of Wales. He learned with anger that the highly respected Labor MP Frank Field had called for a committee of privy councilors, chaired by the prime minister, to oversee the upbringing of Princes William and Harry, and although—unsurprisingly—nothing came of this suggestion, it was yet another shot across Charles's bows. To have a parliamentarian accuse him of being an unfit parent simply added to his public humiliation.

The previous month Charles had been on an official visit to Southwark, South London, to meet workers involved in the Gateway Project, an enterprise designed to provide accommodation and job training for the homeless and unemployed. When he arrived on 8 December, the street was empty. Newspapers the following day carried a tally of people who'd come to see him: photographers—thirteen; reporters—ten; members of the public—two. "He's obviously as unpopular as everyone makes out," said the crowd-control policeman, whose skills, perforce, went unused that day. When finally he found himself indoors, Charles, with his usual panache, tackled twenty-one-year-old Barry Holden, who told him that one of the reasons he'd ended up homeless was that his parents separated when he was six years old.

"Really?" said his royal inquisitor. "Why did they divorce?"

"It was due to my dad going out with another woman behind my mum's back," came the reply. Charles smiled wanly. It was time to move on.

Diana, meanwhile, was in Belfast on one of her last public engagements. Although, for security reasons, her visit went publicly unannounced, the newspapers made another tally: photographers—thirty; reporters—ten; members of the public—one hundred and sixty. No wonder Charles could not wait for his wife's enforced retirement, for it was clear he was now being threatened with the worst fate that any king-to-be could face—he was in grave danger of being ignored by his future subjects.

In Australia, a nation whose political leader, Paul Keating, had already signaled that becoming a republic was not a matter of if but when, Charles arrived to barely veiled indifference and sparse crowds. Reports suggested that advisers had to work hard to get Charles to go to Australia at all, but a major public-relations victory was needed, and could more easily be won abroad.

On his arrival in the last week in January, Charles had with him a portfolio of justificatory speeches designed to catch whatever mood he and his advisers could sense and turn to their advantage. But despite this extensive groundwork, no plans had been laid to cope with what came next.

His first major engagement was at Tumbalong Park in Sydney. A police band played "Waltzing Matilda" and "I Still Call Australia Home." On stage the prince prepared to present prizes to a group of schoolchildren. Before him in the arena was spread a genial crowd of fifty thousand or so, but as Charles stepped forward for the prize-giving, one spectator, a twenty-three-year-old anthropology student, David Kang, stood up and pulled out a gun. He sprinted toward Charles, firing in the air. For a moment no one took in what was happening and Charles failed to react, merely fiddling with his cuff links. With a leap up the steps Kang was on the stage, firing again. Then he tripped on a microphone cable and crashed to the floor. He was overpowered, aptly enough, by a man who had just been named Australian of the Year, yachtsman Ian Kiernan.

The gun had contained only blanks; Kang had been making an ill-considered protest about the Cambodian boat people. He made his point, but more effectively it instantly brought a sharper focus to Charles's visit. Those who had viewed it with contempt or indifference found themselves impressed by the way Charles brushed it aside, and his comments that such alarms were all part of the job. He added wryly to the still stunned audience: "It's all right for you, at least you've all had a drink."

Two days later an opinion poll was published as the royal road show hit Perth. Charles was given a rapturous reception by a newly respectful public as the poll revealed that now 63 percent of Australians believed him fit to be king. Only one in five thought he was doing a bad job, and 53 percent thought he set a good example. Compared with the findings of the poll back in Britain, this was a remarkable turnaround.

Suddenly there was a new impetus to the royal tour, given extra thrust by the rekindled enthusiasm of ever-increasing crowds.

So what happened next would seem to many to be a logical step. Royal reporters accompanying the tour had been given unofficial briefings by courtiers who labeled it the "Tippex (erase) the Tampax" tour: Australia was the chance of a new beginning for the prince, a chance to put the past behind him.

Until the gun attack, that had seemed a pretty forlorn hope, but in the wake of it, and assisted by some eulogistic analysis pieces by British journalists, maybe this was the moment to move things up a notch.

Whatever the reasoning behind it, and whatever the source, on 30 January the London *Mail on Sunday* newspaper ran as its front-page lead a story headlined: PRINCE CHARLES SEVERS ALL LINKS WITH CAMILLA PARKER BOWLES: MY DUTY BEFORE LOVE.

Under this dramatic headline ran a story by Nigel Dempster which stated that Charles had "renounced" his friendship with Camilla.

"He has decided to sacrifice his close friendship with the

mother of two for the sake of his duty to the country," wrote the journalist.

"The prince has resolved, after months of heart-searching, to remove any obstacle to his succession by finally severing their twenty-four-year relationship. According to a royal confidant the prince has come to an 'irrevocable decision' on the matter."

The article went on to quote the unnamed source as saying: "The prince says he has every intention of becoming king in the fullness of time and, as long as that is his intention, there is no room in his life for Mrs. Parker Bowles."

Dempster continued: "Now Prince Charles has decided they must lead separate lives, which cannot cross at any point.

"Camilla is said to be 'frantic' over her rejection.

"The source said: 'Camilla has found that the prince is no longer taking her calls and is very unhappy about it.' "

If she was, she had a remarkable way of showing it. Confined to the shadows for many a long month by a self-imposed purdah to beat the press's unquenchable thirst for more information about her, she emerged from her house—confident that the world's press was waiting for her—and took coffee to workmen chopping logs in the grounds. She spent long enough in their company for photographers to get the pictures they needed—of a Camilla utterly at ease with herself and wreathed in smiles. One of the coffee mugs she bore out to the workmen carried the word LOVE in large print on its side: a not particularly coded message which would wing its way to the other side of the globe.

Nonetheless, the British press believed they had a story—and a historic one at that. Some papers talked of the "months of heart-searching" by Charles "to remove any obstacle to his succession." While this was palpable nonsense, since nothing short of premature death could stop Charles coming to the throne, there was a belief—buoyed up by who knows what— that there was substance to the story. As is often the case among headstrong editors, the desire to see a story in print sometimes has the blinkering effect of pushing away all contrary arguments.

Some sections of Fleet Street saw the parallels between Edward and Mrs. Simpson and Charles and Camilla slipping away. Instead they portrayed a prince determinedly walking away from his nemesis. An unnamed cabinet minister was quoted thus: "This decision is a clear indication that he takes his future responsibilities very seriously. It is entirely right that he should put his duty first, and he should be respected for this decision."

It did not take long for the dream to evaporate. By the following morning a very strong counter-argument was running—that Charles and Camilla's love was as strong as ever, that the prince resented this new interpretation of his attitude to her, and that everything was as it had been.

To this end, a stray piece of information surfaced—that Charles and Camilla had enjoyed a lengthy telephone conversation while he was actually undertaking his Australian tour—which demonstrated more implacably, and more than any other single piece of information in the months since the publication of the Camillagate Tapes, that the couple were still deeply involved.

The call came to Charles at his official residence overlooking the Sydney Opera House. Camilla made it from the home of a family friend somewhere in the south of England—and a place unlikely to be bugged. Other calls followed, and the ongoing relationship continued without a hitch. Those who enjoy such parallels would later recall that after King Edward VII was shot at (a recurrent problem, apparently, to successive princes of Wales) as he passed through Brussels in 1900, he immediately telegraphed to Alice Keppel in Weymouth that he was unharmed. It is fair to suppose his successor instantly made a similar, though technologically more advanced, communication with Mrs. Keppel's great-granddaughter.

The scoop of the year evaporated as quickly as morning mist. One source told the *Daily Mirror*'s James Whitaker: "These two are in love. And even if the affair had cooled down, which it hasn't, the prince is not the sort of person to dump friends. He is immensely loyal and it is insulting to his integrity to suggest he now won't take Camilla's calls."

This theme was taken up by another well-sourced journalist, who wrote: "One friend who regularly has the prince's ear complained during a New Year house party in the Caribbean that, for all his endeavors, Charles and Mrs. Parker Bowles seemed determined to carry on."

He quoted a singular exchange which demonstrated the depth of Charles's loyalty. The prince told a companion: "I would never treat anyone like my great-uncle did Mrs. Dudley Ward." This was a reference to David Prince of Wales's treatment of his mistress Freda Dudley Ward once he took up with Mrs. Simpson: he cast her aside by the simple expedient of ordering the Buckingham Palace switchboard that she was not to be put through to him anymore.

Apocryphal maybe, but this anecdote does demonstrate Charles's lasting qualities. Though in truth there was another, glaringly obvious reason why he could not give up Camilla—he could not do without her. So why the sudden rush of blood to the head which had the world's press believing that Charles had just thrown away a love affair which had lasted over two decades?

The prevailing theory as to the placing of the leaks was

that well-meaning friends felt his already high profile in Australia would be given an upward nudge and increase his slowly rising popularity back home. Brightly, they thought up a "Ditch the Bitch" campaign to strengthen Charles's hand; it was as ill-conceived a notion as was possible and led to further humiliation. After initial incredulity that the prince would let it be known he had dumped Camilla, there was the predictable backlash: One newspaper headline read, HE BEDS THEM THEN HE BETRAYS THEM, a reference to both Diana and Camilla.

Charles's most prominent biographer, Anthony Holden, tartly alluded to "the different ambitions of his so-called 'friends', anxious to be associated with a future king rather than another Duke of Windsor." And he accused Charles's friends of telephoning the press with the information in an attempt to force the prince's hand on the Camilla issue.

"There was general agreement that the prince himself was unaware the leaks were taking place. He was outraged at their effect. In making his painstaking preparations for the Australasia tour, 'Tippexing the Tampax' meant eradicating all references to his relationship with Camilla—he did not want his name in any way connected with hers at a crucial time in his repairing fortunes. He was furious."

Disinformation spread alarmingly in the ensuing witch-hunt. In a quick backtracking movement it was suggested that the friends planted the information not because Charles had dumped Camilla, but because the physical side of their relationship was over and the world would feel more comfortable knowing that. This was yet another version, as risible as those that preceded it. According to these sources, the couple had not been lovers since November 1992, a month before Charles and Diana separated. It was all over, and the "obstacle" of adultery could therefore no longer be part of the debate about Charles's fitness to be king.

This logic had the distinction of being both ingenuous and disingenuous. It was intensely stupid of Charles's friends to suppose that, simply because he and Camilla were no longer in an adulterous relationship, the Church of England could ignore the two decades of adultery which had already taken place. When it came to their deliberations on Charles's fitness to head the Church, whether the relationship was active or passive would make very little difference.

And there was something deeply suspicious in the scenario which was created by those friends: "They mutually agreed to cool it but remained in close touch," said one. Then, shortly before Christmas 1993, elaborated the friend, the couple took the final step to stop their regular telephone calls.

The fact that Camilla called Charles in Australia twenty-four hours before the gun incident, and that this should be leaked to the press accompanying the royal tour, effectively destroyed that testimony. Charles and Camilla were talking, were seeing each other, and if the physical side of their relationship had become nonexistent it owed more to the passage of time than to any conscious decision by the parties involved. But, as the days wore on, even that one seemed increasingly unlikely.

In the midst of this confusion came a moment of light relief as a popular novelist, Una-Mary Parker, dipped her toes into the already muddied pool.

Her qualifications for speaking about the royal marriage were based on her marriage to the society photographer Archie Parker. Parker, along with Andrew Parker Bowles, was descended from the sixth Earl of Macclesfield, whose long-suffering wife produced for him a record eleven sons and four daughters.

But Una-Mary's marriage to Parker had foundered some years earlier and, in any event, he was dead and thereby unable to quiz his distant cousin on the latest turn of events. Nevertheless Mrs. Parker saw this as no bar to her deliberations and proclaimed that Charles was considering making a new start with Diana for the sake of their children. Referring to the press reports, she declared: "It is part of a master plan in which Diana and Charles are working for a reconciliation."

This was greeted with hoots of laughter back in Australia by the royal camp.

As spring approached there were, of course, no sightings of Charles and Diana together. Despite her emotional announcement that she wanted to quit public life, Diana was not very often out of the newspapers: Photographers captured her on an almost daily basis taking out her sons, shopping, emerging from a restaurant after lunch, diving into a Chinese foot-massage parlor. After over a decade of public work, it could be argued, it was only right that she should take time out to reorder her life and reconsider her priorities. But it soon became plain that she had walked into a vacuum and that, stripped of her duties and with no great hobbies or pursuits to indulge, she had nothing to do. There were an awful lot of pictures of a woman with nothing to do that spring.

Soon after Charles arrived back from Australia, his campaign managers pleased with the overall success of the feel-good tour, it was revealed that he had been in touch with Camilla to discuss the success of his trip: His call to her was confirmed by the same source which revealed how Camilla had telephoned Charles in Australia. At the same time it emerged that Diana had told friends that she had never accepted that her husband's relationship with Camilla had ended: She was convinced it was still on. In that, she was entirely correct, even if the frequency of the lovers' meetings had been scaled down.

Life went on: Charles and Camilla both continued to hunt with the Beaufort, though they now chose alternate days so that they should never be seen together. As the summer approached, Charles took up polo again and Camilla tended her garden. His anxiety over coping with Prince William and Prince Harry when he had them to stay was overcome by the appointment of a "surrogate mother," Alexandra Legge-Bourke, who had previously run a London nursery school called Mrs. Tiggywinkle's: The boys took to her instantly. After a tumultuous two years, life was beginning to return to normal, though it would never be the same again: Events that Camilla would once have attended without a second thought—the wedding of a friend, the annual National Hunt Festival at Cheltenham—she now chose to avoid. The public were naturally fascinated to see the woman whom the Prince of Wales truly loved, and for many years yet she would be an object of fascination to millions.

In February, Charles's private apartments in St. James's Palace were burgled and a quantity of jewelery, including a number of sets of cuff links, was taken. Immediately palace officials were asked whether the thief had stolen Camilla's famous cuff links, the ones with the entwined Cs which the prince so foolishly wore on his honeymoon.

They never existed, came back the stony answer. The officials had got out their correction fluid again, trying desperately to put over their message to the outside world—*this woman does not exist, she has never existed, please forget about her.* But theirs was a hopeless task, for it would take years for the nation to forget Camilla Parker Bowles; indeed, having over-come the initial shock of her existence, the public felt, rather encouragingly, very much less antagonistic toward the idea of her.

Meanwhile the rehabilitation went on apace: Charles turned out for a Status Quo concert at the Royal Albert Hall. This, in a previous life, was the sort of event he would leave to his wife—on the odd occasion when he did turn out he would make no secret of his discomfort, like the Live Aid concert in 1985 when he wore a suit while everyone else did not. His interest in rock music, never strong, was over by 1967 when the Troggs, already chart toppers with "Wild Thing" and "I Can't Control Myself," invited the prince to accom-pany them on their next hit with his cello. He declined, and from then on immersed himself in music from the classical and baroque periods. Now he was back, tapping his feet to the Quo as they explored the limits of their three-chord repertoire, and smiling a great deal. It required an enormous effort.

But there was a greater challenge ahead. A year before, in April 1993, Charles had found himself floundering in a welter of criticism and abuse for the way he had handled himself after the shocking death of two young boys, Johnathan Ball and Tim Parry, who died in an IRA attack on the northern town of Warrington.

The boys' death touched a nerve in the nation. A tele-vised memorial service was arranged, which the prime min-ister, the leader of the Opposition, and the president of the Irish Republic all agreed to attend. The question was then asked: Which member of the royal family will be there?

Charles was the obvious candidate, since he had paid a fleeting visit to the town immediately after the bomb and Warringtonians had been pleased by his apparent concern.

But on the day of the memorial, Charles was in Spain attending the funeral mass of Don Juan de Borbon y Battenburg, the father of the king of Spain.

There was little purpose in his presence, though his critics claimed that he did not like missing the opportunity of rubbing shoulders with Europe's crowned heads: It made him feel superior. If anyone should have represented the British royals in Spain, it should have been Prince Philip, whose mother was a cousin of the don: Charles, as a cousin twice removed, may have looked resplendent in his naval uniform in this Ruritanian procession in the Spanish sun, but in the chill and rain of Warrington they waited for him in vain.

The MP Ian McCartney declared: "As the king-to-be, he should have known that his place was with his future subjects at such a traumatic time." Nobody disagreed with that. Where the dissension began was when the townspeople of Warrington discovered that, while Charles would not be attending the memorial, he had banned his wife from attending either. The Princess of Wales had expressed an urgent desire to go to Warrington, and had spoken at length on the telephone to the mother of one of the dead boys. But Diana fell victim to Charles's determination to marginalize her, and a nation chafed at the ineptitude of the House of Windsor at such a time: If politicians could bury their differences to mourn the dead—and make the considerable journey from London— why couldn't Charles?

The best that can be said is that overenthusiastic courtiers offered faulty advice, and Charles took it. But it was a mistake he could not afford to make; and in his stride forward to public acceptance was a major setback.

When in March 1994 there was a chance to redress the balance, an older and wiser Prince Charles did not fail. At the Hall Garth School at Acklam, near Middlesbrough, a masked, knife-wielding gunman burst into a mathematics classroom on the second floor and ordered the pupils to kneel down, shouting: "They have killed me; now they have killed all of you." He stabbed to death twelve-year-old Nikki Conroy, and injured two other pupils, Emma Winter and Michelle Reeve, before being tackled and disarmed by two members of the staff.

The nation was in a universal state of shock, not only for the loss of a bright and pretty child, but also from the realization that no school was immune from the dangers of sudden attack. Into this scenario came the Prince of Wales, who was on a tour of the Cleveland area which incorporated Middlesbrough.

He arrived at Hall Garth School bearing a wreath of yellow and white carnations, lilies, and roses, to which he had attached a handwritten card saying: "In deepest sympathy, Charles." He gathered around him the children and staff who had witnessed the attack and addressed them gently. In a ten-minute conversation he spoke of his own pain, anger, and grief at the loss of Earl Mountbatten, murdered by the IRA in 1979, and he urged the children to talk to each other about their feelings and about Nikki.

The school's headmaster, Peter Smith, said: "They were friends together and the prince made it very easy. We were very touched by the whole visit and the trouble he has obviously gone to try to make it right." And a sixteen-year-old pupil, Claire Barry, added: "I think it's good that he came here. It's not just Prince Charles coming to see us—it's more important than that. He represents the whole country."

The country took his decorous behavior, so very different from the previous year, to its heart. It was even ready for another earful of Prince Charles on the dreaded subject of architecture.

In March, Charles launched his own architectural magazine, *Perspectives,* with a celebrity-laden (and shrewdly rehabilitative) launch party at St. James's Palace. *Perspectives* was never likely to be a publication to send the nation rushing to the bookstall: But everyone was polite about it. It was lightweight, and seen to be so, but that did not stop Charles inveighing against other planners and developers. In May he sounded off against the Russians for attempting to build a high-rise block to kick-start the dormant economy in St. Petersburg. What was charming about Charles was that some things in his life were immutable: Architecture and polo were two. Mrs. Parker Bowles was another.

And suddenly there was Mrs. Parker Bowles playing— without any great seriousness, it has to be said—the power game which the Princess of Wales had enjoyed so much in her heyday.

San Lorenzo, the renowned Knightsbridge restaurant which plays host to the likes of Eric Clapton, Dustin Hoffman, Joan Collins, and a host of rich and famous who like to pay a lot to eat not very much, was the headquarters for Diana during her ill-starred love game with James Gilbey. Its Italian proprietor, Mara Berni, became one of Diana's closest friends and, during the height of her clandestine liaison with Gilbey, would lend the key to her family house around the corner so that Diana and Gilbey could retreat there to be alone. Moreover the restaurant was used as a dead-letter drop during the period when Diana—with or without justification—believed that her mail at Kensington Palace was being intercepted.

But now, in May, all that had changed. Camilla Parker Bowles, not renowned for her lunching activities, suddenly made an entrance. And just as suddenly she was clasped to the ample bosom of Mara Berni. To the jet set, this simple gesture was a sign that they had arrived. But to Camilla, it meant no more than another kick back at her rival.

As part of his fight back, Charles launched a sustained attack on the fashion of political correctness, which he said was destroying much of the fabric of British society. It was a sweeping condemnation of fashionable theories, from child care to education and literature, in which he urged ordinary people to resist "intellectual fanaticism" and stand up for well-tried principles. But the ordinary people he spoke for were just as interested in the fact that Charles had lost his Jack Russell terrier, Pooh, somewhere on the Balmoral estate. And even more fascinated when they discovered that Pooh's sister was owned by Camilla, and that she had commiserated with the prince over the loss of the dog. Human-interest stories, especially with an animal thrown in, were as likely to touch their hearts, and bring Charles the support he so desperately sought, as the high-minded lectures he delivered for the greater good.

From this, at last, Charles should have been able to see something which had so far evaded him: that royalty, for the masses, does not exist at street level but hovers somewhere high above and out of reach. That makes the loss of a prince's dog a matter for concerned discussion, where the loss of a hundred other dogs would pass without remark; equally it means that any debate instituted by him will be treated, by the majority, in the same otherworldly way. Not being taken entirely seriously is a burden he has to bear, even though he has devoted his career to being accepted as a credible figure.

It was time for a reappraisal of his merits.

Chapter Eleven

"What Lady Chatterley Enjoyed"

Agonizing over this dilemma Prince Charles sought, through the early months of 1994, a grand design—something which would draw a line under his quarter-century as Prince of Wales, marking its triumphs, while simultaneously rubbing balm into the nation's wounds regarding Mrs. Parker Bowles.

There was a commendable logic to this. Sooner or later he had to make a fresh start with his public—and so it seemed—some explanation for his past behavior was required in order to achieve that aim. With his popularity still at an all-time low, the question was: How?

About this time the prince was approached by Penny Junor, a writer and TV presenter whose authorized biography *Charles* had been published to much acclaim in 1987. On that occasion the prince had cooperated with Miss Junor by providing substantial interview material. Would it not make sense, she now argued, to make a two-pronged attack on his critics via the very different mediums of television and the printed word? As his celebrated biographer and as a seasoned TV presenter, was she not the ideal candidate to put over the message Charles so desperately wanted to convey to the outside world?

The prince withdrew to mull this over. It was the last Miss Junor was to hear on the subject until she learned that a combined TV documentary and authorized biography of the Prince of Wales—her very idea—would be coming out in the latter part of 1994. The author and presenter would not be Miss Junor but Jonathan Dimbleby, of the well-known British broadcasting dynasty. She took this snub with good grace and sat back, along with the rest of the nation, to await the revelations in store. They were not long in coming.

In early October a memorial service was held in London for Camilla's mother, Mrs. Rosalind Shand. Following the first part of the Wales/Dimbleby charm offensive—a lengthy, often tedious TV documentary broadcast in the summer of 1994 which touched on most aspects of the prince's life but which most famously had the interviewer asking his subject about his marital infidelity—the nation was curious to see how Charles would respond to this event. He had now publicly acknowledged the deepness of his friendship for Camilla; would he do her the honor of appearing at her mother's memorial service?

In the end he devised a neat compromise. The prince sent as his emissaries his friends the Earl and Countess of Shelburne, dispatching then to St. Paul's, Knightsbridge, where Bruce and Rosalind Shand had married in 1946, in his official Bentley. "Mrs. Shand," explained a palace spokesman tautly, "was a friend of the Prince of Wales." The occasion was one where Mrs. Shand's stiff-upper-lip dictum on the Charles/Camilla imbroglio was recalled with satisfaction: "None of us has ever broken ranks. I think Camilla has done remarkably well considering some of the terrible things written about her."

Later that month came the more substantial apologia: the publication of Jonathan Dimbleby's book *The Prince of Wales.* While much of the narrative dealt ably enough with the milestones in Charles's action-packed life, it was less than robust when it came to detailing Charles and Camilla's relationship.

"It was not until late 1986 or 1987, when he and the Princess of Wales had begun to lead separate lives, that the prince's friendship with Camilla was renewed," wrote Dimbleby disingenuously. "Now, in the search for support, he once again began to talk to Camilla on the telephone and they started to see each other at Highgrove. She usually came with either her husband or some of the prince's other close friends, and the opportunities to be alone with her for any length of time were infrequent."

Herein lay the whole project's innate weakness. Public opinion—or at least a sizable chunk of it—judged that Charles had a right to a private life, insofar as it did not destabilize his position or that of the monarchy. Perhaps more importantly Mrs. Parker Bowles—who had remained silently, blamelessly, tantalizingly out of reach of the inquiring eyes and ears of the press during the sullying war of words between the Waleses—also had that right.

The choice, it seemed to the interested parties, was either to tell all, or in the immortal words of Camilla's father, Major Bruce Shand, keep their traps shut. Charles, assisted by his eager Boswell, Jonathan Dimbleby, did neither. Nor, in this official confession of his affection for Mrs. Parker Bowles, was he scrupulous with the facts—indeed, the phrase coined by former British Cabinet Secretary Lord Armstrong, "economical with the truth," springs to mind. Not because the prince lied, but because a partial picture of the relationship was presented as the whole; and in the end, readers of Charles's fully sanctioned biography will have learned considerably less about his all-consuming love affair than was their due.

Dimbleby characterized the couple's early relationship from late 1972 as a conventional love affair which, had things gone differently, might have resolved itself in marriage; the emotional mine-field Charles was forced to traverse from then until his 1981 wedding could have been avoided, the writer implied, if only he had had the presence of mind to make his feelings for Camilla clearer before he set off on his eight-month voyage on HMS *Minerva*, leaving her to succumb to Andrew Parker Bowles's proposal of marriage.

This is patent nonsense. As is made clear in the early chapters of this book, Camilla, by the time she cemented her relationship with Charles, was set on a resolute course: that of marriage to her cavalry officer. This had been her purpose for the previous six years, and now her goal was within sight. She, and Charles, both knew their relationship could not be sanctified in marriage for all the reasons laid out in previous pages: She was no longer a virgin, neither had Andrew Parker Bowles been her only conjugal partner. Her lineage, while indisputably aristocratic, was not sufficiently grand in those far-off days for her to qualify as a serious contender for the prince's hand. And, though her bearing and looks bore the indelible stamp of the upper classes, they fell short—in courtiers' minds at least—of the fairy-tale princess they would like to see adorning the nation's stamps and coins and, ultimately, the throne.

The book's apparent candor masked a wealth of suppressed detail. Charles was said to have turned over 10,000 personal letters for Dimbleby's perusal, as if in some way this guaranteed a portrait that was whole and complete; it did not. No mention was made of the resumption of their affair soon after Camilla's marriage, and interested parties seeking a more precise portrayal of events during this period were forced to rely on the testimony of a butler at Hall Place, West Meon, the home of Camilla's grandmother Sonia Cubitt, to shed some light on the reheated affair.

The unnamed butler served Mrs. Cubitt during the 1970s while Charles was a Royal Navy officer based at HMS *Mercury* and Camilla was the mother of a toddler son, Tom. The couple would meet at Hall Place, a short drive from the naval base at Portsmouth, on a regular basis. The servant recalled: "I well remember the first time the prince came to Hall Place. He arrived at 6:00 P.M. and after a few minutes talking to Mrs. Cubitt he vanished into thin air with Camilla.

"She had been wandering around all day wearing a pair of jeans with no zip—the flies were held together with a safety pin. This sort of behavior shocked Mrs. Cubitt and she demanded to know whether Camilla was going to change into a frock before the prince's arrival. 'I can even see your drawers, Camilla,' I heard her bellow," recalled the servant. "Camilla's reply was, 'Oh, Charles won't mind about that.' The manner of her reply indicated that it didn't matter because he'd seen it all anyway."

His account was filled with the kind of detail that would be often repeated, with great relish, below stairs. On one occasion Charles's detective went looking for his master. "I told him not to worry—that they were out in the garden taking a stroll, and I persuaded him not to go looking. He'd have been very embarrassed if he had—they were up against a tree doing what Lady Chatterley enjoyed best. I saw it myself. As soon as they went into the garden they headed straight for the avenue of beech trees and into the shadows— they were oblivious to everything around them."

These recollections related to a period when Prince Charles was still a bachelor but Mrs. Parker Bowles was a newly married woman, a period glossed over in Dimbleby's version of the couple's love affair. Soon after came another memoir, this time from a former employee, Brenda Stronach, which even more directly challenged the Dimbleby version.

In it she recalled that Prince Charles "had been visited by women at Highgrove years before . . . 1985." She added: "It was a deceitful and cruel conspiracy. Everyone at Highgrove knew he had been having an affair, from the most junior footman upward—everyone, that is, except the princess. Everybody living on the estate knew about the prince's nighttime visits to Mrs. Parker Bowles's home, it was a standing joke."

It is fortunate for the principals involved in such scandals that few people take lasting account of the tittle-tattle of servants, however authentic their recollections, and the early reaction to Charles's apparent candor in admitting adultery with Camilla was favorable, even though rather more informed readers wrinkled their noses at Dimbleby's assertion that Charles had had three separate affairs with Mrs. Parker Bowles. Instant polls commissioned by various media, involving the canvassing of the opinions of tens of thousands of people, tended to come down on the prince's side.

Doubtless encouraged by this, the prime minister, John Major, hoisted the prince's love life from the realms of gossip into the public arena, declaring that divorce would not stand in the way of his becoming king. A Downing Street statement made plain that even if the prince divorced and remarried, it would have no effect on the succession.

The timing of this statement, so soon after the first airing of Charles's confession of adultery, was crucial. All constitutional experts remained convinced that Charles's right to succession was unaffected; there was no need for a reaffirmation of the statement made in the House of Lords in 1992 by Dr.

John Habgood, Archbishop of York, in which it was made clear that neither divorce nor remarriage would keep Charles from the throne. It was just that, at this juncture, Charles could use all the official support he could get and Downing Street, like Barkis, was willing. The *Times* ran the item as their front-page lead.

Though delighted by this apparent public relations coup, Charles and his private secretary, Commander Aylard, were forced to acknowledge that whatever the opinion polls were saying, the combined book and TV onslaught would not be without its downside. Charles having had his say, the commentators would feel free to have theirs, and so it was. Quite soon the question was being asked—this is all very well for Charles, but what about Camilla?

For his confessions of adultery affected not only her, but her family. That included not only her children but also her husband, a man who for more than a year had been forced to bear the brunt of public curiosity and endure more than his fair share of ribaldry.

There was never any chance that he, or Camilla, would speak out against the prince's self-serving candor. But suddenly in November came a sudden, chill, clarion call from Australia. On a visit there Andrew's brother Simon—the man who all those years ago worked for Bruce Shand at his Mayfair wine merchant's and introduced the major's daughter to Andrew—suddenly launched a broadside. Camilla had been "dropped in a heap" by the Dimbleby book's revelations, he said. His view was that the prince blamed everyone else for his shortcomings, disappointments, and failures, yet at no stage was prepared to accept blame himself.

Speaking to an Australian magazine, Mr. Parker Bowles confessed that he felt pain when people asked him "how poor Charles copes with the publicity every day.

"I'd be more inclined to say 'poor old Camilla,'" he declared. "Prince Charles does not have our sympathy at the moment. You can't go back and blame your upbringing, or your parents, as he has done [for his unhappy life]. That is wrong and very hurtful. Even if you feel it, you don't go around talking about it, particularly if you are a member of the royal family.

"Let's face it, that generation, just like my family, did not show their emotions like people show them nowadays. They were not as involved with the children as we are today. You can't just go back over old ground and say, 'Well, the reason I had an unhappy schooltime was . . .'"

This was a calculated broadside against the prince, albeit launched from the other side of the globe. But Mr. Parker Bowles, proprietor of one of London's most sophisticated restaurants, Green's in St. James's, was not finished. He felt that something was wrong with Charles. "He is very mixed up. It must be very heartbreaking for the queen, who has really done her job so well."

His wife, Carolyn, daughter of the Australian banker Sir Ian Potter, added that Charles's confessions in the Dimbleby book were ill judged: "It is all right to talk to Camilla, but to tell the world is an entirely different matter."

These comments will almost certainly have reflected the view of Brigadier Parker Bowles, who had not been consulted on the question of his wife's adultery being aired in the prince's book—but they may, too, have reflected those of Mrs. Parker Bowles herself.

Many observers saw a very clear application of the laws of cause and effect in what happened next. On 10 January 1995 came the quite unexpected announcement that Brigadier and Mrs. Parker Bowles were to divorce; it appeared that

Charles's public humiliation of Andrew Parker Bowles, intentional or otherwise, had proved the final straw.

The divorce petition had been filed on 14 December 1994—less than two months after the publication of Dimbleby's all-revealing book. A statement was released on behalf of both parties by their solicitors, which read:

> The decision to seek an end to our marriage was taken jointly and is a private matter, but as we have no expectation that our privacy will be respected, we issue this statement in the hope that it will ensure that our family and friends are saved from harassment.
>
> Most especially we ask that our children, who remain our principal concern and responsibility, are left alone to pursue their studies at what is clearly a difficult time for them.
>
> Throughout our marriage we have always tended to follow rather different interests, but in recent years we have led completely separate lives. We have grown apart to such an extent that, with the exception of our children and a lasting friendship, there is little of common interest between us, and therefore we have decided to seek a divorce.

What astonished observers was the advanced stage of the proceedings. A petition had been filed a month before, it was said, yet those responsible for reporting the divorce courts had curiously failed to notice that very distinctive surname in the lists. Furthermore, though it was acknowledged by their friends that Camilla and her husband pursued the separate lives referred to in their statement, it was generally thought that their relationship had remained amicable and stable enough to prevent the trauma of an irrevocable split.

Now, barely a week after the shock announcement was made by Brigadier Parker Bowles and his wife, the divorce case was heard in London. On Thursday, 19 January, the public was to learn with astonishment that Camilla and her husband had been living apart for more than three years; this, not adultery, was the cause of their mutually agreed divorce. While none would challenge, either in court or in print, their declaration that the brigadier had spent no more than ninety nights at their home, Middlewick House, since February 1992, more cynical followers of the story found that hard to swallow, declaring that on the basis of this divorce going through, any disaffected traveling salesman could, in an instant, secure an end to his marriage because he was only home at weekends.

The marriage which had started in such style twenty-one years before, with a crowded Guards Chapel and serried ranks of royals and upper echelons of aristocracy moving sedately on to a sparkling reception at St. James's Palace, could not have ended more drably. The action between Camilla Rosemary Parker Bowles, petitioner, and Andrew Henry Parker Bowles, respondent, was one of a list of thirty-two such cases heard in Court Two of the High Court Family Division at Somerset House in the Strand. A scruffy list fixed by a drawing pin to the door of the court was the only advertisement of this small footnote in history.

Judge Gerald Angel asked an empty courtroom: "Does any party or person wish to show cause against the decree being pronounced?" and with no reply forthcoming, the decree nisi was granted. The judge rose, gathered his papers into a bundle, and left. The hearing to decide the end of a twenty-one-year marriage—one, latterly, of the most celebrated in the land—took just three minutes.

The trauma was not over yet, however. For in contrast to

the stillness and quiet of the courtroom, outside there was uproar. The consequences of Mrs. Parker Bowles's divorce were clear for all to see: Within the space of six weeks and one day, when the decree became absolute, Camilla would be free to remarry. With the Prince of Wales already two years into an official separation from his wife and, according to some, preparing for his own divorce, would Charles and Camilla do what until this very minute had seemed unthinkable, and marry?

Once again Charles came under attack. Some felt that, despite his apparent openness about the state of his love life, he and Camilla were working to a hidden agenda. Were they secretly planning to marry? Was Charles about to abrogate all responsibility and flee the country with his divorcee, exactly mirroring what his predecessor David, King Edward VIII, had done half a century before? The sense of frustration and, indeed, anger at the Parker Bowles divorce and what it appeared to conceal rebounded heavily on the prince. The promonarchist magazine *Majesty* polled its readers to discover they believed him to be emotionally weak, demanding, and indecisive. Only half those polled believed that he should be the next king, and nearly two-thirds took the view that his public standing would never be restored after admitting his adultery with Camilla.

All this might have been predicted. Charles's breast-baring exercise, via Jonathan Dimbleby, was always going to be a risky undertaking; and it was still too soon to judge the long-term effects of his forthright confession. It was only a year since Charles's popularity had broken through the pollsters' aggressive questioning to show that, after the gun attack at Tumbalong Park in Sydney, 63 per cent of mainly republican Australians believed him fit to be king. Courtiers and royals alike take a longer view of history than most: If even

Australia, under the yoke of a monarchy which based itself half a world away, could smile on Charles, then the readers of *Majesty* magazine would come around in due course.

Sanguine as they were in this knowledge, their confidence was only partially dented by two other polls which endorsed the public's dissatisfaction with the prince: One poll, published in *Today* newspaper, demonstrated that 84 percent believed that Charles had damaged the royal family's image by publicly confessing his relationship with Camilla Parker Bowles. Rather more alarmingly, another poll in the *Guardian* showed that half Britain believed the monarchy would not last longer than fifty years.

But, courtiers would reason, polls tend to swing like weathervanes in the wind. What they could not have predicted was what was to happen next.

On 15 January 1995, Prince Charles's valet of the past fifteen years, Ken Stronach, decided to betray his master to the *News of the World*. Under the headline CHARLES BEDDED CAMILLA AS DIANA SLEPT UPSTAIRS, Stronach delivered some of the most damaging information yet published regarding Charles and Camilla's intimate life. The front-page headlines were accompanied by a photograph of Camilla, smiling on a garden seat, which was said to have pride of place on the night table in Charles's bedroom at Highgrove. In the background of the photograph, taken at Birkhall on the Balmoral estate, sits Prince William, apparently at ease in the company of his father's mistress. The newspaper's royal editor, Clive Goodman, wrote: "It tells a story the Princess of Wales understands all too well—and it will cut her to the quick.

"If they are all at Birkhall, the Queen Mother—powerful guardian of family values within the royal circle—must approve of the close relationship. The fact that Prince William is there too suggests that the Queen Mother believes that a blissfully happy Charles can only be good for her great-grandson."

The valet, who claimed he had wearied of his master's ill treatment and was disillusioned with Charles's public confession of adultery, revealed that the prince had removed himself from the marital bedroom after Prince Harry's conception, preferring to sleep in a brass bed in his dressing room; but since the departure of Diana from Highgrove, had returned to the principal bedroom.

His testimony, like that of the butler at Hall Place, was riddled with belowstairs gossip. One of Stronach's duties was to scrub the green grass stains from the knees of his master's pajamas. "There was mud and muck everywhere," he declared. "They'd obviously been doing it in the open air."

During the period when the Waleses were both still occupying Highgrove, Camilla would arrive when Diana was absent and stay overnight as part of a small house-party. Though assigned a separate bedroom, she would spend the night in the prince's bed after he had switched off the intruder alarms which protected his room. "It was a big risk," observed the valet. "There had been intruders before. It was a stupid thing to do—but he is blind to everything where the lady is concerned."

Stronach was encouraged by the prince to participate in the subterfuge: In the mornings he would provide fresh pillows and new sheets for the royal bedroom to mislead other household staff. "It was very elaborate, but it didn't fool anyone for a minute," he observed. He added that he would also cover up for the prince when he went to spend the night at Middlewick House: To make it seem as though Charles had remained at home watching television, the valet would take a pen and circle programs listed in that night's *Radio Times,* leaving the magazine beside Charles's chair or in his bedroom in order to mislead the Princess of Wales.

Hard upon these revelations came more, from the *News of the World*'s sister paper, the *Sun*. This time they were unsourced generalities, but photographs which accompanied the text revealed Mrs. Parker Bowles's bedroom and four-poster bed; other pictures clearly purloined from a family album showed Charles and Camilla informally together on a variety of occasions. Light was being shone on all corners of Charles and Camilla's secret life: It was a secret no more.

An instant gagging action was taken by courtiers against the various royal servants who had sold, or were trying to sell, their stories to the tabloid press, but the damage was done. Charles's petulant, sometimes violent temper—an aspect of his personality hitherto obscured to the public gaze but obligingly reminiscent of his grandfather King George VI— had been vividly portrayed. The more risible aspects of his marital subterfuge were exposed. The compliant part of Mrs. Parker Bowles, a frequent hostess at Highgrove dinner parties, was laid bare. While it made for fascinating reading, it did nothing to raise the public's opinion of Charles and Camilla.

Nonetheless their relationship remained unaffected by the brouhaha. In December, Charles had been spotted visiting Camilla at Middlewick House, arriving with his detective Superintendent Colin Trimming, at 8:30 P.M. and leaving four hours later, hidden from view. At about the same period Camilla had been seen riding out on the Highgrove estate. With many opportunities to meet away from the public gaze, these occasional sightings were treated by the press as the tip of the iceberg. It was generally agreed that the relationship was as strong as ever, and that sooner or later the world would be treated to a curiosity they had long waited to see: a picture of the Prince of Wales with the woman he loved by his side.

But it would take a violent death and a nation's tears to bring that about.

Chapter Twelve

Death in the Night

The uneasy truce which followed could not last. Diana had secured the moral high ground after Charles's confession of adultery, but was unable to leave well alone—in secret she arranged with a BBC reporter, Martin Bashir, to make her own public confession on the much-respected program *Panorama*.

During the highly charged interview, the princess was evidently on the verge of tears and appeared in front of the cameras wearing heavy eye makeup and dark clothing. It was all too obviously stage-managed; so too were the phrases which tumbled from her lips in this apparently extempore confessional. She had "adored" James Hewitt, she confessed, but he had let her down. Then she came out with a phrase which resonated across the world. . . . "There were three of us in this marriage," she declared, "so it was a bit crowded."

Despite the fact that she later said something much more damaging, that she doubted that Charles was fit to be king, or would be king, this was the phrase which caught the press's imagination, once again propelling Camilla into the spotlight. According to Charles's biographer Penny Junor, Camilla was "shattered" by Diana's words.

Revenge was swift but not particularly effective—Charles and Camilla's longtime friend Nicholas Soames, grandson of Winston Churchill and now Armed Forces minister in the Tory government, went on television to state in forthright terms that Diana had "endured a period of unhappiness that led to instability and mental illness." Warming to his theme, he then accused her of being "in the advanced stages of paranoia." In the moral switchback which the royal marriage had become, the brief advantage that Charles had held—with Diana's own confession of adultery—was lost again. The public did not like the idea of their princess being traduced by a pompous and insignificant figure like Soames.

But the worldwide shock waves created by Diana's confession, in November 1995, and the dirty row which followed, were too much for the queen. After speaking to the prime minister and the Archbishop of Canterbury, she wrote separately to Charles and Diana ordering them to divorce. An unseemly squabble followed relating to the terms and conditions of the final settlement, but eventually Diana walked away with a package thought to be worth more than £17 million.

Charles was angry at the vast sum involved, but was warned to make no statement or action which could be interpreted that way. By now he was acquiring a more media-savvy group of courtiers around him, notably Mark Bolland, who had come from the Press Complaints Commission and was possibly the first person inside palace walls ever to really know how the bloodthirsty British press operated. Bolland and others were instructed by their royal master that Camilla would, one day, stand alongside the prince and be acknowledged by the nation for the help and support she had given through his bumpy and often unhappy life. It was their job to make Camilla acceptable to the public.

It might have been easier to ask them to walk on water. By the time Charles and Diana divorced in August 1996, Camilla Parker Bowles was, in the British nation's eyes, Public Enemy Number One. A supporter of hers who spoke up during a live television debate on ITV was howled down by the angry audience and the producer was heard to say, "If Camilla walked through the door right now they would string her up by her heels." Anger and confusion reigned in the months after the divorce, but Charles was adamant—the door should be opened, and Camilla must be allowed in out of the cold.

There followed a series of attempts to gauge public opinion. In the week the divorce was finalized, a grainy long-distance photograph of Charles and Camilla—the first of them together for over twenty years—appeared in the *News of the World*. It was no accident. The couple were staying at Glyn Celyn House, the Welsh home of Nic Paravicini, Camilla's former brother-in-law, a place so isolated in the Welsh countryside and so unlikely a venue that not even the most determined news-hound would have been there that day to record Charles and Camilla's presence had they not been tipped off.

As part of the subterfuge, officials from Charles's office expressed horror and disgust at this intrusion into Charles's private life, but few observers were fooled. The photograph was the start of a long—and as yet unfinished—process to gradually introduce Camilla to the wider world as the Prince of Wales's next wife.

If this was an exercise in gauging the public mood, Charles did not have long to wait to discover how successful it had been. Within two days of the Glyn Celyn picture, one which said boldly "Charles and Camilla are together, forever," a broadside was launched by the Church. A survey of its members—from the bishops down to the congregations—showed that at all levels, more than half thought that a remarried prince should not become king, or head of the Church.

It was a shaky start to Camilla's rehabilitation, and soon it was learned in the courtiers' offices in St. James's Palace that things would have to change faster. An early victim of this policy was Charles's private secretary Commander Richard Aylard, who had taken the full force of the attack after Charles's disastrous involvement with the broadcaster Jonathan Dimbleby. It was Aylard who had suggested that Charles confess his adultery on television, Aylard who had failed to consult with Camilla to see what the effect would be on her and her family, Aylard who had gradually sealed off all lines of communication to the prince except through him. It may also be that Aylard took exception to the ideas of Mark Bolland, a maverick who already felt at home within the palace walls and who was ready to brief the press with stories in a way which was unprecedented and highly risky. So despite eleven years of devoted, if sometimes misguided, loyalty to the royal house of Wales, Commander Aylard was sacked.

About this time the phrase "nonnegotiable" was coined on Charles's behalf. Soon it was to become a mantra, repeated every time anyone tried to suggest that Charles would be much better off living a celibate life. "Mrs. Parker Bowles is a nonnegotiable part of his life" became the stock phrase from St. James's Palace, as though the prince were prepared to barter anything else in return for hanging on to her. But with that proviso established, Charles began 1997 in a buoyant mood, allowing it to be known that he had adopted a formal campaign strategy to restore his public standing.

Charles and Camilla were now effectively living together as man and wife at Highgrove, though Camilla returned often to her home Ray Mill House at Raybridge in Wiltshire. The choice of this house after her divorce from Andrew Parker Bowles initially confused observers, since its relatively modest size and awkward positioning hardly reflected her new status as Prince Charles's official lover, or *maitress en titre* as one newspaper now started to label her. But it was intended merely as a staging post, a temporary roost, until public opinion swung sufficiently in her favor.

To this end, Camilla was now ready to dip her toe into the same water where Diana already effectively ruled the waves—that of charity work. Courtiers reasoned that Camilla needed to have some public profile, and that by attaching herself to a charity, she could be seen by the populus apparently going about doing good works. While recognizing that this was the area where Diana reigned supreme, there was little alternative—Camilla had no passions of her own beyond her children, her support of the Prince of Wales, and hunting: She had to be seen somewhere, doing something.

The charity chosen was the National Osteoporosis Society, and with good reason. Both her mother and grandmother had died of the bone-wasting disease, and in April 1997 she took up the society's invitation to become its patron. A press conference was arranged where Camilla stood awkwardly among a number of other, more media-seasoned individuals who had also agreed to become patrons. Then she sank from view. Though later she would resurrect her connection with the society to engineer a high-profile public encounter with Charles, Camilla did no further public work for the NOS, nor did she extend her charitable interests elsewhere. Somewhere along the line, the decision was taken that she could not hope to take on Diana and win.

This hesitant step into the public arena, followed by a hasty retreat, would have caused Diana some momentary satisfaction, despite having come to terms, more or less, with her husband's new living arrangements as she herself sought a new life and a new man. Her secret two-year relationship with Dr. Hasnat Khan, a distinguished heart surgeon, was coming to an end: She had wanted to start a new life in Australia with him, an impossible dream, but Khan was too devoted to his work and their aspirations lay in different directions.

Her behavior, outside her relationship with Khan, was becoming more erratic. A stream of staff who had served her devotedly over the years were packing their bags and leaving, some of their own free will, others after being fired. In the year up to February 1997 she had lost eleven staff, from a cleaner all the way up to her personal assistant and her private secretary. Her friend the TV presenter Clive James later observed: "Clearly on a hair trigger, she was unstable at best. And when the squeeze was on, she was a fruitcake on the rampage." A government minister, Earl Howe, described her as "a loose cannon." As the months wore on during 1997, she was getting more edgy.

Camilla was keeping a low profile. That is, until one evening in the spring of 1997 when she was driving from her Wiltshire home to Highgrove for dinner. Rounding a corner on a narrow country road, her car suddenly collided with another coming in the opposite direction. Though the driver of the other car, a woman, was trapped following the collision, Camilla walked away from the scene, calling on her mobile telephone for security officers to come and pick her up. She was whisked away to Highgrove where, much later that night, she was interviewed by police and Breathalyzed.

The occupant of the other car, Carolyn Melville-Smith,

pointed out when asked that Mrs. Parker Bowles had walked away from the scene of the accident without bothering to discover whether she was injured. "I was trapped in my car, yelling for help, and she did not come. I could have been badly hurt and she just left me there."

All members of the British public involved in a road accident are required to stay at the scene until police have arrived, unless they are injured. That Camilla was whisked away by the royal protection squad leaving Miss Melville-Smith trapped and helpless said two things—she was now officially under Charles's protection and, to an extent, above the law: Any police officer will say it is pointless Breathalyzing a driver three hours after the incident. The whole thing was quickly brushed under the carpet and forgotten by all except, one suspects, Miss Melville-Smith, whose injuries, though minor, caused her to be taken to a hospital.

As summer approached, Diana was seen to be increasingly on edge. The press had discovered Charles intended to host a glittering dance at Highgrove for Camilla's fiftieth birthday—a compliment he never paid Diana, incidentally—and Diana expressed the wish to be far, far away when it happened.

Only too willing to oblige, a new friend, Mohamed Al Fayed, the Egyptian-born owner of Harrods department store in Knightsbridge, offered her the use of his house at St. Tropez. By the time 150 guests including ex-King Constantine of Greece and Camilla's father Bruce Shand were sipping their predinner Laurent Perrier champagne, Diana, with William and Harry, was already bronzed by the Cote d'Azur sun.

The boys returned to London but Diana stayed on. A late arrival at the Al Fayed compound had been the tycoon's forty-one-year-old son, Dodi. Though he had met Diana twice before, they were not well acquainted but Dodi, a sometime-successful film producer with credits on the Oscar-winning *Chariots of Fire* and Robin Williams's pirate spoof, *Hook,* was handsome, charming, and a ladies' man. Former dates included Brooke Shields, Joanne Whalley-Kilmer, and the models Marie Helvin and Deneice Lewis: He was unfazed by this thirty-something blonde with a dazzling smile, an almost visible aura, and a hunger to be loved.

Fayed set about wooing Diana in a way she was totally unaccustomed with the previous men in her life. Far more cosmopolitan, much freer with his money, and with infinitely more finesse than the James Gilbeys and Hewits of this world, Fayed moved quickly and conquered Diana's heart. After her initial visit to St. Tropez she returned briefly to London where he bombarded her with flowers, fruit, and a Cartier Panthere watch. He whisked her away for a "mystery" weekend in his helicopter: It was to his father's hotel, the Paris Ritz, where they consummated their love. Within days he had persuaded her to tear up her diary and head back to the Cote d'Azur to board the family yacht, *Jonikal.*

Fayed had too high a profile, too long a track record, for the press not to track down the many women in his life once the romance became known. He left behind a girlfriend, Kelly Fisher, who all too soon claimed that he had proposed marriage, only to jilt her for Diana; there were other similar tales, including talk of his cocaine habit. None of it mattered to Diana, who within the space of days had had an Asprey's cigar cutter inscribed "With love from Diana." More significantly, she gave Dodi a pair of her late father's cuff links. The romance was moving at lightning speed—faster, faster, faster . . .

★ ★ ★

It seemed a very long summer. With Dodi briefly back in Los Angeles, Diana took a holiday in the Greek islands with her close friend Rosa Monckton, daughter of a distinguished aristocratic family and a hugely successful businesswoman in her own right. Flushed with love but still cautious, she worried about Fayed's excessive generosity: "That's not what I want, Rosa, it makes me uneasy. I don't want to be bought, I have everything I want. I just want someone to be there for me, to make me feel safe and secure."

But even in those long sun-kissed days, there was only a moment for introspection. Soon Fayed was back, and Diana boarded the *Jonikal* again for her second holiday with her lover in a month. Photographers soon captured them walking happily across the beach, larking about on a jet-ski, and sharing an intimate moment on deck as the *Jonikal* slipped anchor and headed south through the azure haze of the Mediterranean toward Portofino.

By comparison with all this *grande luxe*—private helicopters, private planes, chauffeured limousines, and expensive presents—Camilla was also off on her holidays. She drove out to Stansted Airport in Essex, London's smallest and least alluring airport, and queued with hundreds of package holiday makers for a cheap flight to Malaga in Spain. The busy backroom boys at St. James's Palace made sure everyone knew that she was paying for her own £145 charter flight ticket, but somehow this stark contrast between earnest penny-pincher and lavish freeloader cut no ice with the British public: They loved to see photographs of a bronzed, laughing Diana having fun in her bikini—they did not care two hoots about Camilla, whom they would never glimpse in a bikini. And anyway, the British public is not so foolish it doesn't know when it is being set up—a woman whose life had been spent in enormous houses in the company of rich men could only be a fool if she wanted to mix with the swirling, suffocating Stansted set. A fool, or someone bullied into a not very good PR stunt not quite succeeding in making a not very effective point.

The paparazzi—those dark outriders of journalism, as Andrew Morton so singularly described them—could not care less about Camilla. Dodi and Diana, tanned, refreshed, ablush with love, were their only target; and when their private jet touched down at Le Bourget airport in Paris, the photographers—so unlike their fictional forbears in Fellini's *La Dolce Vita*—swarmed hungrily around. Dodi, wishing to show himself master of a situation which was new to him, all too familiar to Diana, ordered his driver Philippe Dorneau to drive faster to shake the motorcycle-bound paparazzi off.

Trevor Rees-Jones, the bodyguard assigned to the couple and the only person to survive the horrifying events later that day, recalls the drive into the city center. Under his master's instructions, Dorneau pushed the car faster and faster until it was traveling at 100 mph, Dodi urging him to go faster while Diana began to scream in terror, begging Dodi to slow down. Rees-Jones recalled later: "Dodi was definitely trying to impress the princess, but Diana was angry and scared. By the time they arrived (at their destination) she was flustered and red-faced."

Dodi's father, Mohamed, had put at the couple's disposal the former home of the Duke and Duchess of Windsor, 4 Route du Champ d'Entrainement, a living mausoleum to a dead and discredited king—not perhaps the ideal backdrop for the development of the love affair Fayed *pere* was eager to encourage, but nonetheless a piece of history worthy of a visit. Rees-Jones's colleague Ben Murrell recalled showing a "distraught" Diana into a small office where she composed herself after the terrifying journey. Later she somewhat reluctantly made a tour of the house, looking at the duchess's clothes, now preserved in glass cases.

Murrell recalls noticing the couple's body language as they left after their brief tour: "I followed them at a distance and noticed that they did not hold hands or display any kind of affection. In fact they looked quite distant from each other. On her part, there was no enthusiasm at all."

That was late afternoon. By midnight the couple were once again in a chauffeur-driven car, this time leaving the Ritz Hotel by a back entrance. At the wheel was the hotel's deputy chief of security, Henri Paul, a man who had been drinking pastis and taking the antidepressants Prozac and Tiapradal. Paul, a forty-one-year-old loner, may have worked for the Ritz but drove a Mini: He did not have the special limousine license required under French law to drive high-powered motor vehicles. His job was simply to take Dodi and Diana to Dodi's apartment, avoiding the serried ranks of photographers hanging around the hotel entrances. His instructions were to lose the photographers at all costs. But Paul was three times over the drink-drive limit, the alcohol combining with the drugs in his body, and the car itself, a Mercedes 220SL, had faulty brakes.

The car left the Place Vendome heading for the Place de la Concorde. Paul jumped a red light and was seen by a trailing photographer to be heading for the Place de l'Alma underpass on the north bank of the River Seine at high speed. Diana's biographer Andrew Morton tells the story most graphically: "At around 12:24 the Mercedes, traveling at between eighty-five and ninety-five miles an hour, entered the dimly lit tunnel. Henri Paul lost control, the car colliding head-on with an unprotected concrete pillar, skidding around and coming to a halt facing the wrong way."

The driver and Dodi were killed instantly while the

bodyguard—the only occupant wearing a seat belt, was critically injured, only regaining consciousness two weeks later. Diana died possibly twenty minutes after the crash, long before she arrived at the La Pitie-Salpetriere Hospital, where she was taken slowly and painstakingly by ambulance.

In the dark dead of night the telephone started to ring at Balmoral Castle, where the queen and Prince Charles lay asleep.

Chapter Thirteen

The Fight for Acceptance

———⟨∙⊃◦⊂∙⟩———

What were Camilla's feelings as she watched Diana's coffin travel its silent journey from Kensington Palace to Westminster Abbey? Certainly guilt played a large part in her mixed emotions.

She had, according to the many critics of her behavior within the royal circle—and these included the queen—pursued Charles in the mid-1970s when she was a relatively newly married woman. One such critic told this writer: "She had him in a sexual thrall. She was to him in equal part a mother and lover; he has a mother complex and she was ready to play that part. She knew exactly how to hook him, and hook him she did. After their affair fizzled out, because of her marriage to Andrew Parker Bowles, she always had it in mind to later become his permanent mistress. She knew, from her own family history, how powerful a position that could be. It wasn't difficult for her to achieve, given Charles's sexual inexperience and naivete when it came to women.

"There can be no doubt that she felt a deep affection for him, but some friends felt it was driven by ambition," this critic continued. "She inculcated in him the belief that it would be perfectly acceptable to have a wife *and* a mistress. It did not matter, in a way, who the wife was—because Charles would always have her. It was a neat piece of work."

Camilla's great mistake was in endorsing Diana as Charles's future wife—she had entirely misjudged Diana, labeling her "the Mouse" and failing to look into the character and nature of the woman who was to take the world by storm. The Diana phenomenon had frightened everyone in the royal family, and Camilla—in supporting Charles against Diana—had helped in polarizing the prince and princess's positions. It was, as Diana said, as if there were three people in the marriage.

Camilla watched the funeral, as she had watched the chaotic and hysterical events of the week which followed Diana's death, with alarm and horror. She sat with friends at Ray Mill House, watching the lengthy and sad farewell on television. At one point she is said to have laughed as she viewed the proceedings. But whatever her reaction, she knew—as did Charles—that the process of rehabilitation which had occurred over the past twelve months was on hold. Camilla was back on the outside, out in the cold.

Was Diana pregnant with Dodi Fayed's child when she died? The question was raised even before her funeral. The weight of evidence seems to go against it—her friend Rosa Monckton declared: "I know that it would be biologically impossible for her to have been pregnant at the time of the crash." One of Diana's biographers claimed that she had summoned a doctor over her anxieties about her menstrual cycle—not because she had missed a monthly period but because she was experiencing two a month. And the fact that the idea of her being pregnant was supported by the Al Fayed camp, with their own surrealistic agenda, tended to put paid to what to the general public was a rather unpleasant notion.

On the other hand, the reporters and photographers swarming round Diana in her last days in St. Tropez had noted a change in her body shape. They heard her say to them: "You will have a big surprise coming soon, with the next thing I do." That remark was never explained, and those who were there to hear it still debate its significance to this day. Finally, a close friend of the princess told this writer: "She telephoned Hasnat Khan from the south of France and told him she thought she was pregnant. The relationship still had something going for it and she felt she could still talk to him. He told her to come and see him when she came back to London."

The effect on Charles and Camilla and their public standing would have been huge, whether Diana was dead or alive, if it was discovered she was pregnant. This was a moment when the dark arts practiced by St. James's Palace courtiers could be deployed to great effect—and yet they stayed their hand. No word or hint came from Charles's office to support the notion of Diana's pregnancy; and then it had to be taken into account that her relationship with Dodi Fayed was only six weeks old when she died.

Camilla was all too aware that Diana's death changed, possibly forever, the way the British felt about their royal family. The queen, guided by her private secretary, Sir Robert Fellowes, completely misjudged the public mood and stayed bunkered in her holiday home at Balmoral. It took the intervention of the prime minister, Tony Blair, to force the royals to take a more proactive approach to this national tragedy. Finally, after days of hesitation, the queen traveled south to witness for herself the great carpets of flowers spread in front of Buckingham Palace and Kensington Palace, and to walk among those who had taken it upon themselves to set all-night vigils in memory of this lost icon. Protocol was abandoned and the Union Flag was raised, then lowered to half-mast, above Buckingham Palace. And finally the queen made a televised speech to the nation which, though designed to patch over the wounds her inaction had caused in the past few days, sounded sulky to some.

Though this was a historic royal occasion, the royal family had lost the initiative—it had been snatched from them by Tony Blair and by Diana's brother, Earl Spencer. Dithering by courtiers over what should happen to Diana's body had made up Spencer's mind that she should be laid to rest at the family home, Althorp. Though a state funeral was envisaged, the royals were powerless to stop him claiming the body. His funeral oration to his sister in Westminster Abbey challenged the right of the House of Windsor to claim William and Harry as their own, and promised that he would watch over them as representative of the House of Spencer, a promise, incidentally, which has been kept.

Through all this turmoil Camilla saw her own chances of being accepted by the public receding at an alarming rate. Less than a fortnight after Diana's death it had been planned that she should give a high profile party, "an evening of enchantment, fascination, and the unexpected," at her sister Annabel Elliott's business premises in Dorset. It was canceled. The relationship, wrote Prince Charles's biographer, Penny Junor, was forced back underground.

If Camilla was overawed by the events of the late summer of 1997, the people at the palace were not. Insofar as they were concerned, they had been given a task to make Charles once again acceptable to the British public, by whatever means they saw fit, and they saw no reason to deviate from that. By October, just a month after Diana's death, they had a new strategy in place which in essence meant that Charles would move into all the areas previously dominated by Diana—youth, caring, fun—and wherever possible, try to attract Diana's following to his side.

In November the film *Titanic* had its premiere in London, and though Charles dislikes intensely what he sees as the falseness of such occasions, the film's massive prepublicity was attracting so much press attention that it was clear he could only benefit significantly from appearing in the company of young stars like Kate Winslet and Leonardo DiCaprio. At the last moment, it was decided that no harm could come from Camilla's children—Tom, now twenty-two, and Laura, nineteen—from joining in the crowds. To those who noticed, it would send out a subliminal message that Camilla remained "nonnegotiable." As it turned out, no one missed the point.

Following up on this success, Charles attended the premiere of a film he must have privately loathed, *Spice World,* starring the Spice Girls. He took William and Harry, and arranged for the group to come to tea at Highgrove. All this received maximum publicity, so much so that by December it was felt the right moment for the two princes to be seen following the Beaufort Hunt in which Camilla was participating on horseback. This turned out to be a step too far since Charles's support of fox-hunting is not entirely shared by the general public; and putting that together with the princes and Mrs. Parker Bowles so soon after Diana's death looked suspiciously like a two-fingered gesture to those who continued to say Camilla had no place by his (and the young princes') side. Needless to say, the experiment was not repeated, though the more successful experiment with the Spice Girls was.

Early in 1998 Charles took Prince Harry to South Africa

to see the Spice Girls in a concert attended by Nelson Mandela. It was a no-lose publicity opportunity, giving him the opportunity to be photographed with young pop idols, and one of the free world's greatest heroes. But it was what happened on the airplane on the outward flight which proved to be a turning point in Charles's rehabilitation, for on the flight he was accompanied by several British pressmen, all of whose newspapers had been pro-Diana until her death. Now, there was no more Diana, no more source of spicy stories and beautiful photographs. In the aftermath of the princess's death, the British press continued to print as many photographs of Diana as they could, since in the past these adornments had always boosted circulation, but gradually, over a period of several months, Fleet Street editors came to see that not only was this policy in the worst possible taste, but that a genuinely grieving nation no longer wanted to be reminded every day of someone who had been so cruelly snatched away. There was now a vacuum in the newspapers where Diana had been, and somehow it had to be filled.

Charles had no idea how hostile these pressmen, sitting in the back of his airplane, would be to his appearance with Harry in South Africa. Many of them took great pleasure in sullying Charles's reputation, with information fed out from Diana's camp, during the cold war between the two—in many senses, they were the enemy. But, swallowing hard, Charles made his way to the back of the plane and started to chat with them, and in that instant a new compact was forged. With Diana gone, the press needed Charles just as much as he needed them—the deal was done.

The deal didn't include Camilla. It was evident by the end of the South Africa trip that Charles, William, and Harry would get an easy ride—but as far as Camilla was concerned, that was a separate battle to be fought another day. Nonetheless this new concordat cheered the backroom boys at St. James's Palace and they pressed forward with their Camilla campaign. Soon after, she was to be seen making a stately entry to the wedding of her godson Henry Dent-Brocklehurst at a star-studded occasion featuring Mick Jagger, Hugh Grant, and Claudia Schiffer among the 350 guests. And at the end of July Camilla took a very prominent part in an early fiftieth birthday party for Charles organized by his sons. British actors including Emma Thompson, Stephen Fry, and Rowan Atkinson performed a one-hour revue accompanied by tinkling champagne glasses. In the audience were not only Camilla but her children Tom and Laura.

To coincide with Charles's fiftieth birthday, a new biography by Penny Junor appeared. This author had already written one successful book on her subject, then had been over-looked in favor of Jonathan Dimbleby when her idea of a combined book and video was mooted. Unlike other biographers who had been similarly treated, Ms. Junor maintained her support for the prince and earnestly set about providing what she believed was the definitive portrait to date of the future king.

Guided by courtiers and friends, Ms. Junor accepted what she was told, and passed on her findings unquestioned, but in so doing—her critics later alleged—she failed to utilize the judgment expected of a seasoned biographer.

Universal shock and condemnation greeted Ms. Junor's statement that in 1985 Princess Diana had had an affair with her personal protection officer, Sergeant Barry Mannakee. Grave concern was expressed about the effect this, and other, dubious claims—such as the laughable assertion that Diana was responsible for the broadcast of the Camillagate Tapes—would have on the young princes. Diana's friend Lucia Flecha de Lima said she was "outraged" by the claims and said they could not be true. Her friend Rosa Monckton dismissed the claim and explained that Diana had a close but platonic relationship with Mannakee, a fact well known to Fleet Street royal specialists who many years before had investigated the story and found it to be false.

The book blamed the breakdown of the royal marriage on Diana's "duplicity" rather than Charles's affair with Camilla, and Ms. Junor justified her claims by saying: "A number of his (Charles's) family and friends feel he has suffered enough and believe there should be some attempt to correct some of the misconceptions." But Rosa Monckton parried: "If this is an attempt to relaunch Charles by his friends, they have misjudged the people of this country." She described the book's contents as "cruel, spiteful, and hurtful."

Seeing which way the wind was blowing, Charles swiftly distanced himself from the book's findings. He took the unprecedented step of issuing a joint statement with Camilla saying it was nothing to do with him. The statement came from the selfsame office which had guided Ms. Junor on her way to writing the book.

But the row went on. A fond and loving memory of Diana was still in the air, both in Britain and abroad, and a real sense of anger was generated by other claims by Ms. Junor. These included an allegation that Diana was the first in the marriage to commit adultery, that she had tried to frighten Camilla by ringing her late at night and saying a hit man she had hired to kill her was in the garden, and that the queen had refused to allow Diana's body to rest in the Chapel Royal.

Those promoting the Charles-Camilla cause remained

cheerful despite this universal condemnation. Their next stunt was to engineer a curious pantomime at the wedding of Charles's friends Santa Palmer-Tomkinson and Simon Sebag-Montefiore where Camilla, accompanied by former Royal Protection Squad officers now employed privately by the prince, arrived with her children. Charles, accompanied by Prince Harry, arrived twenty minutes later and sat elsewhere. The couple left the ceremony separately, and arrived at the reception at the Ritz Hotel separately. The effect was to frustrate everyone—for on the one hand Camilla was now famously the "nonnegotiable" part of Charles's life, yet members of the public who were being asked for their support in this union were not allowed to see the couple together. It seemed to many that St. James's Palace's behavior was imperious and high-handed.

If Charles thought he was beginning to win the battle for people's hearts and minds over the Camilla issue he had reckoned without one crucial element—the queen. His plans to have a dazzling fiftieth birthday celebration, including all the crowned heads of Europe, required his mother to be there for the event to be a complete success. But long ago the queen had declared, privately, that she would never meet Mrs. Parker Bowles. As far as she was concerned, Camilla was an adulteress who had wooed her son when she should have known better. The fact that at the time, in the mid-1970s, she was married to a fellow officer compounded the felony.

Despite the fact that Charles had invited Queen Margrethe of Denmark, King Harald of Norway, King Carl Gustav of Sweden, Queen Beatrix of the Netherlands, King Albert of Belgium, King Juan Carlos of Spain, the Grand Duke of Luxembourg, and ex-King Constantine of Greece with their spouses cut no ice with Queen Elizabeth of Great

Britain. She turned down her son's invitation on the very specific grounds that Camilla would be there.

Sensing a growing public frustration, Charles's courtiers deemed it time for the prince and Camilla to appear in public together—but only after an opinion poll by Gallup showed that a majority shared the queen's deeply held conviction that Charles and Camilla should not marry. The occasion chosen was a party for Camilla's sister Annabel at the Ritz Hotel in London's Piccadilly. "Not since the days of Charles's late wife Diana have so many photographers, TV crews, and reporters gathered to record a royal event," gushed the BBC News, conveniently omitting to mention that it was the St. James's Palace press office which had brought them there.

In excess of 200 photographers and journalists waited for the moment when Charles and Camilla stepped out of the Ritz's revolving door and down the steps into Arlington Street. Crush barriers were erected at public expense for this apparently extempore moment, and the whole thing was attended by a heavy police presence—quite a price for tax-payers to pay for something which was, given the private nature of the party they were attending, only to Charles and Camilla's advantage.

The stage-managed exit down the steps was timed to coincide with various TV news bulletins—but here the palace spin-doctors shot themselves in the foot, for such was the ferocity of photographers' flash guns that a strobing effect was created for the TV cameras, and the footage was deemed unusable after the British Epilepsy Association urged broad-casters not to transmit the pictures, fearing it would spark photosensitive seizures in some sufferers.

So far, then, the campaign to rehabilitate Prince Charles and to smoothly introduce Camilla Parker Bowles to the

British nation was, at best, only working fitfully. At the root of the problem was the strategy devised by Charles's private secretary Stephen Lamport and his assistant Mark Bolland, which, to seasoned observers, appeared cynical, opportunistic, occasionally vengeful, and out of step with public desires. By now, news and gossip items were appearing in selected newspapers which could only have come from Lamport and Bolland's office; these items—sometimes later denied by the very same source—manipulated the monopoly situation which Prince Charles now commanded over the media. Those newspapers who "played ball" with the palace were given snippets of information; those which did not were left out in the cold.

This policy had the immediate effect of whipping most newspapers into line, so that now there was very little public criticism of Charles. And yet still it failed to deliver any real returns: The public opinion polls were obdurately refusing to shift in Camilla's favor. She was no longer Public Enemy Number One, but nonetheless a woman eyed with distrust by the majority. In part this was the fault of the image makers, for they were unable to devise a plan where Camilla could mix freely with the public so that they could judge for themselves the merits of the woman Charles held as "nonnegotiable" in his life. The tried-and-tested formula for all royals—visiting hospitals, opening buildings, making short speeches—all seemed too much of a difficulty. She had been called "the prince's kept woman" by the MP Geoffrey Dickens, and this was how she began to be perceived: a woman who was enjoying—very much so—all the privileges of a royal life, with none of the accompanying responsibilities. The idea started to spread that Camilla was idle and uncommitted, for by comparison with any other member of the royal family, her contribution to its cause was minimal and—according to some members of the royal family themselves—negative. Princess Margaret, herself the victim of the family's rules on divorce, was particularly scathing of the Camilla situation.

Added to this uncomfortable impasse now came a new Parker Bowles scandal. Camilla's son Tom, who since leaving Oxford University had led a rudderless existence as he tried to find a suitable job, was revealed to be a habitual user of cocaine. At the Cannes Film Festival in May 1999 he told an undercover reporter from the *News of the World:* "The best place to go (to buy cocaine) is a houseboat. That's what I did last night." Soon after, another newspaper reported an eye-witness account of him taking cocaine at a party.

The *Daily Telegraph's* Robert Hardman, one of the best-informed royal reporters, wrote: "The stories will be of particular concern because of Mr. Parker Bowles's closeness to the young princes. He has often accompanied Prince William to London parties during the school holidays. There is no suggestion that the boys had any knowledge of his use of drugs but both are very fond of him and regard him as something of a confidante and role model."

Damning words indeed—for now the princes, William especially, were being dragged into the scandal. It was the palace spin-doctors who had decided to play up the idea that Camilla's children and Charles's children were unifying, blending into some sort of nuclear family; now this idea, too, had backfired on them. It emerged that while Tom Parker Bowles had been at Oxford he had been cautioned for possession of Ecstasy and cannabis, and fellow undergraduates disloyally hinted at further excesses—this was hardly the ideal "role model" for a future king.

The spin-doctors tried another tack. Princess Diana had taken New York by storm, again and again, during her lifetime. Even Fergie, the Duchess of York, had managed to conquer the Big Apple with her refreshing blend of imperiousness and candor. Their enthusiastic reception there had paid huge dividends back in Britain when the reputations of both Diana and Fergie were taking a pounding back in London. What better than to put Camilla in New York?

Strings were pulled, introductions made—for New York is definitely not Prince Charles's city. Camilla flew into town with Mark Bolland riding shotgun, and they made camp at the Carlyle Hotel. New York, as always, was willing to open its arms and its doors—and the high point of her five-day visit was a lunch given by the ninety-six-year-old Brooke Astor, by common consent the queen of New York society. Among the guests were the designer Oscar de la Renta; Barbara Walters, the TV presenter; actors Michael Douglas and Catherine Zeta Jones; and heavy-hitting businessmen including Mort Zuckerman and Michael Bloomberg.

"Mrs. Astor," declared a columnist, "is a character straight from a Cole Porter song. Her husband's father died on the *Titanic*, smoking his cigar as the ship went down, and she rarely leaves home without her two dachshunds kitted out in sweaters. When she met Mrs. Parker Bowles some years ago she told her she had known her great-grandmother Mrs. Keppel. Camilla, she said in her toast, had done very well by her great-grandmother." But the visit was a flop. The same columnist, Philip Delves Broughton, added: "New York for the most part yawned at this successor to the Princess of Wales." And privately Mrs. Astor asked why she had been asked to give lunch to such an insignificant figure.

By the summer of 2000, only one item was on the royal agenda—the one-hundredth birthday of Queen Elizabeth, the Queen Mother. This doughty and magnificent veteran had returned from ill health in her mid-90s to peak form. Apart from the many triumphs of her long and distinguished life, she could claim to be the oldest woman in Britain to have had two hip-replacement operations. She remained the nation's darling, with old and young alike, and throughout the early summer months the nation looked forward with eager anticipation sharing Her Majesty's most glorious day.

But behind the scenes a historic arm-wrestling match was taking place between Prince Charles and his mother, the queen. The time had come, he told her, for her to recognize Camilla—to meet her face-to-face, to shake her by the hand, to talk to her. It was almost the first time in his life Charles had stood up to his mother, certainly the first time he had challenged her on the Camilla issue.

The queen, mindful of her responsibility as head of the Church of England and as representative of a moral majority which shared her distaste for the whole relationship and its history, continued to refuse. Charles, growing ever more adamant, threatened to boycott the Queen Mother's birthday celebrations unless she relented. He was giving a birthday party for ex-King Constantine of Greece at Highgrove, and she must attend—or face the consequences.

Faced by this neat piece of blackmail, the queen shrugged her shoulders and gave in. The *Daily Telegraph* trumpeted: "The queen has finally acknowledged Camilla Parker Bowles," but the truth was somewhat lamer. The younger woman was introduced again to her sovereign, whom she had not met since the queen issued her ban in the mid-1970s. She curtseyed, the queen acknowledged her presence—and that was that. For the rest of the party they sat at separate tables and did not speak. The queen left without acknowledging her.

It gave the spin-doctors what they wanted. QUEEN

AND CAMILLA MEET AT HIGHGROVE, ran the head-lines. "Prince Philip was not present . . . but he is understood to support the queen's decision to recognize Mrs. Parker Bowles," gushed the *Telegraph*. Nobody cared to look beyond the bulletins to see the pragmatic actions of a seasoned monarch whose forty-eight-year reign had remained beyond controversy. Charles had won the battle—but the queen would never, ever again meet his son's lover. The gesture had been made, selflessly, to spare the Queen Mother.

A few days later, Camilla was at Buckingham Palace on Charles's arm to greet one hundred American guests who came in support of the Prince's Foundation, Charles's chari-table organization. It was also reported that she had been in meetings with Dr. George Carey, the Archbishop of Canter-bury and head of the established Church. There could only be one discussion between these two ill-matched individuals, and that was marriage. No communique was issued and, remarkably, relatively little was made of this portentous en-counter.

In February 2001, a further step up the ladder to public acceptance was attempted by Charles and Camilla. Once again picking an event off the rack as if it were an item of clothing in a store, they chose the tenth anniversary of the Press Complaints Commission, a not wholly successful media watchdog whose head, Guy Black, happened to share an apartment with Charles's assistant private secretary Mark Bolland.

Once again, as with the Sebag-Montefiore wedding many months before, a complex ritual was arranged whereby the event—heavily covered by the media—would allow Charles and Camilla in the same room without their arriving or leaving together. But though the event was attended by Prince William and Charles's brothers Andrew and Edward as

well as a number of well-known actors and politicians, it pro-
voked fury among the public that the elaborate game of
hide-and-seek with Camilla continued: She arrived in a separate car, and left separately. The couple were in the same
room, but took care not to be photographed together—even
though by now the St. James's Palace press office had given
up all pretence and openly acknowledged that Charles and
Camilla slept together at the palace and at Highgrove.

The high-profile events continued, specifically tailored, or
so it seemed to more cynical observers, to the tabloid and
glossy-magazine reader. In March 2001, Mick Jagger, Elton
John, and eighty other high-profile guests turned out for a
twenty-fifth-year birthday party for his charity, the Prince's
Trust. And a few weeks later came what Charles's spin-
doctors considered to be their greatest coup—the first public
kiss between Charles and Camilla.

It was at yet another birthday party—this time the fifteenth anniversary of the foundation of the National
Osteoporosis Society, the charity which had not benefitted
from any publicity from their association with Camilla since
she was made its patron in a high-profile flurry of headlines
four years previously.

Suddenly the charity, a modest and unassuming organization, was being given a party at Somerset House, the ancient
Thameside palace in central London. No doubt bewildered
by this lucky turn of events, they did not question whether
the party had been organized specifically to advance the
interests of their patron and her companion. The patron wore
a lilac chiffon cocktail dress by Anthony Price and, on this
occasion, appeared to be the host of the event. The guest of
honor, naturally, was Prince Charles—and the world's press
was there with the promise of a kiss.

When it came, drowned by the clatter of flashguns, it was

formal and passionless—a light touch on both cheeks so far removed from the tender kiss Charles gave his bride on the Buckingham Palace balcony twenty years before as to be beyond comparison. The Somerset House party—filled with celebrities, as observers have come to expect these days when the occasion contains both Charles and Camilla—had been designed around The Kiss.

It was a renunciation of the past, a promise of the future.

When the World Trade Center in New York was attacked on 11 September 2001 civilization came to a standstill. In the aftermath a new way of thinking was born; much of what had gone before was reevaluated. Yet there were places, even in this deepest and darkest hour of despair, where it was business as usual: Cynical men, whose only thought was to capitalise on the moment and to turn it to their advantage, went quietly about their work.

Two days later, in the leafy quiet of Grosvenor Square in London, many Americans gathered. They had walked in procession from Buckingham Palace where they heard the band of the Coldstream Guards play "The Star Spangled Banner." With mourning etched on their faces, they moved slowly and silently through the square's somber gardens, lighting candles, laying wreaths, leaving letters and poems and messages in a cellophane-and-flower carpet.

It was a historic moment, one in which the mighty roar of London's traffic was stilled, in recognition of the grief of those exiles who sought to make contact with their homeland in the only way they could. At that hour, two nations were joined as one.

Into this intensely private scene stepped a strange and alien figure—that of Camilla Parker Bowles. Dressed brightly in a lilac suit, she walked hesitantly through the square accompanied by William Farish, the United States ambassador to Britain. Though she behaved with complete decorum, American citizens who recognized her asked themselves why she was there, for Camilla is not part of the royal family. Her presence was not an official visit, nor could she claim any close personal involvement with the American nation beyond a recent lunch in New York with a society queen.

She was there for what is described, in journalistic parlance, as a photo opportunity. And, next day, among acres of press coverage of the tragic and disturbing visions of the violated New York streetscape, one British newspaper devoted a large amount of space to pictures of Camilla in Grosvenor Square. To many, it was as absurd as it was insulting to the memory of those thousands who had died in the World Trade Towers—but so what? In the subterranean world occupied by those who believe it is their mission to promote the cause of Charles and Camilla, it was an opportunity not to be missed. That her presence in Grosvenor Square on a unique day of grief could be construed as tasteless and irrelevant would mean nothing to them—if one or two heads in Britain were turned by the vision of a "caring" Camilla, then their job would have been done and they could go home happy.

Chapter Fourteen

Road to Redemption

<hr />

Three years, and more, had passed since the death of Princess Diana, yet like a man stumbling across the desert toward the horizon, Charles never got any closer to achieving his goal of public acceptance for the non-negotiable part of his life. Other aspects of his princeship were utterly praiseworthy— his charities continued to provide money and job opportunities for the young and underprivileged, his public utterances on such issues as GM crop exploitation continued to find favor. In all aspects but one, he appeared to be an exemplary prince, an apprentice whose spadework had more than prepared him for kingship.

But on the one issue—Camilla—he was unable to budge public opinion. Poll after poll came back with the same story, that Britain was prepared to smile kindly on their future king, but wanted nothing to do with his mistress.

In large measure this was to do with the public relations campaign being waged on the couple's behalf. There had been too many staged appearances where Camilla would tantalizingly appear, then be whisked away before the public could grasp her hand, make eye contact, engage in small talk.

After the glamorous ubiquity of Princess Diana, this was not only a disappointment, but there lurked a growing suspicion among ordinary folk that they were in some way being used to promote Camilla, and propel her forward. Nobody seemed very keen to do that apart from the few self-serving individuals who, at public events, took to calling her "Ma'am" and curtsying as though the royal ermine was already tucked firmly around her shoulders.

If this was the very visible tip of the iceberg, under the waterline rather more reconstructive work was going on, most especially between Charles and his sons William and Harry. In the days before Diana's death, his parenting of the young princes had become a now-and-then thing, causing one former courtier to blurt out as the news of her fatal crash spread across the world, "How will he cope with the boys? He had them to stay for less than thirty days last year, he hardly knows them anymore."

This shocking truth was withheld from the public domain, but is the final evidence that in the days before her death Diana had won the war over possession of the children. Earlier, living in the *rallentando* of her marriage at Highgrove, she would take them to bed to keep them at arm's length from their father. Now, she had created a gulf between father and sons. "I don't want to win," was her disingenuous confession to the then-editor of the London *Daily Telegraph*, "But I am absolutely determined to see William succeed the Queen." What disinformation she whispered in her elder son's ear at this time we shall probably never know, but in her hurt and rejection she was as dangerous as a wounded tiger. Certainly, she had isolated her boys geographically from their father; whether she had done so emotionally seems likely but impossible to prove.

Perhaps through fear for his sons' equilibrium, perhaps

because he had been outsmarted, Charles allowed the distance to grow. When he had them to stay he would use a friend, often Emilie van Cutsem, to act as surrogate mother even though the hours allotted for their stay whistled past at an alarming rate. Now, in the years since their mother's death it was Charles's duty to rediscover his children and ease his way back into their lives.

At the time of her death, William was fifteen, Harry approaching his thirteenth birthday. Such intimate accounts as exist of the princes' reaction to their mother's violent demise tend to suggest they swallowed their grief, rather than talk it through; certainly it would have been difficult, at the beginning, for them to articulate their innermost feelings to a man who had been demonized so comprehensively by their mother.

The vulnerable one turned out to be Harry. He had already started drinking and smoking, before this teens, while on a Greek-island-hopping holiday with friends. During such holidays, it was claimed later, the young people were left to their own devices, and there were reports of wild parties with vodka and tequila. Whatever tendency Harry had toward wayward behavior, it was exacerbated by his mother's death.

In the tight-knit circle that surrounds the British royal family, there were enough people acquainted with the next peril, drugs, for Harry to have been familiar with their use from the earliest adolescence. Apart from Tom Parker Bowles, caught red-handed in his cocaine use, there was also Tom's cousin Emma, who had been treated in the United States for addiction to drugs and drink. The grown-up daughter of Charles and Patti Palmer Tomkinson appeared on a British television show quite evidently under the influence of drink and drugs and shortly afterward was hustled onto a plane to take her to Arizona to find a cure for her addictions. Lord Frederick Windsor, son of Prince and Princess Michael of Kent and near-neighbor of the young princes during their Kensington Palace days, was similarly captured by the media and bound to confess his use of cocaine. One more name to add to the list of shame is that of Nicholas Knatchbull, great-grandson of Lord Mountbatten and Prince Charles's godson, who preceded Prince William through Eton and acted as his mentor, and who twice found refuge in the United States while he sought a cure for hard addiction. It was hard to deny the existence of such temptations.

Whether William succumbed to the ever-present peril of drugs, we do not know, but it seems highly unlikely: too many of his well-heeled friends were making fools of themselves at Eton and, possessed of that ingrained sense of duty that runs through his father, he steered clear. Certainly there has been nothing erratic in his behavior to suggest that he is anything other than a healthy and intelligent young man who saw the dangers clearly enough to successfully sidestep them.

But Harry was a weaker vessel, and by 2001 his errant behavior was starting to break surface. There were allegations that he had on several occasions become so drunk at private parties that he vomited: certainly at a grand affair given by Britain's richest aristocrat, the Duke of Westminster, he was seen throwing up in the bushes. By the summer, he was in Spain attending the Sotogrande Copa de Plata polo cup on the Costa del Sol, and later witnessed smoking and drinking in the nearby nightclubs of Marbella. He had already torn up the turf of a nearby golf course, turning it into a makeshift polo pitch and using golf buggies for ponies. On vacation in Rock, in the British west coast county of Cornwall, he incurred the wrath of several mothers whose daughters were subjected to a hitherto-unseen arrogance in the young prince, not yet sixteen. "He seemed to think he could do whatever he liked because of who he is," one complained.

The final unmasking came after an incident at the Rattle-bone Inn, a sixteenth-century pub in the village of Sherston, not far from Highgrove, later in the summer of 2001. It had become a regular meeting-place for young men of rich families in the area and though two years under the legal age limit, Harry soon joined in the thirsty, noisy drinking sessions that occurred most nights. What turned his youthful high spirits into a national talking-point, however, was when he was involved in a brawl during one of the many after-hours bingeing sessions that went on. It later emerged that it was Harry's habit to return to Highgrove with his friends where, in a basement disco rigged up by the royal brothers some time before, Harry and friends would listen to techno and garage music while smoking marijuana and drinking even more.

When this behavior was exposed by the tabloid newspapers, the talk among the columnists was of a boy cruelly robbed of his mother at a crucial stage in life, and with Harry eating a suitable amount of humble pie, including publicly visiting a drug rehabilitation center with his father, the story seemed to go away.

Meanwhile, addressing his own issues, Charles was keeping up the pressure for greater recognition of Camilla. One day in December they were apparently discovered strolling together through Green Park, which separates the royal palaces from the Ritz Hotel, on their way to the annual St. James's palace staff party. The weather was cold enough, and the journey far enough, to justify the use of a limousine but Charles had another purpose in mind: his spin doctors had alerted their favorite press photographers and another photo-op was underway, just to remind the world, in case anyone had forgotten, that Charles and Camilla were still an item. In a heavy news agenda that fall, the couple were in danger of being lost to view and this was their attempt to maintain the advantage. "The prince has walked through Green Park before on his way to the Christmas party, and Mrs. Parker Bowles has also been a previous guest," warbled the publicity machine. Neither statement was true, but nobody bothered to check.

It was inevitable that at the age of 101 the Queen Mother could not go on forever, and from Christmas through the bleak winter and into spring, reports emerged from Windsor that she was nearing her end. In the last days of March she was visited daily by her niece, the Honorable Margaret Rhodes, as she lay in repose at Royal Lodge in Windsor Great Park. When the final hour of that great life arrived, Mrs. Rhodes, a complete stranger to the cameras and the media world in general, emerged to describe what she had seen with great clarity and decorum. It was a moment for reflection on a life so vigorously lived and with such a high moral code attached to an unswerving sense of public duty: TV newsreels accompanied Mrs. Rhodes' words with footage of the Queen Mother greeting the veterans of two world wars outside Westminster Abbey on a freezing winter's morning a matter of weeks before. None but the most hardbitten republican could refrain from expressing amazement at a life so richly led.

For Prince Charles, his grandmother's passing opened the door to a number of possibilities. He inherited both her houses—Birkhall on the Balmoral estate in Scotland, and Clarence House on the Mall near Buckingham Palace. This would, in due course, allow Camilla to play a more equal role at his side, albeit away from the cameras, but also it lifted whatever lingering inhibitions he may have felt about making a last dash for marriage with his long-term mistress.

After Diana's death, Charles, close to a nervous break-down, spent many long hours in the Queen Mother's company, for she was indeed his surrogate mother and had been nearly all of his life. But her standards of behavior were forged in the Edwardian era and the one thing she could not countenance was a marriage between a Prince of Wales and a married woman—it had happened once in her lifetime, sixty years before, to devastating effect; it was not to happen again. Now that she was gone, the most significant hurdle to Charles and Camilla's marriage had been cleared away.

People often commented on the similarities between grandmother and grandson and in the wake of her passing, one houseguest of the prince felt able to make comparisons: "His grandmother encouraged him to indulge himself, to be really royal in the old style, and he does." Describing the house party, the guest recalled: "To start with, there must have been twenty or thirty servants. Everybody had their own individual maid or valet and each evening, as we came down to dinner, our jaws dropped open at the splendor of the table, the silver, the decorations, the flowers, the statues and the lighting. It was different on each of the three nights—an unbelievable display, absolutely dazzling. He's got the same incredible instinct for style as the Queen Mother, but she never went over the top. He does."

Camilla was present at the Queen Mother's funeral, but then nobody expected it to be otherwise. By this stage Charles was beginning to gain the upper hand in the Machiavellian dealings that now characterized his only contact with Buck-ingham Palace—"the enemy," as one departing courtier de-scribed it. Just before the Queen Mother's death, a gala concert to celebrate the life of the cellist Mstislav Rostropovich was arranged at Buckingham Palace and it was announced that both the Queen *and* Camilla would attend:

by a process of attrition Charles had gotten his mother and his mistress in the same room again, and though their contact was once again perfunctory, the tabloids had a field day, wildly suggesting that with such regal endorsement, a marriage could only be around the corner. The truth was a whole lot frostier than that, however.

But now Charles headed north to inspect his inheritance, an imposing 1715 mansion on the Balmoral estate north of the River Muick, which was in virtually the same state as when the Queen Mother, as Duchess of York, had redecorated it in 1931. Time had taken its toll on Birkhall, and in those first few days, as the spirit of its former owner gradually departed, Charles and Camilla set about devising a program of works to restore the house while maintaining its essential character. As elsewhere, notably the Sandringham Flower Show—an insignificant affair in the global scheme of things, but a must-do in the British royal calendar—Charles now stepped into his grandmother's shoes. He took his house party, including Camilla, Princess Margaret's daughter Lady Sarah Chatto, and Camilla's friend from those long-forgotten days in Ebury Street Virginia Carington, to Crathie Kirk where his presence—and that of Camilla—was greeted with great warmth. The Scots are far less judgmental when it comes to royal love affairs than their southern neighbours.

If Prince Harry had caused his father considerable anguish in those years since Diana's death, what of Prince William? Remarkably, he seemed to remain untouched by the turmoil which overshadowed his formative years—marital discord, divorce, death—and despite his mother's dynastic ambitions, did not appear to harbor a lust for kingship ahead of his father. His years at Eton had passed smoothly enough, in part because he was equal to the school's academic demands, unlike his younger brother. Having found an outlet in water polo— an exhausting, dangerous, but thoroughly exhilarating sport— a great deal of his teenage angst was dispelled in the pool.

For the rest, he made sure he avoided doing anything that would draw attention to himself. His head-down marches through Eton High Street, avoiding all eye contact, effectively created a *cordon sanitaire* which all but the most foolhardy learned to respect. In his last year, he became a member of Pop, Eton's self-electing elite whose distinctive badge is a self-designed silk waistcoat under the habitual tailcoat. He won the school cadet force's Sword of Honor. He grew, his shoulders broadened, and manhood descended upon him. He looked, said every woman who cast eyes on him, simply stunning.

By the middle of 2002, William had completed his first year at St. Andrew's University, a seat of learning founded in 1411 and situated on the remote east coast of Scotland—a long, long way away from where the paparazzi like to play. Here, among a broader group of young people, he was allowed to develop social skills previously denied by reason of privilege and security, and his horizons expanded accordingly: here, Diana's wish that he should not be separated from ordinary people was as near coming to pass as it was ever likely to.

His degree course was in the history of art, a congenial and one might assume not unfamiliar subject to one whose houses are stuffed with the very subject he was studying. Nonetheless, the prince found the going tough and, frustrated by his comparative lack of progress, was ready to quit at the end of his first year. All the more credit to him, then, that at the year-end in the summer of 2002, he agreed to undergo some tentative royal duties.

Pressing the flesh at a royal garden party held at Holyroodhouse, the House of Windsor's Scottish version of Buckingham Palace, he found these duties delightful and rewarding—a surprise, since rumor had it everywhere that he was a reluctant royal and wanted to stay as far away from the public and the press for as long as possible. Another hurdle to overcome was that this early outing was also attended by Camilla in an attempt by Charles once again to forge some apparent connection between his mistress and his son. Outwardly, the thing was choreographed well enough for William's frustration not to show: inwardly, while pleased by the crowds, he was less thrilled by being used as a tool in his father's public relations game.

But the Camilla issue was pushing aside all other considerations: it hung in the air, unresolved and apparently irresolvable, coloring all judgment of Charles and his doings. The tabloids, discarding other more serious matters in royal and national affairs, nagged away at the Camilla problem and yet Charles and his advisors, the only ones capable of forcing change, seemed becalmed and bemused. Help was at hand, however, and it came in the shape of the newly-elected Archbishop of Canterbury, Dr. Rowan Williams, who quite unexpectedly gave his blessing to new rules governing the remarriage of divorcees in church.

Without further opposition from the church, a weakened but still powerful force in British opinion, the barriers to marriage could now be expected to be quickly swept away. It could no longer be claimed that such a marriage would trigger a constitutional crisis, the fallback position of so many who still did not want Charles to marry Camilla. A senior aide to the Archbishop said the matter had already been addressed and in the future if the couple wanted to get married, they would be treated the same as any other couple in a similar position.

While this was perhaps a trifle optimistic—the church adores anything royal—it was significant that the Archbishop had, in his previous incumbency, approved the marriage of divorcees in church. Significantly, he was willing to give his consent even when one partner was responsible for the breakdown of his previous marriage.

Emboldened, Charles took Camilla and her father Bruce Shand to the Sandringham Flower Show, an innocuous enough event except that a military band played God Save the Queen and—uncaptured by the cameras—for the first time ever, the couple stood side by side in this most formal celebration of royalty. It was a picture, perhaps, of things to come.

Retreating to Birkhall for the traditional summer Scottish break, the couple were able to inspect the progress of its refurbishment. Together they paid a visit to the Castle of Mey, the Queen Mother's sixteenth-century retreat on the northernmost shores of Scotland, which had been bequeathed to a trust, and this was followed by a visit to the nearby Highland Games. Subtly, on these two public engagements Charles *and* Camilla were stepping into the Queen Mother's shoes, a duo where before there had been only one, and people were not objecting.

Among the glitterati, Camilla was already more than acceptable. During their Scottish holiday the couple attended the sixtieth birthday celebrations of the comedian Billy Connolly at his Aberdeenshire castle, mixing happily with the likes of Steve Martin, Robin Williams, Paul McCartney, Whoopi Goldberg, Rod Stewart, Ewan McGregor, and Pythons Michael Palin and Eric Idle.

At about this time—helpfully or not—it was revealed to what an extent Charles now prized the company of his consort:

she was turning out to be a very expensive luxury with chauffeurs, bodyguards, personal assistants, a gardener, a groom, domestic help, odd-job men, PR guidance, and a secretariat suddenly sprouting where none had been before. All these people required salaries, cars, and the ancillary benefits that go with working for the royal family even if their new boss wasn't royal, just yet. Charles was more than happy to dip into his pocket, not so surprisingly since the income from his Duchy of Cornwall estates exceeds $25 million a year, quite apart from a personal fortune—made up from family and private bequests—which probably tops $75 million.

He had made it his personal quest to find and buy back as many pieces of jewellry as could be identified as having been given by his forbear King Edward VII to her forbear Alice Keppel. In addition, a friend, Blondel Clough, was advising Camilla on the purchase of lesser pieces. Royal milliner Philip Treacy was supplying hats, with couture clothes being provided by British designers Anthony Price, Paddy Campbell, and Robinson Valentine. Oscar de la Renta, whose clothes Diana wore, expressed surprise and pleasure at Camilla's new-found *chic,* but after a brief flirtation with Versace she realized that the gap between them was unbridgeable.

Dressing Camilla like a princess would not come easily: only by a process of trial and error could she work her way toward something approaching a personal style, and mistakes were made along the way—though friends say that Camilla is harder on herself than anyone else when it comes to her public appearance.

Those observers most closely watching the Camilla campaign had come to the conclusion as long ago as 2001 that somewhere in St. James's Palace there existed a sheet of paper on which was typed the announcement that the Prince of Wales and Mrs. Parker Bowles would marry. All that was left blank was the date. They theorized that Charles—desperate to move to the next stage—was waiting for a window of opportunity sufficiently large to spring his news on the British nation. A lift in the opinion polls would do it, or one of those moments which arrive unheralded in Britain when the royal family is suddenly, and for no particular reason, seen to its best advantage. This often follows a ceremonial occasion when the men look handsome in their uniforms and the women dazzling in their hats and jewels.

But curiously, as the year wore on, no such opportunity presented itself. The Queen's Jubilee, celebrating fifty years on the throne, had come and gone. During the four-month lead-up there was a tacit understanding that the Camilla issue would be shelved: it had had the effect of pushing every other royal off the front pages as the Queen, as Sovereign, made it clear that for once nothing should deflect from her moment of glory. The following year—2003—would be dominated by the twenty-first birthday celebrations of the future king, William, and thus those who were running the Charles-Camilla campaign were squeezed into an autumn slot if they were to get the announcement out at all.

It might have happened, but for the re-emergence of a ghost from the past. In October Paul Burrell, a forty-four-year-old former butler to Princess Diana, suddenly appeared in the dock at the Old Bailey courthouse in London, accused of stealing 310 items, allegedly the possessions of his royal mistress. He vehemently denied the charges.

The case followed a raid on Burrell's house in the north of England after a mysterious tip-off. Though no special emphasis was laid on it at the time, it became clear later that when police barged through Burrell's front door they were looking not for the 310 items, but one. They wanted to locate the tapes of a conversation that Diana had recorded in 1996 between her and a royal valet called George Smith. In the conversation, Smith had accused a member of Prince Charles's staff of subjecting him to a homosexual rape.

Thus the theft charges were but a means to an end. Soon stories started to appear that police, eager to pursue their target, had informed Prince Charles that Burrell, a bisexual, had dressed himself in one of Diana's ball gowns and swanned around a party attended by other royal servants. No evidence was ever offered in court to substantiate this wild claim, but when presented to the prince it had the effect of recruiting his support of the police's pursuit of the butler.

Burrell it was who had attended the dead body of Diana in Paris, clothing her in the last garments she would ever wear. In the aftermath of her shocking death he became a celebrity by default—he talked while others held their tongues. Much was made of the fact that Diana was said to have described Burrell as "my rock," though later it emerged that she used this description of a number of people who helped her in her last years; but the point was that Burrell had behaved honorably during his years with, and after, Diana— and he did not steal the so-called "rape tape," had not worn her dress, had never sought to sell or make capital out of the artefacts he had stored in his attic, and was to all intents and purposes just another sad casualty of the Diana cult.

As the case progressed it became clear that in mixing in the highest social circles, the police were out of their depth. There was conjecture that it was Diana's sister Lady Sarah McCorquodale who had set them on to Burrell, and that her motives were not entirely pure: both she and Burrell had sat on the Princess Diana Memorial Fund board, but it was clear that Lady Sarah—once herself courted by Prince Charles in the pre-Diana days—felt uncomfortable sitting at a table on equal terms with an ex-butler. She may also have been motivated, entirely understandably, by the fact that Burrell had gone on to make a career out of his years with Diana, while people from her own background had always been taught not to talk publicly about private matters.

Whatever the motivational thrust behind the prosecution, it became clear as the lawyers made their opening statements that something very nasty was about to emerge from the woodwork. For the next eleven days as the trial lumbered on, more and more embarrassing information came to light, including the fact that Diana's mother and sister Sarah had moved into Kensington Palace at the earliest opportunity and started to shred her private papers: under the bright light of cross-examination, nobody emerged without blemish.

Then something very strange occurred. Just as Burrell was preparing to step into the witness box, the trial was halted. After a lengthy delay, it emerged that no less a personage than the Queen had come forward to offer the revelation that, after Diana's death, Burrell had had a meeting with her in which he stated he had taken possession of some of Diana's things.

Well, said the judge, Mrs. Justice Rafferty, that nullifies the prosecution. Burrell walked away from the court for a champagne luncheon with his lawyers, saying "The Queen came through for me," and that was the end of the matter.

Except that it wasn't. While the lawyers seemed satisfied that justice had not only been done, but had been seen to be done, the public and press took a very different view. The Queen's intervention in the process of her own court was decried, since until this point it had always been assumed that she was above the law and therefore not able to participate in its workings.

Worse, the press had an inkling of what Burrell might have said when examined in the dock. The inner workings of Kensington Palace, its relationship with Buckingham Palace, the private life of Princess Diana, her relationship with Charles both before and after their divorce, intimate details of Charles's relationship with Camilla, the truth about Prince William and Prince Harry—all these, and much more, were likely to spill forth in the course of Burrell's testimony. That the powers-that-be had taken so long to wake up to this possibility merely added to the contempt being poured on all participants in this sorry affair—all, that is, except Burrell. For once the Queen, traditionally immune to criticism, came under fire for having meddled in the judicial process; but far worse was the backlash on Prince Charles, for during the course of evidence some light was shed on the arcane practices which passed for daily life in the House of Wales.

The public were shocked to hear that gifts sent in good faith to the prince, if unwanted, were privately sold, with royal servants and Charles himself sharing the proceeds. Worse, those which could not be easily disposed of ended up in the garbage dump: a wedding gift of a carved table from South Sea islanders had been sent to be burned on a bonfire. Coupled with an apparent cover-up over the male rape— Fleet Street knew the name of the alleged attacker but because no legal moves were made, were unable to name him—anger grew over the apparently casual and possibly corrupt way Charles was running his fiefdom. The Camilla campaign was back on ice, indefinitely.

In an attempt to head off criticism, it was announced that Charles's private secretary, Sir Michael Peat, would investigate the way the palace was being run: most people assumed that any conclusions Peat arrived at would be covered by a thick coating of whitewash, and so it proved. Within Charles's circle there was a glum acceptance that, once again, the prince had fallen in public esteem and another long haul would be required to bring him back to acceptability.

Virtually the only casualty within Charles's household, following Peat's inquiry, was Michael Fawcett. At forty-one, Fawcett had spent more than two decades in his master's service, starting as a valet and now occupying an unspecified position which seemed to range from squirting the tooth-paste on Charles's brush to choosing the menu at official dinners and masterminding décor changes at Highgrove. He became known as "Fawcett the Fence" after disposing of unwanted gifts and allegedly pocketing $150,000 in a single year. However, the style of the departure of this sacrificial lamb—a farewell party, and a freelance contract with the prince worth as much as his salary—demonstrated that in terms of courting public opinion, Charles had learned nothing. A Golden Jubilee year, a year marked down to compare favorably the work of Britain's monarch with that of her forbear Queen Victoria, ended with a low-key dinner at the Ritz Hotel in London, and humiliation.

In the early months of 2003, a fresh scandal emerged, relating to Princess Diana's will. Her former private secretary, Patrick Jephson, questioned why the executors ignored her instruction to leave her godchildren a quarter of her possessions.

The bequest, spelled out clearly in a letter of wishes by the princess in 1993, was overturned by a court order soon after her death at the request of her two executors—her sister Sarah, and mother Frances Shand Kydd. The decision was legal since the letter of wishes was unenforceable, but slowly the parents of Diana's godchildren, among them the former King of Greece, the Duke of Westminster, and broadcaster Sir David Frost, allowed their anger at the high-handed manner of the two women to surface.

Their views were summed up by Jephson, who himself had been briefly an executor of the will. It was said that under the terms of her letter, the godchildren could have expected to inherit as much as $500,000 each; instead they were given what was described as "tacky mementoes," including a china rabbit and a framed picture from the budget store Argos. Lady Sarah's justification of her action was that "there were not many paupers" among the beneficiaries and their families, but upon investigation, this was found not to be entirely true. Once again, the Spencer women were demonized in the press for their arrogance and mean-spiritedness; furthermore, questions were raised over the decision for Diana to be buried on an island at Althorp, the Spencer family seat: "It was not what she wanted," said a friend, emphatically.

But for this one brief resurgence, the memory of Diana was slowly fading to proportionate levels, and by the spring of 2003 it was felt that Camilla could once again be let out of the shadows. When Charles was admitted to hospital for a hernia operation she publicly accompanied him, taking full advantage of a press-call to show a new ease with the cameras. When that faithful stand-by the Sandringham Flower Show came around again in July, she posed happily with bunches of flowers given by members of the public, for all the world a full-blown member of the British royal family.

And yet the deed was not done: Charles had yet to declare his intention to marry Mrs. Parker Bowles, though the British public were perfectly aware of his desires and, in opinion polls, expressed no particular opposition to it. His procrastination called to mind the dithering of another prince, Hamlet of Denmark, but in part it may have been inspired by the knowledge that the vast majority, while perfectly content with Camilla as his wife, did not want to see Camilla as his queen.

The road to redemption has been long and hard, a path trodden with weary fortitude by Charles and with no end in sight. By the fall of 2003 he had established himself as one-half of a modern live-in couple, with Camilla acting as his official hostess at St James's Palace, Clarence House, Birkhall and Sandringham, and yet there was something still missing— marriage.

He once complained bitterly: "Nobody but me can understand how absolutely bloody it is to be Prince of Wales." Given his riches, his privilege, and his life of ease, people laughed at this self-centered pronouncement. But, given all that he has been through, and all there is yet to come, there is perhaps more than a grain of truth in what he says.

For a sneak peek at

DANCING WITH THE DEVIL
by Christopher Wilson

Now available from
St. Martin's Press

Just turn the page. . . .

No particular attention was paid to the departure of the RMS *Queen Mary* on 24 May 1950 as it slipped its moorings at Pier 90 on New York's East Side and headed down the Hudson River, out past the Statue of Liberty towards the Atlantic Ocean. Of its 1,754 passengers there were few to excite the interest of the dockside reporters. They had seen the Duke and Duchess of Windsor too many times; there was no other celebrity of note aboard. Having scoured the first-class passenger list they had found nothing more than a smattering of well-heeled manufacturers and City men with addresses in Belgravia and the deeper reaches of the British Home Counties. Most travelled with their wives, some with their mistresses, a few with their valets. A J. P. Donahue appeared among the fourteen first-class passengers travelling with a valet, but his name raised no special interest.

For the Windsors, the *Queen Mary* was one link with a kingly past that no one could take away. Named after the Duke's mother, the Cunarder made her maiden voyage in those fleeting few months when David was King. He had taken a childlike interest in the liner's construction and had been on a stem-to-stern inspection of the ship which had taken all day. To the Windsors it was 'their' ship, and the Cunard line were happy to concur with this particular fantasy. Each time they sailed in her, the large outboard suites assigned to the royal couple were repainted, re-hung with new curtains, re-laid with new carpet. At sea the Duchess favoured a shade of grey in which no other suite was allowed to be decorated; flowers specially chosen by the ship's gardener, Davis, were changed daily, the bed linen twice daily.

The Duke loved seaboard life: its bell-ringing luxury, the panoply of his surroundings, the pleasant mental torpor it induced and the sense of removal from everyday concerns. He made a particular friend of the *Queen Mary*'s captain, Commodore Harry Grattidge, and took pleasure in being lured onto the bridge and into the engine room. The Duchess cared for none of these boyish attractions, though as far as is possible the *Queen Mary* was the marine embodiment of her personality and spirit and appearance; an Art Deco masterpiece, a spectacular palace where dreams were born among the ebony, jacaranda, zebra wood and calamander-lined rooms, in the shadows of its bars, in the hidden corners of its decks, and on its dance-floors late at night.

It was here, on the high seas, that the Duchess of Windsor fell in love with Jimmy Donahue. He was thirty-four and she was fifty-four.

'Make no mistake, it was Wallis who made the running,' says one of the Windsors' intimates. 'Jimmy cannot have anticipated what was going to happen, much less manoeuvre himself into the position where he, a homosexual, was going to make a play for a woman. Heaven knows what drove the Duchess to do it—anger, frustration, boredom with her lot in life? The onset of the menopause? No one has adequately explained it—but it happened on board ship, on the way from New York to Cherbourg. When they got on board they were friends. By the time they disembarked, they were lovers.'

The cars at Cherbourg took them in convoy, but separately, to Paris. The Windsors in their Rolls Royce to the Rue de la Faisanderie, Jimmy in his black Cadillac to the Ritz in the Place Vendôme. Within minutes the lovers were on the telephone to each other, whispering, conspiring. A couple of days later the Windsors and Donahues arrived together at the first big ball of the Paris season at the Hotel Lambert on the Ile St Louis. Barbara Hutton, wearing an enormous emerald necklace, was accompanied by Prince Igor Troubetzkoy and among the other guests were Henry Ford, Cecil Beaton, Lady Diana Cooper, the Duc and Duchesse de Brissac, Margaret Biddle and the Baron de Cabrol. 'The setting was absolutely beautiful,' recalls one guest. 'The main hall, where the orchestras were, was decked out in antique red velvet. On the higher surrounding floors were the boxes, occupied by the chosen few—the Windsors and Donahues among them. There was a beautiful garden, buffets with magnificent food, and champagne flowing like water, and on the top floor there was a night club which stayed open till 8 a.m.' The Duke left at midnight. Two of the last guests to leave, it was noted, were Jimmy and the Duchess.

A week later Barbara returned the compliment, hosting her own ball at the Cercle Interallié with 500 guests and the hostess appearing in a pink Indian sari and the famous Hutton ruby necklace, each stone the size of a large grape. Once again the Duke retired early, his wife and escort staying until dawn rose on the City of Light.

In the beginning, the Duke was almost as taken with Jimmy as Wallis was. Jimmy's jokes, his risqué anecdotes and his eagerness to pay a restaurant bill were new, fresh, deliciously acceptable to both Duke and Duchess. Her biographer Stephen Birmingham observed: 'With each successive rebuff from Downing Street and Buckingham Palace, the Duke had become gloomier and harder to divert, and trying to penetrate his sadnesses and dark moods had become increasingly difficult. With Jimmy Donahue it was just the opposite . . . he even helped her by sharing the burden of cheering up the Duke. Then there was the Duke's tightfist-edness, which over the years became a considerable cross for his wife to bear. When the bill arrived at a restaurant when they were entertaining guests for dinner, it was often down-right embarrassing to watch the Duke gazing balefully at it, fingering its corners suspiciously, then pushing it away from him just slightly, obviously in the hope that it would go away or someone else would pick it up. With Jimmy Donahue in tow, there was *no* such problem, it was *always* his treat.'

There was a madness about Jimmy and Wallis in the early stages of the relationship. The staff in Barbara Hutton's suite, observing with fascination the state of the bed linen, took note of what was described as 'activity' in Jimmy's room. At the Rue de la Faisanderie, Jimmy would leave evidence of his nocturnal play with the Duchess. He would dip his fingers in the icing of a cake and scrawl on the kitchen mirror: 'Dear Chef, we love you.' Soon they were to be seen *à deux* at all the fashionable night clubs.

Very quickly the press picked up on this new friendship, though with Jimmy's extravagant mannerisms it was quite clear he was gay, so little more was thought of it. Still, as one columnist observed: 'Jimmy escorts the D and D everywhere and stays up playing cards with the Duchess long after the Duke has retired.'

The writer Charles Murphy, engaged to ghost the Duke's memoirs, *A King's Story,* was in Paris at the time and noted later: 'They danced together. They sang duets of the sentimental song hits of the season: "La Vie en Rose" and "Autumn Leaves," "If I Were a Bell" and "C'est Si Bon." If they did not happen to be seated side by side, they wrote notes to each other and passed them behind the intervening chairs, and each's languishing glance seldom left the other's face.'

Jimmy celebrated his thirty-fifth birthday on 11 June with a dinner at Maxim's; his guests of honor were the Windsors. Contrary to popular belief, Jimmy received no $15 million ($103.5m) inheritance on his thirty-fifth birthday with which to fund his costly adventure with the Windsors. Instead he received the small portion of Jim Donahue's estate, a negligible sum, which had been held in trust since his father's suicide in 1931. The next four years of wining and dining, sybaritism and seduction, were paid for, like everything else in her sons' lives, by the omnipresent Jessie. Many believed that Frank Woolworth had made individual provision for his grandchildren, but his estate passed in its entirety to the three daughters and, in Jessie's case, she never let go. Nonetheless, when it came to the Duke and Duchess, Jimmy rarely found himself short of cash: 'Jessie's purse is as wide open as her heart,' write Maury Paul.

When Jimmy's affair with the Duchess of Windsor became known among their circle—and, once it took hold, neither was in the mood to hide it—several people admitted to having introduced them; for to have triggered this most extraordinary of marital deceptions was to lay claim to a piece of history.

For a sneak peek at

THE DUCHESS OF WINDSOR:
The Uncommon Life of Wallis Simpson
by Greg King

Now available from
Citadel Press

Just turn the page. . . .

"With touching simplicity," wrote Arthur Bryant of the King's abdication in the *Illustrated London News,* "he made his renunciation, and nothing in his whole brilliant and generous career of service became him like the leaving it."

Not all opinion, however, was as generous. The abdication was a great shock. Only a week earlier, almost no one in England outside of government, aristocratic, and court circles had known who Mrs. Simpson was. A few individuals with friends and relatives on the Continent or in America had read news clippings outlining her story, but the great majority of the King's subjects remained ignorant of the relationship. The feeling of loss and betrayal, therefore, was all the greater when they learned that their beloved King had abandoned them. It was even worse that he had left owing to his desire to be with a twice-divorced woman he could not live without. The lower and working classes on the whole supported the King and would likely have remained loyal to his cause had the issue come to its divisive head; the middle classes, however, opposed the relationship on moral and religious grounds. To them, Wallis, in the words of Caroline Blackwood, "symbolized sex and evil."

The aristocracy and members of the court greeted the abdication with relief. They owed their allegiance not to the sovereign but to the continued existence of the throne; it is no surprise that they readily abandoned the King for his brother. As Harold Nicolson noted on December 9: "What is so tragic is that now the people have got over the first sentimental shock they *want* the King to abdicate. I mean opinion in the House is now almost wholly anti-King. 'If he can first betray his duty and then betray the woman he loves, there is no good in the man.' "

The American consul in Plymouth reported to the secretary of state that it was not a question of Wallis being an American or even "the inherent distaste for divorce" that turned the British people against the marriage. Rather, he declared, "the people here consider the proceedings leading up to the second divorce were too much of a farce for them to endure." It was "the middle class, which includes the dyed-in-the-wool non-conformists and the greater part of the Church of England adherents" who had objected most strongly. Many of the latter "stated openly that it would be quite all right if the King were to follow the example set by some other Kings in the past, and make Mrs. Simpson his mistress. They appeared incapable of realizing the hypocrisy of this view, and find no difficulty in saying, almost in the same breath, that the King must set a moral example for his people."

Public acclaim seemed to fall to Baldwin. After the abdication, Alan Lascelles wrote to the *Times* that "the King had no more loyal and devoted subject than Mr. Baldwin then or at any other time." And Sir Eric Mieville, the private secretary to the Duke of York, recalled: "It is totally unfair and untrue to say that Baldwin had stage managed the whole thing to get rid of the King. A sentimental man, he was just as upset as everyone else. He hated every minute of it."

Abroad, the reaction was mixed, and many believed that the abdication might have been forced on the King. Certainly, this was the view in Germany. On January 2, 1938, Ribbentrop reported to Hitler that "Edward VIII had to abdicate, since it was not certain whether, because of his views, he would cooperate in an anti-German policy." Hermann Goering told his wife that Mrs. Simpson had only been used as a pretext for getting rid of the King. Hitler thought the "real reason for the destruction of the Duke of Windsor was . . . his speech at the old veterans' rally in Berlin, at which he declared that it would be the task of his life to effect a reconciliation between Britain and Germany."

In America, copies of the abdication speech were being sold at a rapid pace, but there was a curious prohibition of sales in England. John Gunther wrote: "It is somewhat shocking . . . that a country which traditionally prides itself on free speech and fair play should submit to the stupid censorship which prevented phonograph records of this speech being bought anywhere in England. Of course, the ruling classes, trying desperately to 'build up' the Duke of York, did everything possible to bury Edward and his memory at once."

Novelist Upton Sinclair was unstinting in his praise for the King: "You have, by one magnificent gesture, done more to dignify womanhood and give woman her rightful place, than many great people have been able to do by long and laborious effort."

America was enraptured by the Romeo and Juliet quality of the romance of a King giving up his throne for love; and the fact that Wallis was an American. Crowds watching newsreels of the participants the week of the abdication at the

Embassy Theatre in Times Square in New York City report-edly made their feelings quite clear, as a writer from *Time* magazine noted: "Prince Edward (cheers); Mrs. Simpson (cheers); her first husband Commander Spencer, U.S.N. (boos); her second and present husband Mr. Simpson (cheers and boos); the Archbishop of Canterbury (boos); new Crown Princess Elizabeth (boos); new King George and Queen Elizabeth (boos); Prime Minister Baldwin (prolonged catcalls and boos); King Edward and Mrs. Simpson bathing in Mediterranean (cheers)."

Among those who had known Wallis, reaction to the abdication was also mixed. Chips Channon wrote: "I really consider that she would have been an excellent Queen. . . . She has always shown me friendship, understanding, and even affection, and I have known her do a hundred kindnesses and never a mean act. There is nothing sordid or vulgar in her make-up, but she is modern certainly. . . . She would prefer to be grand, dignified and respectable, but if thwarted she will make the best of whatever position life gives her."

Others were not as supportive. In London, Emerald Cunard and Sir Philip Sassoon, among others, quickly backed away from their former friends; even before the abdication, this disreputable flood began. On December 9, Harold Nicolson noted of Lady Cunard: "She came to Maggie Grenville and said, 'Maggie darling, do tell me about this Mrs. Simpson—I have only just met her.'"

In February 1937 the Winston Churchills were present at a dinner party given by Chips Channon. Clementine Churchill, who had disagreed with her husband over support of the King, shared, however, his view of those who now turned their backs on the former sovereign. Chips wrote: "Lord Granard tactlessly attacked the late King and Mrs.

Simpson to his neighbor, Clemmie Churchill, who turned on him and asked crushingly, 'If you feel that way, why did you invite Mrs. Simpson to your house and put her on your right?' A long embarrassed pause followed. . . ."

The most famous chronicle of this disassociation was a small poem written by Osbert Sitwell. Called "Rat Week," the verse was a stunning indictment of these former friends and supporters and began:

> *Where are the friends of yesterday*
> *That fawned on Him,*
> *That flattered Her;*
> *Where are the friends of yesterday,*
> *Submitting to His every whim,*
> *Offering praise of Her as myrhh*
> *To Him?*

Sitwell was no fan of either David's or Wallis's, and the undercurrent of his poem was criticism not only of their friends but ultimately of the pair at the center of the crisis. Copies of the poem were privately printed and circulated with much glee among London society, particularly by Mrs. Ronald Greville, the dedicated enemy of the King and Wallis and great friend of the new King and Queen.

The most hurtful *volte face* came from the Royal Family itself. When he left England, David carried letters of support and love from many members of his family, including his sister-in-law, the new Queen Elizabeth. Only Queen Mary appeared unmoved, releasing a message to the British people:

> *I need not speak to you of the distress which fills a mother's*
> *heart when I think that my dear son has deemed it to be his*

duty to lay down his charge, and that the reign, which had begun with so much hope and promise, has so suddenly ended. I know that you will realize what it has cost him to come to this decision; and that, remembering the years in which he tried so eagerly to serve and help his Country and Empire, you will ever keep a grateful remembrance of him in your hearts. I commend to you his brother, summoned so unexpectedly and in circumstances so painful, to take his place. . . . With him I commend my dear daughter-in-law, who will be his Queen.

On Sunday, December 13, the nation gathered in their churches and cathedrals for the first time since the abdication. While most religious figures concentrated their sermons on the future, there were several exceptions where Christian charity was notably absent. The Archbishop of York referred to the "sad, humiliating story" of the King's decision to give up the throne for "another man's wife." Then he added, "A man of honor would have acted differently." The Bishop of Portsmouth, Dr. Frank Patridge, declared: "Events have shown the soundness of the English temperament and its aversion from evil things. Almost universally there was a shudder at the indecency and impropriety of wild conduct that knew no law, of which there had been such plain signs. English people would not stand it. They hate Pharisaism and cannot abide smugness. They have a sense of propriety in great places and in great affairs, and will not tolerate headlong slips into the abyss of shamefulness."

The most virulent denunciation, not surprisingly, came from Cosmo Lang, Archbishop of Canterbury, who had been one of the King's most vocal enemies. The Archbishop declared of the King:

From God he had received a high and sacred trust. Yet by his own will he has abdicated—he has surrendered the trust. With characteristic frankness he has told us his motive. It was a craving for private happiness. Strange and sad it must be that for such a motive, however strongly it pressed upon his heart, he should have disappointed hopes so high and abandoned a trust so great. Even more strange and sad is that he should have sought his happiness in a manner inconsistent with the Christian principles of marriage, and within a social circle whose standards and ways of life are alien to all the best instincts and traditions of his people. Let those who belong to this circle know that today they stand rebuked by the judgment of the nation which had loved King Edward.

He ended melodramatically by saying, "The pity of it, O, the pity of it."

Although the public might have been critical of the King's abdication, few thought the Archbishop correct in abusing Edward VIII in such a public manner. His official residence, Lambeth Palace, was flooded with angry letters, all of which took great umbrage at his condemnation of the former King.

The Royal Family, however, appeared to support this very public humiliation, providing some evidence that they were quite out of touch with the general mood of the nation. Queen Mary wrote to the Archbishop immediately, congratulating him on the speech.

Despite the very warm letter she had written to David when he left England, Queen Elizabeth quickly turned on him. Undoubtedly, in this she was influenced by Queen Mary, who remained at the center of the House of Windsor. Queen Elizabeth was particularly supportive of the almost universally condemned speech by Lang. She wrote to Victor Cazalet: "I don't think you need feel the Archbishop failed to express the right thing. *She* [Queen Mary] felt he said exactly what he should and was grateful to him. All the family feels the same. I think the nation vaguely *felt* it, but *he* put the issue clearly and as no one else had the right to do. Nowadays we are inclined to be too vague about the things that matter, and I think it well that for once someone should speak out in plain and direct words, what after all was the truth. . . ."

This reaction became typical for the Royal Family. David's elderly aunt, Queen Maud of Norway, wrote of Wallis: "Wish something could happen to her!" She described Wallis as "one bad woman who has hypnotized him." She concluded: "I hear that every English and French person gets up at Monte Carlo whenever she comes in to a place. Hope she will feel it." And David's great-aunt Princess Louise, Duchess of Argyll, took great delight in repeating a joke to her brother that Wallis must spend lots of time in the bathroom, since it was the "only throne she would ever sit on."

Index